Financial Vipers of Venice

*Alchemical Money, Magical Physics, and Banking
in the Middle Ages and Renaissance*

The sequel to *Babylon's Banksters*

Financial Vipers of Venice

Alchemical Money, Magical Physics, and Banking in the Middle Ages and Renaissance

JOSEPH P. FARRELL

FERAL HOUSE

Financial Vipers of Venice: Alchemical Money,
Magical Physics, and Banking in the Middle
Ages and Renaissance
© 2010 by Joseph P. Farrell

A Feral House book
ISBN 978-1-93623-973-3

Feral House
1240 W. Sims Way Suite 124
Port Townsend WA 98368
www.FeralHouse.com
Book design by Jacob Covey

10 9 8 7 6 5 4 3 2 1

Above all, to

SCOTT DOUGLAS de HART:
You are a true

For all the shared bowls and walks and talks and so many brilliant insights
in so many conversations through the years, anything I could say,
any gratitude I could express, is simply inadequate.

GEORGE ANN HUGHES:
Dear and good friend:
You are a constant encouragement; thank you,
but again, it seems so inadequate.

DANIEL R. JONES:
Good friend, who has seen the full implications of the Metaphor,
and given numerous and priceless insights:
Thank you is, in your case as well, inadequate.

BJK, BAS, "BERNADETTE," PH,
and all the other "extended Inklings" out there:
Many thanks for continued and consistent friendship through the years.

And to

TRACY S. FISHER,
who with love and gentle prodding encouraged me to write:
You are, and will always be, sorely missed.

"I met Murder on the way—
He had a mask like Castlereagh—
Very smooth he look'd yet grim;
Seven bloodhounds followed him:

"'Tis to let the Ghost of Gold
Take from toil a thousand fold,
More than e'er its substance could
In the tyrannies of old:

"Paper coin—that forgery
Of the title deeds, which ye
Hold to something of the worth
Of the inheritance of Earth."

—Percy Bysshe Shelley, from *The Masque of Anarchy*

TABLE OF CONTENTS

ACKNOWLEDGEMENTS

Like all authors, I remain indebted to a few good friends with whom conversation so often brings insights and inspirations, and among these, I must particularly acknowledge a grateful debt to George Ann Hughes, to Daniel A. Jones, and especially to my dear friend of almost twenty years, Dr. Scott D. de Hart, whose eyes and comments on this manuscript were, as always, timely, and as I have come to expect, brilliant. Thank you George Ann, Daniel, and Scott, so very much.

Finally, a word of gratitude to Mr. Adam Parfrey of Feral House. Finding publishers willing to tackle such books as this, both controversial, arcane, and risky, is a rarity, and I have consistently found Adam both willing and eager to do so. Thank you again, Adam!

This book, like all my books, is dedicated to my many readers, whose countless letters and emails of support, of prayerful good wishes, and many suggestions, are hereby gratefully acknowledged.

ᥲ Preface ᥲ

∵

"Before coinage, there was barter."
—Murray Rothbard[1]

"In fact our standard account of monetary history is precisely backwards. We did not begin with barter, discover money, and then eventually develop credit systems. It happened precisely the other way around. What we now call virtual money came first. Coins came much later, and their use spread only unevenly, never completely replacing credit systems. Barter, in turn, appears to be largely a kind of accidental byproduct of the use of coinage or paper money ... "
—David Graeber[2]

THERE ARE TIMES when I wish that I had been born in seventeenth century Berlin or London, or that I could transplant their literary style and diction to the twenty-first century, so that I could indulge my taste for explanatory titles of books, those long titles that are part title, part sub-title, part academic abstract, and part table of contents, such that one could, in many

---

1   Murray Rothbard, *The Mystery of Banking* (Auburn, Alabama: Ludwig von Mises Institute, 2008), p. 3, emphasis in the original.
2   David Graeber, *Debt: The First 5,000 Years* (Brooklyn: Melville House Publishing, 2011), p. 40.

cases, read the title without having to read the book. In that case, the title of this book would be:

Babylon's Banksters, the Financial Vipers of Venice,
the Annuitary Asps of Amsterdam, the Collateralized Cobras
of the City of London, and the Weasels of Wall Street:
In One Stupendous Volume,
BEING
An Objective, Dispassionate and Encyclopedic Discourse and Assaying
Essay Upon the Marvelous Magick of the Metaphor of the Medium,
Money, Alchemy, Metaphysicks and the Darke Secrets, Mysteries
and Miserific Witchery of Banking, Bullion Brokers,
and Corporate Personhood
&
Upon the High Crimes and Misdemeanors of Banksters From
The Bardi, Perruzi, Cerchi, Fuggers, Contarini, Dandoli, Mocenigi,
D'Estes, Welfs, Orange-Nassaus, Saxe-Coburg und Gothas, Medicis,
and Borgias, Contarini, Mocenigos, and other Assorted Miscreants
Downe to Our Own Time
&
Upon the Excesses and Babelish
CONSPIRACIES,
CABALS,
CONGRESSES,
CONVENTIONS
&
CONVENTICLES
of the Rottenchilds, Rockefailures, Wartburgs, Schiffen, Kohns, Luhbs,
Leymanns, and Lees
With Modeste Proposals for Their
SOLUTION.
Heady and Harrowsgate
Geoffrey Codswallop & Sons, Ltd. London
MMXII

All of this would, of course, be encased in the florid filigree of a baroque cartouche, with fat cherubs seraphically strumming lutes and lyres, with a scene of Christ chasing the money-changers from the Temple, while berobed onlookers, clutching their frocks anxiously around them, warily eyed the whole proceeding.

Well, unfortunately (or perhaps, fortunately), times and literary tastes have changed, and publishers like quick alliterative sound bites for titles, with the contents of the book being in the actual book and not the title, and they prefer breaking up such essays into one or more volumes, rather than publishing ponderous one-volume tomes.

Thus, all humor aside, this book is conceived as the second in a series I had planned beginning with *Babylon's Banksters: The Alchemy of Deep Physics, High Finance, and Ancient Religion.* But the title of it—*The Financial Vipers of Venice: Alchemical Money, Magical Physics, and Banking in the Middle Ages and Renaissance* —is somewhat misleading, for this book is about more than Venice, or for that matter, the Middle Ages or Renaissance. It is as much about our own "feudal" age as a former one, and as much about ancient times as about medieval ones.

I begin with Venice, and its persecution of the famous Renaissance magus Giordano Bruno. I intend both Venice and Bruno's martyrdom to function as the twin icons of a system, and of the tremendous change in cultural debate that occurred because of what both the Venetian system, and the magus, represented. Like its predecessor volume, therefore, this is an extended essay on the relationship between metaphysics, physics, alchemical magic, and finance, and, as we shall also discover, apocalyptic speculation.

Why apocalyptic speculation?

For a very simple reason.

We tend to take many of our social conventions, including our institutions of finance and credit, for granted, assuming their implicit permanence without realizing that they arose from a certain complex constellation of cultural factors—from medieval metaphysical and philosophical speculations and doctrines on the nature of debt and personhood, from alchemical metaphors of the transmutative physical medium, from varying notions of what actually constitutes money, credit, and debt—that were hardly permanent. From the High Middle Ages ca. 1400 to the establishment of the Bank of England in 1694, the meaning of "money" fluctuated back and forth from virtual credit and local private "currencies," to securities, to bullion, and back again, in just three hundred years.

We likewise tend to wonder—with some justification—how an excursion into such magical medieval matters could possibly shed light on the contemporary debate on finance, commerce, credit and debt taking place around the world. Some might argue that there is no resemblance between the Middle Age and Renaissance economies and institutions and our own. After all, ours is a truly global economy. With our modern lights, the Middle Ages and Renaissance seem not only half a world away, but hopelessly arcane and irrelevant to our own time.

As will be seen in these pages, however, the modern global economy, with its bonds, annuities, bills of exchange, alchemical paper "fiat money," bullion, wage-slavery, national debts, private central banking, stock brokerages and commodities exchanges, in a sense *began* in the Middle Ages, for quite perceptible and specific reasons. The debates we are having now over corporate responsibility to the public good, and over the proper role and influence of private corporations within public government, all occurred in the Middle Ages and Renaissance as well.

The Daddy Warbucks, Little Orphan Annies, the rags-to-riches heroes of nineteenth century American pulp fiction, the corporate heroes—the Carnegies, Fords, Rockefellers—of yesteryear were once lauded, and now, as circumstances have changed, are excoriated. The same, as we shall see, is an old debate, and corporations—corporate *persons*, the *persona ficta* of medieval jurisprudence—at varying times and for varying reasons, were held now as responsible for risks, and now as insulated from them, now as responsible for and to the public good (and hence punishable, even by death, for infractions of it), and now as not.

The centerpiece in this debate, then as now, was, of course, money: What, and who, does it really represent? And how did it manage to begin as a purely metaphysical phenomenon, with deep ties to a cosmological and indeed topological and alchemical metaphor of the physical medium, then to transmute itself into the conception that money is bullion, and then once again to transmute itself back into a purely metaphysical construct of credit and debt denominated on tokens of paper? To phrase the questions in this fashion is once again to point out what I argued in *Babylon's Banksters*, namely, that there is a deep and abiding relationship between a culture's view of physics and cosmology and its views of finance and credit. Nowhere is this complex relationship rendered more clearly than in the Middle Ages and Renaissance.

The centerpiece here is, of course, Venice, and the rather "conspiracy theory" view taken of its activities. On the internet there are a variety of articles purporting to show that Venice's dark and hidden hand lay behind the demise of the great Florentine international "super-companies," the Bardi and Peruzzi companies, and in some cases, this scenario is extended to even broader theories of deliberate Venetian involvement in the importation of the Black Plague, and so on. For myself, the central and most interesting part of these internet theories has always been the demise of the great Florentine super-companies, and that will eventually be our focus here. These articles, while often *referring to* scholarly academic works that can—and as will be seen here, do—make the case for such a role for the Venetian financial oligarchy, seldom *cite* those studies with anything approaching academic rigor, a problem that so often surfaces in the alternative media and research community. And the citation of such academic sources, even if only in general terms, often disguises a methodological problem, namely, that the argument for such a conspiratorial view must be made by combining such sources, taking note not only of Venetian banking and exchange practices, but also taking note of the structure of its government agencies and its noble families and financial classes. Academic histories of Venetian monetary policy tend to ignore such features, or, if they approach it at all, only suggest it briefly, thence to quickly shuffle on—"nothing to see here folks, move along"—while political histories of the Venetian shenanigans abound, but *they* tend to be decoupled from the underlying trading and monetary aspects. The attempt of this book is to fill in that void, albeit in a necessarily cursory and synoptic fashion.

This work is consequently only an *essay,* an argued speculation, or perhaps better put, a *meditation,* on this complex constellation of concepts, for as anyone who has researched any of these individual components is aware, a vast and specialized literature exists for each of them. I have attempted, therefore, to restrict myself to citations from sources more readily available, though in a couple of instances, specialized—and quite expensive—references were unavoidable.

(As an aside here, so expensive were two of these sources that my utilization of them would not have been possible without the generous support of my readers, some of whom donated the funds to purchase them. While trying to find them—one of which I had been seeking for some years until I finally found a rare book dealer with a copy for sale at the "reasonable" price of $325!—I had, and still have, the impression that these books, essential sources for any monetary and financial history of the high Middle Ages and Renaissance in Italy, were deliberately bought up, leaving few circulating copies on the market. The reasons for my suspicion will, I suspect, become abundantly clear to the reader in the main text of this book. In a word, techniques are clearly shown, and in a few [*very* few] instances, names are named that provide connections to modern history and what the old news commentator Paul Harvey called "the *rest* of the story … ")

In any case, the complexity both of the concepts and of their interrelationships can be revealed by considering just one of the components, a strange, wonderful, and mysterious fact: we humans tend to couch our language of love in terms of the language of debt, of a transaction, and even of sacrifice. We say, for example, that we are indebted to a loved one. "I am forever in your debt," we say to a lover, a friend, a brother, a sister, a parent. Parents speak of "owing" their children a decent life, love, a happy home. Children speak of "owing" their parents respect, honor, love. In short, the language of debt, of finance, transaction, contract, and commerce, are a part of our vocabulary of love, even of our religion and culture. Christ, for example, is called the Redeemer, yet another term of transaction. The *Pater Noster*, in one well-known English translation, has the petitioner saying "Forgive us our debts, as we forgive our debtors," even though the idea of a general debt forgiveness in the society at large *praying* this prayer was quite unthinkable. The question is, why? And when did this association of love, transaction, credit, debt, and religion first begin?

Here, the execution of Giordano Bruno by Roman authorities becomes an iconic portal, a gateway into the profound mysteries of alchemical money, magical physics, and banking. For here we find a clash of worldviews on religion, physics, and finance, combined with different interpretations of an ancient metaphor, a metaphor for whose implications Bruno was both murdered ... and martyred ...

Joseph P. Farrell
From Somewhere
2012

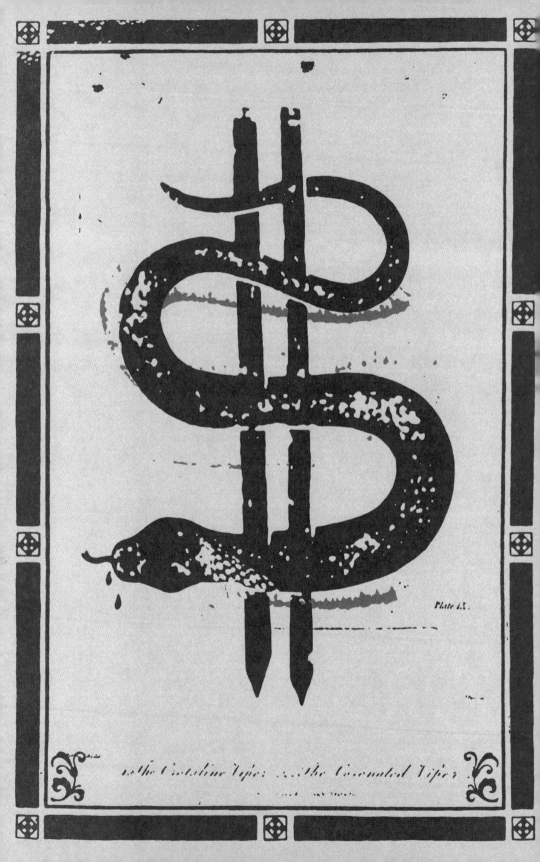

1. the Cristaline Viper; 2. the Coronated Viper

Financial Vipers of Venice

I

THE MARTYR, THE METAPHOR, AND THE MERCHANTS

"… Hermeticism is once again relevant, this time to the realm of quarks, M-theory and DNA. As science itself becomes more magical, Hermeticism's time has truly come."

—Lynn Picknett and Clive Prince,
The Forbidden Universe: The Occult Origins of Science and the Search for the Mind of God, p. 210.

One

MARTYR TO THE METAPHOR:

Banksters, Bishops, and the Burning of Bruno

∴

"We here, then, have a Jove, not taken as too legitimate and good a vicar or lieutenant of the first principle and universal cause, but well taken as something variable, subject to the Fate of Mutation ... "
—Giordano Bruno[1]

ON ASH WEDNESDAY in the year 1600, a man who was a constant irritation to Churchianity—and to its hierarchy preaching more than hypocritically about the God of Love—was led through the arched corridors of various buildings into a public square, where he was tied to a stake at which cords and bundles of wood were thrown at his feet. When this was done, the man was most likely brushed with tars and oils according to the practice of the period, and flame was put to the bundles of wood. The flames and smoke rose, boiling and baking the skin, perhaps amid cries of anguish and suffering, until, overcome with pain, he finally lapsed into unconsciousness and death.

This burnt offering of a man had made his way to France, thence to Geneva, back to Paris, onward to London and Oxford, back to Paris, to Germany and Bohemia, and finally back to his native Italy. Along all these travels, he had managed to anger the Anglican doctors and dons of Oxford,

---

1   Giordano Bruno, "Explanatory Epistle" in *The Expulsion of the Triumphant Beast*, trans. from the Italian by Arthur D. Imerti (Lincoln: University of Nebraska Press, 1992), p. 75.

the Puritans of Cambridge, the Calvinists of Geneva, and of course, the Lutherans of Germany and the Catholics of France and his homeland.

After the burning was complete, the red- and purple-robed authorities breathed a sigh of relief. The ideological threat the man posed had brought them perilously close to losing not just power, but centuries of status and standing. They were, however, but agents for deeper, murkier powers, powers whose long-term plans and goals were very directly threatened by the man and his ideas.

Those powers were Venice and the Vatican.

And the man's name was Giordano Bruno.

Bruno was a martyr to a Metaphor, to a way of thinking and viewing the cosmos that he—most definitely not alone—had come to hold and to champion. His martyrdom to that metaphor is an icon of a tremendous clash of forces that was transforming his world and time, forces deeply embedded in religion, alchemy, money, magic, and even, as we shall see, physics.

However, to understand how Bruno came to such a tragic fate, and why this brilliant man could symbolize such a constellation of forces, we must first look deeper into his life, and into the powers that conspired to end it. We must look into the Hermetic Metaphor by which he lived and for which he died, and into the tremendous threat it posed to the financial power of Venice and the religious power of the Vatican (and for that matter, to the Protestant world as well). Accordingly, in this chapter we will explore Bruno's life and doctrine, in the next chapter we will explore the Hermetic Metaphor itself and its relation to Bruno's doctrine, and in the third and fourth chapters we will explore Venice's financial doctrine and power. These three chapters in turn will afford the portal of entry into a deeper exploration of medieval jurisprudence, philosophy, physics, and finance in the subsequent sections of this book.

A. Bruno's Life and Wanderings

Though the exact date of his birth is unknown, it is known that Giordano Filippo Bruno was born in the year 1548 in Nola, within the then-Kingdom of Naples. Throughout his life, he and others thus referred to himself as "the Nolan." He received what was then a traditional education, and entered the Dominican order at the Naples monastery of San Domenico Maggiore at the age of seventeen, taking for his ecclesiastical and monastic name "Giordano, after Giordano Crispo, his metaphysics tutor."[2]

---

2   "Giordano Bruno," http://en.wikipedia.org/wiki/Giordano_Bruno. For a less publicly available treatment of Bruno's life and travels, see Bruno, *The Expulsion of the Triumphant Beast*, pp. 3–20, 47–65.

He was ordained a priest in 1572, and early in his life showed a remarkable ability with memory, even journeying to Rome to demonstrate his memory system to Pope Pius V. However, it was also during this period that his tendency to think "outside" the box of ecclesiastical doctrine and dogma took hold, manifest in his reading of banned works of the North European humanist Erasmus, in his rejection of images of the saints, and in his defense of the Arian doctrine, that is to say, the doctrine that Christ was a mere man and not the second person of the Trinity. Learning that an indictment was being prepared against him by the local Inquisition, Bruno laid aside his monastic frock and fled Naples for the city-states of northern Italy, including Venice and Padua. At Padua, he encountered fellow Dominicans who encouraged him to wear the Dominican habit once again.

From there, Bruno wandered across the Alps into France and eventually ended up in John Calvin's (1509–1564) Protestant Geneva in 1579, where he adopted secular dress in order to move freely within the city. However, Bruno, never one to hold his tongue or pen, soon ran afoul of the Calvinist authorities, and fled Geneva for France once again, finally taking his doctorate at Toulouse, and attempting yet again, unsuccessfully, to return to the Church. When strife broke out in Toulouse, Bruno made his way to Paris, where his feats of memory brought him to the attention of King Henry III. It was here that Bruno published his first work on the art of memory, *De Umbris Idearum,* "The Shadows of Ideas" (1582). As we will discover in the next section, Bruno's art of memory is deeply tied to his views on magic and the cosmological Metaphor for which he gave his life.

In the year 1583 Bruno journeyed to England as a guest and under the protection of the French ambassador Michel de Castelnau, and it is here that Bruno entered into the first public controversies with the authorities that would eventually bring about his trial and execution. He did so by delivering a series of controversial lectures at the University of Oxford, in which he defended Nicholas Copernicus' then-controversial theory that the Earth revolved around the sun, with George Abbot, later the Archbishop of Canterbury, taking the opposing view. It was during this period in England that Bruno wrote many of his most famous, and as we shall see, scandalous works, among them *Lo Spaccio della Bestia Trionfante* (*The Expulsion of the Triumphant Beast*), a work that Karen De León-Jones has described as being part of a trilogy on "the ethics of mutation,"[3] and *On Cause, Principle, and Unity,* two works we shall examine in more detail in the next section. It is even speculated that while Bruno was staying in London under the French ambassador's

---

3 Karen de León-Jones, foreword to *The Expulsion of the Triumphant Beast* by Bruno, p. vii. The other books of this trilogy are *The Cabala of the Pegasean Horse* and *The Heroic Furors* (p. vii).

protection, he was also spying on Catholics for Sir Francis Walsingham, Queen Elizabeth's famous Secretary of State and spymaster.

Bruno returned to France in 1585, but found a reception less warm than before, since his relentless attacks on the cosmology and physics of Aristotle—the reigning cosmology and physics of the Roman Catholic Church—plus his open endorsement of the Copernican theory had earned him the ire of Catholic authorities. Thus, by 1586 he had departed for Germany, where he was able to land a teaching position at the University of Wittenberg. Here he remained for two years, until once again, changing academic climates forced him to flee to Prague, and then to flee yet *again* after being excommunicated by the Lutherans there for his controversial views. It was, however, during this period that he composed and published several works in Latin (among them *On Magic*) which, as we shall discover in the next section, were guaranteed to upset both Catholic and Protestant orthodoxy, on account of the very tight blending of magical philosophy with the broader Hermetic cosmology he had come to adopt as his personal religion. Bruno promoted this new Hermetic religion because he believed it could unify the growing religious divisions within Europe.

1. The Return to Venice, and a Mystery

By 1591 Bruno had landed in Frankfurt, and his life took the turn that would eventually lead him to the stake, for it was here that he received the invitation from the Venetian nobleman Giovanni Mocenigo to come to Venice and instruct him on the secrets of his art of memory. Mocenigo had acquired a copy of Bruno's *De Minimo* and was so impressed with its references to the art of memory that he wrote to Bruno asking him to come to Venice, where he would pay him to tutor him in the art.[4]

It's here that we begin to sense the discomforting possibilities of a mystery and of a conspiracy. Arthur D. Imerti, whose superb translation of *The Expulsion of the Triumphant Beast* we shall rely on in this section, puts it this way:

> It is difficult to understand why the philosopher decided to return to Italy, whence he was a fugitive from both the Neapolitan and Roman Inquisitions. Perhaps the author of (*The Expulsion*) believed that his heretical philosophical and religious ideas might meet, if not with acceptance, at least with toleration in the Republic of Venice … [5]

---

4 Arthur D. Imerti, "The Making of a Heretic," in *The Expulsion of the Triumphant Beast* by Bruno, p. 16.
5 Ibid.

But the mystery only deepens when one considers the views on wealth and property Bruno himself stated in the second dialogue of *The Expulsion.* There, Bruno advocates that "tyrants be deposed" and "republics be favored," certainly no threat to the *Serenissima Republica* of Venice. But then, without so much as a pause for breath, Bruno urges that "the indolent, the avaricious, and the owners of property be scorned and held in contempt."[6]

Imerti observes that these words "might be construed as socialistic"[7] and such a direct assault on property and wealth could hardly be palatable to the views of the Venetian republic, founded as it was on an empire of merchant banking and mercenary military force. One is dealing with the possibility, therefore, that Bruno was simply tricked into returning to Venice. (And there are *other* possibilities, as will be seen in section two.)

This possibility grows when one considers Mocenigo's actions toward Bruno. Initially, he showered Bruno with "numerous acts of kindness" to the extent that Bruno was apparently taken in by Mocenigo, eventually divulging "many of his heretical ontological and epistemological views,"[8] the very cosmological views that were the basis both of his art of memory and its corresponding philosophy of magic. The Venetian nobleman, however, quickly became disenchanted with the progress of his studies with the Nolan, and "accused Bruno of not teaching him all he knew about the arts of memory, invention, and geometry, threatening repeatedly to denounce him to the Holy Office if he did not teach him what he had promised."[9] The Venetian disclosed Bruno's views to his father confessor, who urged him to denounce the Nolan to the Venetian Inquisition. More on this in a moment.

2. Disturbing Testimony and a Deepening Mystery: Bruno's Secret Society, the Giordanisti

When Bruno, blissfully unaware of the nobleman's intentions, told Mocenigo of his own intentions to return to Frankfurt, the latter acted. Tricking Bruno and locking him in an attic, on May 22, 1592, Mocenigo betrayed him to the Venetian civil authorities, who in turn handed him over to the Venetian Inquisition.[10] According to the English scholar Frances A. Yates, Mocenigo told the Venetian Inquisition that Bruno's views were clearly directed at the whole power structure of the Inquisition itself:

---

6   Bruno, *The Expulsion of the Triumphant Beast,* p. 145.
7   Imerti, "The Making of a Heretic," p. 39.
8   Ibid., p. 16.
9   Ibid., p. 17.
10   Ibid.

The procedure which the Church uses to-day is not that which the Apostles used: for they converted the people with preaching and the example of a good life, but now whoever does not wish to be a Catholic must endure punishment and pain, for force is used and not love; the world cannot go on like this, for there is nothing but ignorance and no religion which is good; the Catholic religion pleases him more than any other, but this too has need of great reform; it is not good as it is now, but soon the world will see a general reform of itself, for it is impossible that such corruptions should endure ... [11]

What did Bruno mean by this?

During his stay in Frankfurt, he had disclosed to the Venetian Giovanni Battista Ciotto—through whom Mocenigo had originally arranged for Bruno's journey to Venice—that "he knew more than the Apostles" and that "if he had a mind to it, he could bring about that all the world should be one religion,"[12] a religion, as we shall see, neither Protestant nor Catholic, nor even Christian, but "hermetic."

How did Bruno think he could possibly have achieved such a feat?

Again, a hint is provided by Mocenigo in his testimony to the Venetian Inquisition:

I have not heard him (Bruno) say that he wanted to institute a new sect of Giordanisti in Germany, but he has affirmed that when he had finished certain of his studies he would be known as a great man ...[13]

Clearly, the Inquisition had *some* cause for concern, for the "Giordanisti" were revealed to be a new secret society Bruno intended to found:

In Mocenigo's delation to the Inquisition against Bruno, he reports him as having said that he had intended to found a new sect under the name of philosophy. Other informers made the same insinuation, adding that Bruno had said that the sect was called the "Giordanisti" and appealed particularly to the Lutherans in Germany.[14]

Putting this together with Bruno's travels throughout Italy, France, England, Switzerland, and Germany reveals the concerns not only of the Anglican and

---

11   Frances A. Yates, *Giordano Bruno and the Hermetic Tradition*, (London: Routledge, 1964), p. 340.

12   Ibid.

13   Ibid., p. 5, citing the *Sommario* of the Venetian Inquisition, pp. 57–58.

14   Ibid., p. 312.

Protestant authorities that Bruno encountered, but also of the Catholics, for it is possible that Bruno was planting the seeds of his secret society and "hermetic revolution" during all his travels.

Frances A. Yates poses the problem this way:

> It has occurred to me to wonder whether these rumored "Giordanisti" could have any connection with the unsolved mystery of the origins of the Rosicrucians who are first heard of in Germany in the early seventeenth century, in Lutheran circles.[15]

As Yates herself understood, the answer to this question lay in Bruno's art of memory, the very art whose secrets Mocenigo had lured the Nolan to Venice to learn![16] Bruno "may be the real source of a Hermetic and mystical movement which used, not the real architecture of 'operative' masonry, but the imaginary or 'speculative' architecture of the art of memory as the vehicle of its teachings."[17] Noting that early Rosicrucian documents speak of "mysterious *rotae* or wheels, and of a sacred 'vault' the walls, ceiling and floor of which was divided into compartments each with their several figures and sentences,"[18] these are, as we shall discover in the next section, the *exact* mnemonic devices used by Bruno to construct both his magic and his art of memory, and indeed, his hermetic cosmology. Bruno's denunciation to the Inquisition, plus his own statements regarding his founding of a secret society to spread "philosophy," i.e., hermetic teaching, would account for why his "secret," which was "the combination of the Hermetic beliefs with the techniques of the art of memory,"[19] went underground in the increasing religious intolerance of the late sixteenth and early seventeenth centuries.

3. The Roman Inquisition and Bruno's Execution

But before we turn to the substance of Bruno's doctrine, and why it posed such a threat to the financial powerhouse of Venice and the religious powerhouse of the Vatican, we must deal with the final grisly details of his trial before the Roman Inquisition, for as we shall see, there are further clues to be found there. By the end of his trial before the Venetian Inquisition, Bruno had recanted "all of the heresies of which he was accused and threw himself on

---

15   Ibid., pp. 312–313. See also Yates, *Selected Works of Frances Yates*, Volume III, *The Art of Memory* (London: Routledge, 2001), p. 303.
16   Yates, *The Art of Memory*, p. 304.
17   Ibid.
18   Ibid.
19   Ibid., p. 305.

the mercy of the judges."[20] But he still had to be handed over to the Roman Inquisition and to its own trial.

While the documents concerning Bruno's Venetian and Roman trials are somewhat lacking (due to reasons we shall explore in the appendix to this book), one Gaspar Scioppus was a witness to Bruno's execution. Scioppus details an interesting list of the points for which Bruno was condemned and executed by the Roman Inquisition:

> ... that there are innumerable worlds; that magic is a good and licit thing; that the Holy Spirit is the *anima mundi*;[21] that Moses did his miracles by magic in which he was more proficient than the Egyptians; that Christ was a Magus.[22]

Yates notes, however, that the evidence remaining for the reasons for Bruno's condemnation and execution are threadbare.[23] We do know that the famous Jesuit Inquisitor, Robert Cardinal Bellarmine, the same Bellarmine who examined Galileo, drew up a list of eight formal charges Bruno was required to recant, which, of course, the Nolan refused to do.[24] It does appear, however, that Bruno's condemnation was for specific conflicts with Catholic doctrine—including the deity of Christ—and that his Hermetic philosophy and support of the Copernican heliocentric theory were also at the root of it.[25]

Indeed, in his letters to the Venetian Inquisition—and we must assume these became part of the testimony against Bruno in Rome—Mocenigo drew up an astonishing list of complaints against the Nolan. According to the nobleman,

> Bruno maintained that the Catholic faith is "full of blasphemy against the majesty of God"; "that there is no distinction of persons in God,"

(A difficult proposition to believe, as we shall discover in the next section and more fully in chapter two.)

> ... "that the world is eternal"; "that there are infinite worlds"; "that all the operations of the world are guided by fate";

---

20 Yates, *Giordano Bruno and the Hermetic Tradition*, p. 349.

21 *Anima mundi* or ψυχη κοσμικη, i.e., the "World Soul" of the Neoplatonists.

22 Yates, *Giordano Bruno and the Hermetic Tradition*, p. 354.

23 For a consideration of the peculiarities and implications surrounding the evidence of Bruno's Trial, see the Appendix, "The Missing Documents of Bruno's Trial: Napoleon Bonaparte, Pope Piux IX (Giovanni Cardinal Mastai-Ferretti), and the Implications."

24 For Yates' complete recounting of the Roman trial, see *Giordano Bruno and the Hermetic Tradition*, pp. 349–356.

25 Ibid., p. 355.

(A proposition having some credence, given Bruno's heavy reliance upon astrological imagery and his belief in a multitude of inhabited worlds.)

> ... and that "souls created through the operation of nature pass from one animal to another." In other accusations Mocenigo charged that Bruno affirmed that "Christ was a rogue" and ... that "the miracles of Christ and His disciples were 'apparent'"; and that He and His disciples were "magicians."
>
> [Mocenigo's letters to the Inquisition] further reveal that Bruno severely criticized monastic institutions, branding all monks as "asses," and Catholic doctrines as "asinine"; that he considered a blasphemy the Catholic teaching that bread is transmuted into flesh; that he disapproved of the sacrifice of the Mass, stating that "there is no punishment of sins"; that he denied the possibility of the Virgin Birth ... [26]

and so on. In this list, we see Bruno following out the logical implications of his hermetic and magical system with a degree of rigor and personal abandon not shared by most other Renaissance Hermeticists.

A list of eight charges were drawn up against Bruno, extracted from his publications,[27] and Bruno refused to recant or retract them, though he did throw himself on the mercy of Pope Clement VIII. The pope proved to be anything but clement, handing Bruno to the secular authorities on January 20, 1600 for "extreme measures."[28]

On February 8, 1600, the Roman Holy Office, i.e. the Inquisition, after reviewing the findings of the Roman trial, decided that Bruno was "'pertinaciously' persevering in his 'errors,'"[29] and even mentioned that while in England Bruno had been "considered an 'atheist'"[30] for his publication of *The Expulsion of the Triumphant Beast*. On February 16, 1600, after being given eight days to recant, Bruno was led to the Campo di Fiori to be burnt alive. "Before being given to the flames, he was shown the image of Christ, from which he disdainfully turned his gaze,"[31] the torch was set, and after a few agonizing moments, the Nolan was no more.

So what was it, precisely, about this man's philosophy that posed such a threat to financial Venice, Oxford Anglican dons, Geneva Calvinists, German

---

26   Arthur D. Imerti, "The Heretic and His Trial," in Bruno, *The Expulsion of the Triumphant Beast*, p. 48.
27   Ibid., p. 63.
28   Ibid.
29   Ibid.
30   Ibid., pp. 63–64.
31   Ibid., p. 64.

Lutherans, and the Vatican? What was it that allowed him to be accused of promoting a new religion in the guise of a secret society, one which he hoped would sweep Europe both of Protestantism and Catholicism, one in which he himself defended theism, but which also earned him in England the title of atheist? How does one reconcile all of this?

To answer these questions, we must examine his doctrine much more closely, and in doing so, an astonishing set of implications—both very ancient in their Hermetic roots, and very modern in their physics corollaries—will emerge.

B. Bruno's Doctrine and the Ancient Metaphor
1. The Expulsion of the Triumphant Beast

Bruno's *The Expulsion of the Triumphant Beast* was published in London in the year 1584, and it was "the only work of Bruno's to be singled out by the Roman Inquisition at the summation of his trial."[32] For indeed, it was "owing to its daring ethical and epistemological speculations, its philosophy of nature, of religion, and of history," that the work was "the embodiment of all that is most heretical in the philosopher's thinking."[33] We get some measure both of the man and the work's "irksome" heretical contents with Bruno's reference to the crucifixion of Christ as "a cabalistic tragedy."[34] *The Expulsion* is thus, in a certain sense, Bruno's declaration of war against Christianity itself.[35]

But the Nolan does not stop there.

For example, in the "Explanatory Epistle" of the work, Bruno boldly declares that man is "a citizen and servant of the world,"[36] a political view that would reemerge almost two centuries later with the credo of Adam Weishaupt and the Bavarian Illuminati, and therefore hardly a view to endear him to the political authorities of his own age. Indeed, if Frances A. Yates is correct in assuming that there is some connection between Bruno's secret society, the Giordanisti, and the emergence of the Rosicrucian Fraternity in Germany, there may be even deeper connections between Bruno, his secret society, and the Illuminati of the eighteenth century than scholarship has hitherto assumed.

The connection with the doctrines of the Illuminati is made even more cogent when one considers Bruno's conception of revealed, or "positive," religion, as Imerti explains:

---

32 Arthur D. Imerti, "*Lo Spaccio*, Its Fortunes, Literary Aspects, Allegory, and Summary," in Bruno, *The Expulsion of the Triumphant Beast*, p. 21.
33 Ibid.
34 Ibid., p. 146.
35 See Imerti's remarks in "The Making of a Heretic," p. 9.
36 Bruno, *The Expulsion of the Triumphant Beast*, p. 72.

Bruno's concept of the Deity as pure rational principle, and as both cause and effect, made all positive religions, with their emphasis on the anthropomorphic attributes of God, repugnant to him … his sly references to monks, monasteries, and relics hint at his disapproval of some of the basic tenets of Catholicism. His ironic allusions to the New Testament, and particularly his satire of Christ, whose life on earth he allegorizes in Orion, and whose "trinitarian" nature, in Chiron the Centaur, are an implied refutation not only of Catholicism but of Christianity itself.[37]

Compare this summary of Bruno's doctrine to the summary of Weishaupt's doctrine given in the late eighteenth century by the French priest Abbé Augustin Barruel:

The Religion of Christ is represented as a medley of the reveries of Pythagoras, of Plato, and of Judaism. It is in vain for the Israelites to believe in the unity of God, in the coming of a Messiah … he will declare in his *corrected Code*, that the Religion of the Jews was but a modification of the reveries of the Egyptians, of Zoroaster, or of the Babylonians. To *correct* his adepts, he teaches them to cast aside the Creation as a chimera unknown to antiquity, and to reduce all Religion to two Systems—The one, that of matter co-eternal with God, a part of God, proceeding from God, cast forth and separated from God, in order to become the world—The other, matter co-eternal with God, without being God, but worked by God, for the formation of the universe.[38]

Clearly, Weishaupt's Illuminism, as Barruel recounts it, is suffused with Hermetic views that are, in the final analysis, almost identical with Bruno's, making it possible that Bruno was successful in establishing his "Giordanistas" in Germany, and that they may have had some deep connection to the subsequent emergence of Rosicrucianism and Illuminism in that land.

As we shall discover momentarily, however, Imerti's statement that Bruno rejected anthropomorphism is not entirely correct, for in Bruno's hands, such anthropomorphism becomes the signal of a profound underlying metaphor of *physics, mind, memory, and the operations of magic.* Nonetheless, it remains true that Bruno's hermeticism was the repudiation of all revealed religions.[39]

---

37 Imerti, "The Heretical Premises of *Lo Spaccio*," in Bruno, *The Expulsion of the Triumphant Beast*, p. 41.

38 Abbé Augustin Barruel, *Code of the Illuminati* (Hong Kong: Forgotten Books, 2008), p. 135.

39 Imerti, "The Heretical Premises of *Lo Spaccio*," in Bruno, *The Expulsion of the Triumphant Beast*,

The reason for this repudiation may not be entirely clear until one recalls that Bruno, like many Hermeticists of the High Renaissance, viewed the origin of all positive or revealed religion as being from Egypt. As Imerti explains:

> In his interpretation of the Old Testament Bruno's views clash with both Christian and Jewish teachings. He regards its stories as fables, or metaphorical representations of history, passed on from the Egyptians to the Babylonians and then to the Hebrews. He adduces as evidence of his premise the "metaphor of the raven," which, he declares, was "first found and developed in Egypt and then taken by the Hebrews, through whom this knowledge was transmitted from Babylonia, in the form of a story … "
>
> Bruno is struck by the variations of the Osiris myth in the ancient Mediterranean civilizations, to which he makes a brief allusion. However, he specifically points out analogies between such Greek myths as that of Apollo and the Raven and the biblical Noah and the Raven, between Deucalion and Noah, and between Cerus and Jonah and the Whale.
>
> The source of the myths shared by the Greeks with the Hebrews, he insists, is not Hebrew but Egyptian. Egypt, indeed, is for Bruno the source of all the myths and fables of the Mediterranean world, all being poetical representations of events dating back to the dawn of Western civilization.[40]

As we shall see, this "Egyptian monogenesis" also included a doctrine of a primordial trinity, such that Bruno came to the conclusion that its ultimate origins were not in revelation, but in reason. Hence, unlike most Hermeticists of the High Renaissance who were busily trying to *reconcile* elements of Hermetic doctrine with Christianity, Bruno was busily proclaiming their divorce, and with it, repudiating the need for special revelation and authority structures—Protestant or Catholic. To put it succinctly, Bruno believed that once the Hermetic cosmological doctrine was stripped of its religious overlay, religion (in the standard sense) was no longer necessary. We will expand on Bruno's exposition of this metaphor later in this chapter and in the next chapter, but for now, our concentration must remain fixed on *The Expulsion of the Triumphant Beast.*

One implication of this sort of Hermetic interpretation of the Egyptian Monogenesis is that all of nature becomes a manifestation of Deity, thus leav-

---

p. 32.
40   Ibid., pp. 42–43.

ing nature as "the teacher of all rational beings."[41] As a result, the *political*— and therefore, the *financial*—vision that Bruno embodies in *The Expulsion* is:

> a society in which the natural religion of the Egyptians, in its purest sense, and the speculative intellect of the Greeks would coincide in a sociopolitical structure patterned after that of the Roman Republic. The source of the state, which Bruno conceives of as "an ethical substance," is God, "the absolute reality, or reality which is the principle of all realities." The state envisaged by the philosopher would be one containing a unity of law and religion, rather than a separation of "the divine from law and civil life."[42]

While this is true as far as it goes, it misses the point of what Bruno is advocating when he talks about "law" in one important respect: in the ancient Roman Republic, law was an external compulsion backed by the force of the state. With Bruno, law is an interior illumination within individuals, and statute law is its organic outgrowth.

Bruno, in other words, is advocating the *very* revolutionary principle of the sovereignty of the individual person, and this, as we shall see in subsequent chapters, posed a definite threat not only to the religious and political authorities of his day, but to the financial powers—like Venice—as well. The result of this view—and here as elsewhere Bruno traces out all its logical implications without hesitation—is that all the gods, including Jove or Yahweh, should be made to serve man. After all, the gods were but the creations of the ultimate Principle, or nature, and thus were the creations of man himself. It is, says Bruno, "by the grace of the gods" that it is permitted to man to be "at liberty to make them serve us, to take and accommodate them at our convenience and pleasure."[43]

Once again placing the origin of these doctrines in Egypt and its magical science, and not in a special revelation, Bruno calls the Jews "the excrement of Egypt." He holds that Moses' knowledge was not the result of revelation, but of his learning in the ancient magical science, or scientific magic, of Egypt.[44]

Such propositions were, of course, heretical, whether one was a Protestant or a Catholic, and had Bruno ever managed to journey to Orthodox Christian Europe, would have been viewed as heretical there as well. But the catalogue

---

41   Imerti, "The Heretical Premises of *Lo Spaccio*," in Griodano Bruno, *The Expulsion of the Triumphant Beast*, p. 45.
42   Ibid., p. 46.
43   Bruno, "Explanatory Epistle," in *The Expulsion of the Triumphant Beast*, p. 72.
44   Imerti, "The Heretical Premises of *Lo Spaccio*," in Bruno, *The Expulsion of the Triumphant Beast*, p. 42.

we have reviewed above would be incomplete if we did not also mention Bruno's other great heresy—at least as far as *Catholic* Europe at the time was concerned. Namely, his view that the Earth was merely one of innumerable planets, that there were a multitude of *inhabited* worlds, that the universe was teaming with life, and that the Earth did indeed revolve around the Sun.[45] This view, as we shall see in chapter two, is a product of his Hermeticism, for Hermeticism held that the cosmos is literally teeming with life. His scientific and philosophical influence, and particularly his reliance upon a kind of "mathematical magic and philosophy" is even thought to have profoundly influenced Gottfried Leibniz, the inventor (along with Isaac Newton), of integral and differential calculus.[46]

With this background in hand, we are now in a position to examine Bruno's doctrine in detail, concentrating on his works *The Expulsion of the Triumphant Beast, On Cause, Principle, and Unity,* and *On Magic.*

a. *The Contradictory Moral Nature of Yahweh*

Bruno begins *The Expulsion of the Triumphant Beast* with a lengthy "Explanatory Epistle," in which he has the following things to say about Jove, the common name in his time for the God of the Old Testament, Yahweh. Jove, or Yahweh, he explains,

> is introduced, as is vulgarly described, as a god who possessed virtues and kindness, and possessed human and sometimes brutal and bestial dissoluteness, frivolity, and frailty, as it is imagined that he possessed when it is reputed that he changed himself into those various subjects or forms in order to indicate the mutation of the various affects that Jove, the soul, and man incur, finding themselves in this fluctuating matter.[47]

In other words, Yahweh's two-faced moral character, now benevolent, now violent and murderous, is a result of his participation in the mutable, fluctuating world of matter. Because of this, Bruno goes on to note, Yahweh really "represents each one of us,"[48] or to put it differently, the supreme God of the Old Testament is really man, or at least, a representation of man. Given Bruno's hermetic background and familiarity with all manner of hermetic and

---

45   Imerti, "The Making of a Heretic," in *The Expulsion of the Triumphant Beast*, p. 19, and Imerti, "The Heretic and His Trial," p. 51.
46   de León-Jones, "Foreword," *The Expulsion of the Triumphant Beast*, p. xii.
47   Bruno, "Explanatory Epistle," *The Expulsion of the Triumphant Beast*, p. 78.
48   Ibid., p. 79.

alchemical texts, what he is in effect saying is that all the gods are manifestations of ever-transmuting matter, and that Yahweh is, in the final analysis, a manifestation of the Philosophers' Stone. Bruno is, in short, a kind of proto-transhumanist.

This has a social consequence, namely, the standard and endless Yahwist divisions of the social space.[49] In a lengthy diatribe against the Calvinist Protestants, Bruno traces out the morally contradictory character of Yahweh in a review of how this is reflected in Calvinist doctrine and practice:

> And in conclusion, let her see whether, while they utter greetings of peace, they do not carry, wherever they enter, the Knife of Division and the Fire of Dispersion, taking away the son from his father, neighbor from neighbor, the inhabitant from his country, and causing other divorces, horrendous and against every nature and law. Let her see whether, while they call themselves ministers of one who resurrects the dead and heals the infirm, it is they who, worse than all the others whom the earth feeds, cripple the healthy and kill the living, not so much with fire and with the sword as with their pernicious tongues. Let her see what sort of peace and harmony they propose to the wretched peoples, and whether they perhaps want and eagerly desire that all the world agree with and consent to their malicious and most presumptuous ignorance, and approve their wicked conscience, while they want neither to agree with, nor consent to, any law, justice, and doctrine; and let her see whether in all the rest of the world and of the centuries there appear so much discord and dissonance as is evidenced among them.
>
> So among ten thousand such pedants there is not one who has not compiled his own catechism, and who if he has not published it, at least is about to publish that one which approves of no other institution but his own, finding in all the others something to condemn, reprove, and doubt; besides, the majority of them are found in disagreement among themselves, rescinding today what they wrote the day before.
>
> Let her see what success these have, and what customs they inspire and provoke in others in that which appertains to acts of justice and compassion and the conservation and increase of public wealth … let her see whether they are the appropriators of the goods of others or, rather, the bestowers of their own goods; and, finally, let her see

---

49   See Joseph P. Farrell, and Scott D. de Hart, *Yahweh the Two-Faced God: Theology, Terrorism, and Topology* (Las Vegas: Periprometheus Press, 2012), pp. 23–36.

whether those who side with them increase and stabilize public wealth, as their opponents and predecessors used to do, or, rather, together with these, dissipate, dismember, and devour it; and whether, while they belittle good works, they extinguish in people all enthusiasm for the construction of new works and the preservation of the old.[50]

Note Bruno's indirect attack on Calvinism's approval of interest-bearing debt and its relationship to "the public wealth," in itself an attack that would be of great concern to the merchant bankers of Venice and northern Italy. It is but one aspect of the schisms in the social space induced by the alliance between Yahwism and such financial practices, producing, as Imerti observes, "an insecure individual, convinced that only wealth and power can give him a sense of security."[51] For Bruno, championing the individual as a direct manifestation of Deity, a just social order could not come about without converting these desires into temperance and reason, without the expulsion of vices, represented by the "triumphant beast," Jove.[52]

Bruno does not stop merely with attributing mutability to Yahweh, nor with attacks on the growing schisms of the social space it produced in its Protestant forms, but even puts the mutable character of Yahweh into a speech that Yahweh himself delivers to the council of gods, a speech in which Yahweh points out his own moral schizophrenia. "Justice," says Yahweh,

> by which Fate governs the rulers of the world, has completely deprived us of that authority and power which we so badly employed, our ignominies being revealed and laid bare before the eyes of mortals, and made manifest to them; and it causes heaven itself, with such clear evidence, as the stars are clear and evident, to render us testimony of our misdeeds. For there are clearly seen the fruits, the relics, the reports, the rumors, the writings, the histories of our adulteries, incests, fornications, wraths, disdains, rapines, and other iniquities and crimes; and to reward ourselves for our transgressions, we have committed more transgressions, elevating to heaven the triumphs of vice and the seats of wickedness, leaving virtues and Justice banished, and neglected in hell.[53]

Yahweh, in other words, had "for a long time led a life of dissoluteness, devoting

---

50 Bruno, *The Expulsion of the Triumphant Beast* (Second Dialogue, First Part), pp. 150–151.
51 Imerti, "*Lo Spaccio:* Fortunes, Literary Aspects," Gordano Bruno, *The Expulsion of the Triumphant Beast*, p. 25.
52 Ibid., pp. 25–26.
53 Bruno, *The Expulsion of the Triumphant Beast* (First Dialogue, Second Part), pp. 106-107.

himself almost exclusively to amours and to warlike enterprises … "[54] Determined to repent for such behavior, he summons the council of the gods on the Feast of the Gigantomachy[55]—or War of the Giants and Titans in Greek mythology, a point by which Bruno subtly stresses the idea that Yahweh's behavior is no less a moral reflection of human passions and contradictions than that of the myths of the gods of the Greeks.

As such, Bruno speaks in the first part of the second dialogue of *The Expulsion of the Triumphant Beast* of the love "of the Divinity which is above all Joves and all heavens,"[56] indicating that it is Yahweh himself who is the "triumphant beast" to be expelled from society, along with the vices he represents, which are to be expelled within man himself.

To sum up, thus far Bruno has accomplished the following:

1) Critiqued the Yahwist moral contradiction;
2) Exposed it as the basis for (endless) divisions of the social space (in its Protestant and Calvinist form);
3) Noted that, since such mutable behavior is evident, that Yahweh cannot logically represent the divine order of "mutable permanence";
4) Noted that the real origin of various doctrines comes from Egypt, and that therefore,
5) No positive or special revelation is needed, since nature reveals itself to one and all immediately; and thus,
6) Challenged the religious authority of elites based on that revelation, while
7) Championing the idea of man as a "citizen of the world," thus challenging political elites; and finally,
8) Subtly challenged the Calvinist doctrine of debt-interest in the hands of a private monopoly by distinguishing it from "the public wealth," which is, in the final analysis, a not-so-subtle attack on the very idea of private monopoly central banking, that is, upon the banking practices of the northern Italian city-states, Florence and Venice, themselves.

It is little wonder, then, that both Venice and the Vatican determined to end the life of this man, and it is interesting to note that, like the eightfold summary of the implications of Bruno's doctrine above, the final charges brought against him by the Roman Inquisition also numbered eight heresies.

---

54 Imerti, "*Lo Spaccio:* Fortunes, Literary Aspects," *The Expulsion of the Triumphant Beast*, p. 26.
55 Ibid., p. 27.
56 Bruno, op. cit., p. 143.

b. *Yahweh Not the First Cause:*
Man as the Medium and Philosophers' Stone

But the Nolan was just getting started.

In his "Explanatory Epistle" at the beginning of *The Expulsion*, Bruno comments at length on why Yahweh cannot be the First Cause, that is to say the true god, by drawing an astonishingly alchemical conclusion:

> We here, then, have a Jove, not taken as too legitimate and good a vicar or lieutenant of the first principle and universal cause, but well taken as something variable, subject to the Fate of Mutation; he, however, knowing that together in one infinite entity and substance there are infinite and innumerable particular natures (of which he is one individual), which, since they in substance, essence, and nature are one, likewise, by reason of the number through which they pass, incur innumerable vicissitudes and a kind of motion and mutation. Each one of these natures then, and particularly Jove's, finds itself as such an individual, with such a composition, with such accidents and circumstances, having been placed in number, because of differences which arise from contraries, all of which are reduced to one original and first contrary, which is the first principle of all the others, the proximate efficients of every change and vicissitude. Because of this, just as he, from one who at first was not Jove, afterward was made Jove, so he, from one who at present is Jove, finally will be other than Jove.
>
> *He knows that of the eternal corporeal substance (which is not producible* ex nihilo, *nor reducible* ad nihilum, *but rarefiable, condensable, formable, arrangeable, and "fashionable") the composition is dissolved, the complexion is changed, the figure is modified, the being is altered, the fortune is varied, only the elements remaining what they are in substance, that same principle persevering which was always the one material principle, which is the true substance of things, eternal, ingenerable, and incorruptible.*[57]

The alchemical conclusion of the second paragraph in the above quotation is important, for it is clear that Bruno envisions a kind of perpetually transmuting "something" that underlies all existence, and ascribes to it the incorruptibility and indestructibility that alchemists ascribed to the Philosophers' Stone.[58] So a closer look at this unexpected alchemical turn is in order.

---

57   Bruno, "Explanatory Epistle," *The Expulsion of the Triumphant Beast*, p. 75, italicized emphasis added.
58   See Farrell, *The Philosophers' Stone: Alchemy and the Secret Research for Exotic Matter*

This eternal, yet information-creating, transmuting substance or substrate is viewed by Bruno as inhabiting the entire universe, in a fashion analogous to the soul inhabiting the body. "In short," says Arthur D. Imerti, summarizing Bruno's views, "it is, according to the philosopher, the 'substance which is truly man.'"[59] Man, in other words, *is* that eternal, transmutative substance, *is* the Philosophers' Stone, a view which anticipates by almost three hundred and fifty years the debates within modern physics over the Anthropic Cosmological Principle. In this, Bruno is faithfully reflecting the Hermetic doctrine of man as a microcosm or "small universe," and of the universe as a *makanthropos*, or "great man." [60]

But in order to make these parallels with modern scientific views even more compelling, we must now turn our attention to the Nolan's *On Cause, Principle, and Unity*, and his treatise *On Magic*.

2. Cause, Principle, and Unity, and On Magic
a. The Substrate and Magic

Like *The Expulsion of the Triumphant Beast*, Bruno's *On Cause, Principle, and Unity* was written and published in England in 1584, and thus may function as a kind of philosophical commentary on the more popularly-written *Expulsion*. In it Bruno outlines "his vision of an infinite universe in which he sought to re-unify terrestrial physics with celestial physics on the basis of a principle of universal becoming."[61] This principle of universal becoming—or to put it into more modern physics terms, perpetual creation of information—is of course the same philosophical cosmology that underwrote alchemy with its emphasis on the Philosophers' Stone as a transmutative information-creating medium. In Bruno's hands, however, it also functions, as we have seen in our examination of *The Expulsion of the Triumphant Beast*, as the basis for his assault on all revealed, positive religion, i.e., on Judaism and Christianity (and by implication, Islam).

As we saw previously, by equating the physical medium with mankind himself, or rather by understanding it as a kind of "great man" or *makanthropos*, the entire system of theology, and what Bruno understood by the term "God" is completely reoriented. With it the meaning of human life, and

---

(Port Townsend, WA: Feral House, 2009), pp. 63–79.

59   Imerti, "The Heretical Premises of *Lo Spaccio*," *The Expulsion of the Triumphant Beast*, p. 34.

60   See Farrell and de Hart, *Transhumanism: A Grimoire of Alchemical Agendas for the Transformation of Man* (Port Townsend, WA: Feral House, 2012), chapter 1.

61   Alfonso Ingegno, introduction to *Cause, Principle, and Unity and Essays on Magic*, by Giordano Bruno, ed. Richard J. Blackwell and Robert de Lucca (Cambridge: Cambridge University Press, 1998), p. vii.

how we approach God, is also wholly transformed,[62] a transformation that is in *itself* alchemical. Bruno's claims for his magical and hermetic philosophy-religion are thus quite sweeping.

> He claims that this new vision will reconcile us with the divine law which governs nature, and free us from the fear of imaginary divinities, cruel and unfathomable, who look down from heavenly heights, controlling the sublunary world in a mysterious way. Human beings believe that they are enclosed in an inferior world subject to generation and corruption, but this is a simple illusion.[63]

Because this world of becoming is viewed by Bruno as an illusion, one is tempted to see in him a Western manifestation of a Vedic outlook, mediated by the Hermetic, Neoplatonic, and magical tradition in which he, like so many other Italian Renaissance Hermeticists, was formed.

For Bruno, there is but one ultimate ground of being, but this is first differentiated into Pure Act, or God, and pure potency,[64] or eternal matter. We may symbolize this ultimate ground of being, this void which is an absolute No-thing, by the empty hyper-set $\varnothing$. By envisioning this No-thing as having undergone some process of differentiation of circumscription—a process we shall symbolize with the paragraph symbol, ¶, to represent the "writing around" or circumscription ($\pi\epsilon\rho\iota\gamma\rho\alpha\phi\omega$)—we may symbolize what Bruno is getting at by calling God "pure Act" and matter "pure Potency" (leaving for chapter two a fuller exposition of this "topological metaphor of the medium"):

$$\P\varnothing \rightarrow \varnothing_1, \varnothing_2$$

But in our previous expositions of this topological metaphor of the physical medium, we have noted that the two "differentiated nothings" that result from this process, $\varnothing_1$ and $\varnothing_2$, share a common surface, denoted by the partial derivative symbol ∂, thusly:

$$\P\varnothing \rightarrow \varnothing_1, \varnothing_2, \partial\varnothing_{1,2}$$

So what is the common surface between the two "differentiated nothings," or God as Pure Act and matter as pure potency, in Bruno's view?

It was precisely through these two eternal principles, pure Act and pure Potency, that it appeared to Bruno "that man, endowed with a rational soul

---

62 Ibid., p. x.
63 Ibid.
64 See Bruno, "Cause, Principle, and Unity," in ibid., p. 65.

and a spirit to mediate between the soul and his elementary body, could link himself to that privileged cosmic point on the boundary between the sensible and intelligible which would allow him to grasp the archetypal forms, the actual generating models of every sensible reality ... "[65] In other words, *man himself was the boundary condition, the common surface, between the two principles.*

It is this fact that forms the basis for why Bruno believed that man could tap into and direct the operations of nature via a kind of natural magic, *by impressing those operations within the human psyche itself via his art of memory.* In fact, Bruno is very direct in his statement on this account in *Cause, Principle, and Unity*, for he states unequivocally that "we can ... grasp the substratum and principle of natural things," i.e., that eternal No-thing, "in diverse ways."[66] And he is equally explicit about the methods that constitute those "diverse ways," for they include "natural and magical methods, and more ineffectively according to rational and mathematical methods."[67] Indeed, as we shall see, Bruno even envisions a kind of "mathematical magic," similar in nature to the kind of simple topological exposition we have given above of his thought.

The attentive reader will have noted that by distinguishing the initial No-thing or $\varnothing$ into differentiated No-things of Pure Act and Pure Potency—$\varnothing_1$ and $\varnothing_2$ respectively—that Bruno has in fact implied that the initial No-thing, prior to its differentiation, contains those contraries. If he or she noted this, the reader is correct, for in that initial No-thing, all contraries coinhere: "There height is depth, the abyss an inaccessible light, gloom is clarity, great is small, the confused is distinct, discord is amity, the divisible is indivisible, the atom is immensity—and all inversely."[68] And of course, this No-thing is also a "great man," and thus a kind of "masculine androgyny," combining the masculine and feminine.[69] Even being and non-being is not, for Bruno, a *real* distinction, for both coincide in that original undifferentiated No-thing, and thus, the distinction between them is only notional.[70] Similarly, since this No-thing—in all its derivative forms—belongs to the nature of the physical medium itself, *none of the specific information content of any individual form derived from it is ever lost:* "Form," says Bruno, "cannot be annihilated."[71] And again, it is the soul, the boundary condition or common surface between all

---

65 Ingegno, introduction to *Cause, Principle, and Unity and Essays on Magic*, p. xii.
66 Bruno, "Cause, Principle, and Unity," p. 7.
67 Ibid., p. 8.
68 Ibid., pp. 11, 21.
69 Ibid., p. 32. For the reason why this androgyny is considered to be a kind of "masculine androgyny," see Farrell and de Hart, *Transhumanism: A Grimoire of Alchemical Agendas for the Transformation of Man*, ch. 8.
70 Bruno, *Cause, Principle, and Unity*, p. 75.
71 Ibid., p. 45.

manner of differentiated No-things, that *is* the Differentiator, as Bruno notes in a passage citing Empedocles.[72]

b. The Medium, The Metaphor, and the Magician

Indeed, it is this "boundary condition" of the soul that is the basis for the Nolan's philosophy of magic. Anticipating the views of the modern biologist Dr. Rupert Sheldrake, again by hundreds of years, Bruno states that "the soul has an immediate and sudden presence with the most distant things, which are not joined to it by any motion … but rather are directly present in a certain sense."[73] To put it in modern physics terms, for Bruno, the soul, the mind, is a non-local phenomenon.[74] In order to understand what chain of reasoning led him to this conclusion, we need to reprise the logic of his argument thus far in a step-by-step fashion:

1) There is an underlying physical medium or substrate, in which all contraries coincide, that is an absolute unitary No-thing or $\varnothing$;
2) Thus, this No-thing has no location, since space, time, and place are all effects of its *subsequent* differentiations, as specific forms or information content of other forms;
3) Possessing all contraries, this No-thing is thus both impersonal and personal, masculine and feminine, and matter, and mind. We shall have more to say about this point in the next chapter.

It is this third point, a No-thing that is also present in some degree in Everything, that allows for the practice of magic, for the magician is nothing but "a wise man who has the power to act."[75] But this "power to act" is understood by Bruno to exist in three distinct kinds of magic, "the divine, the physical, and the mathematical."[76] But what does he mean by "mathematical magic"?

---

72 Ibid., p. 38.
73 Bruno, "On Magic," in *Cause, Principle, and Unity and Essays on Magic,* p. 113.
74 While the complexity of Dr. Sheldrake's thought on biology and the underlying "morphogenetic field" is far too complex to review here, it may be said that Dr. Sheldrake views the individual material *brain* as a kind of transmitter and receiver of a specific *mind* which is non-local in nature, i.e., not imprisoned inside the brain, but outside it. Dr. Sheldrake argues for this position on the basis of the fact that various animal species, unconnected to each other via time or location, seem to somehow learn from each other over vast distances and time. For example, if a species of monkeys isolated on an island learns a particular thing, the same species isolated on another island seems somehow to learn from the first group, even though there has been no actual physical contact between the members of the two groups.
75 Bruno, "On Magic," in *Cause, Principle, and Unity and Essays on Magic,* p. 107.
76 Ibid.

A hint has already been provided by the topological notations of the metaphor, and indeed, for Bruno, such mathematical magic is expression of all the "derivative and differentiated No-things," and is a kind of "reverse engineering" of the process of derivations from the initial No-thing, or ∅:

> ... (Magicians) take it as axiomatic that, in all the panorama before our eyes, God acts on the gods; the gods act on the celestial or astral bodies, which are divine bodies; these act on the spirits who reside in and control the stars, one of which is the earth; the spirits act on the elements, the elements on the compounds, the compounds on the senses; the senses on the soul, and the soul on the whole animal. This is the descending scale.[77]

Note that "God" here designates the primordial substrate or No-thing, while "gods" would include, as Bruno made clear in the *Expulsion*, those higher mutable forms, including Yahweh, derived from it. Thus, the magician *ascends* back up this "descending scale" and operates on its highest levels, in order to affect the lower ones. Putting it into the terms of the mathematical magic or metaphor, Bruno is suggesting that subsequent derivatives from the initial No-thing can be described with the formal explicitness of mathematics. Thus "mathematical magic" resembles what we would call ceremonial magic, but with a difference. "Here," says Bruno,

> the mathematical type of magic is not defined by the usually mentioned fields of mathematics, i.e., geometry, arithmetic, astronomy, optics, music, etc., but rather by its likeness and relationship to these disciplines. It is similar to geometry in that it uses figures and symbols, to music in its chants, to arithmetic in its numbers and manipulations, to astronomy in its concerns for times and motions, and to optics in making observations. In general, it is similar to mathematics as a whole either because it mediates between divine and natural actions, or because it shares or lacks something of both.[78]

Had Bruno lived in a later time, he would have recognized that what he was calling for was a higher order mathematical language, the language of topology.

However, as we have seen, the Nolan also believed that the physical medium was both matter and mind, and this forms the crucial bridge to what he means by mathematical magic, and to his *ars memoriae* or Art of Memory, for

---

77 Ibid
78 Ibid., p. 108.

"Whoever is aware of this indissoluble continuity of the soul and its necessary connection to a body will possess an important principle both to control natural things and to understand them better."[79] In other words, the higher steps of derivatives, those closest to the initial "No-thing," are present within the mind, within the individual soul, and can be used to *order the mind, the psyche, via archetypal forms, and these in turn can be employed to order the cosmos.*

And with that, we arrive at last at:

c. Bruno's Art of Memory

When the Venetian Inquisition, duly suspicious of Bruno and his Art of Memory, questioned him about that subject, the Nolan gave a somewhat evasive response:

> I gained such a name that the King Henri III summoned me one day and asked me whether the memory which I had and which I taught was a natural memory or obtained by magic art; I proved to him that it was not obtained by magic art but by science. After that I printed a book on memory entitled *De umbris idearum* which I dedicated to His Majesty, whereupon he made me an endowed reader.[80]

Bruno, of course, was not being entirely truthful, since in his world view, as is by now evident, there is little distinction between science and magic.

Indeed, Frances A. Yates is quick to point out that the Venetian Inquisitors

> ... had only to look into the *De umbris idearum* to recognize at once ... that it contained allusions to the magical statues of the *Asclepius* and a list of one hundred and fifty magic images of the stars. Clearly there *was* magic in Bruno's art of memory ... [81]

It should therefore come as no surprise that the Venetian nobleman Mocenigo's denunciation of Bruno to the Inquisition came *after* "he had learned the full 'secrets' of his art of memory."[82] It is thus Bruno's art of memory that stands "at the very centre of the life and death of Bruno,"[83] for it is his art of memory that combines his magical practice, his philosophy, and his program for a

---

79 Ibid., p. 116.
80 *Documenti della vita di G.B.,* ed. V. Spampanato, Florence, 1933, pp. 84–85, cited in Yates, *The Art of Memory, Selected Works of Frances Yates,* Volume III (London: Routledge, 2001), p. 200.
81 Yates, *The Art of Memory, Selected Works of Frances Yates,* Volume III (London: Routledge, 2001), p. 200. The "living statues" of the *Asclepius* were statutes that were brought to life by magic.
82 Ibid., p. 201.
83 Ibid.

Hermetic religious revolution. One might go so far as to say that Bruno's Art of Memory *is* his religious revolution, that it *is* his "mathematical magic."

This system is embodied in a complex construction of magical memory wheels, i.e., circular charts, nested one within the other, full of zodiacal, astrological, and magical symbolisms. By rotating these charts, various combinations of symbols, and hence of magical psychic functions, would be created, which Bruno believed potentially encompassed all the major operations or processes within the universe:

> Did he intend that there would be formed in the memory using these ever-changing combinations of astral images some kind of alchemy of the imagination, a philosopher's stone in the psyche through which every possible arrangement and combination of objects in the lower world—plants, animals, stones—would be perceived and remembered? And that, in the forming and reforming of the inventor's images in accordance with the forming and reforming of the astral images on the central wheel, the whole history of man would be remembered from above, as it were, all his discoveries, thoughts, philosophies, productions?
>
> Such a memory would be the memory of a divine man, of a Magus with divine powers through his imagination harnessed in the workings of the cosmic powers. And such an attempt would rest on the Hermetic assumption that man's (mind) is divine, related in its origin to the star-governors of the world, able both to reflect and to control the universe.[84]

The inmost of these embedded, nested wheels of Bruno's memory system represented the Hermetic divine powers: the celestial motions of the stars, the constellations, and planets. The next wheels, moving outward, represented the mineral, the vegetable, and the animal worlds respectively, an exact duplication of the order of descent in the ancient metaphor, for the highest world is the mineral, the next highest, the vegetable, and the lowest, the animal. Note that this order—mineral to vegetable to animal—is roughly that of modern scientific cosmology, which begins with the creation of the elements, then the emergence of simple life, then plants, and finally animals, thus lending some credence to the idea that the ancient Hermetic cosmology might similarly be a legacy of a very high science from High Antiquity. Consequently, Bruno's memory wheels are meant to represent "all arts and sciences" and, as the wheels are rotated, to represent all possible combinations of those worlds.

---

84 Ibid., p. 224.

Again, had Bruno lived three hundred years later, this system of rotation within rotation within rotation, creating ever varied forms, would have been known as dynamic torsion. Memory is thus a Platonic recollection (αναμνη–σις) of the world of forms, of Plato's "mathematicals"[85] and is thus itself yet another alchemical Philosophers' Stone.

The key to this vast astral memory machine is the inmost wheel, representing the motions of the heavens. Bruno is here reflecting his reliance upon Hermeticism, which betrays its Egyptian origins in its, and his, belief that "man is in his origin divine, and organically related to the star-governors of the world."[86] But there is more to this than meets the eye, for in Bruno's memory wheels,

> ... the images of the stars are intermediaries between the ideas in the super-celestial world and the sub-celestial elemental world. By arranging or manipulating or using the star-images one is manipulating forms which are a stage nearer to reality than the objects in the inferior world, all of which depend on the stellar influences. One can act on the inferior world, *change the stellar influences on it, if one knows how to arrange and manipulate the star-images.* In fact the star-images **are** the 'shadows of ideas,' shadows of reality which are nearer to reality than the physical shadows in the lower world.[87]

The stars, in other words, like man himself, are the boundary conditions, the common surfaces, between two worlds, and as such, there is an intimate relationship between them and man, such that man, by manipulating their forms or images in the psyche, can manipulate their influences in the real world. Again, Bruno is maintaining that there is a direct relationship between the mind and the physical medium.

It is important to pause here, and reflect why this one fact alone would have been perceived as such a threat to the financial and banking powers of Venice, for as I pointed out in the previous book in this series, *Babylon's Banksters: The Alchemy of Deep Physics, High Finance, and Ancient Religion*, the connection between astrology, religion, and private banking is an ancient one, and to some extent, the astrological influence over finance is a well-known "secret."[88] Bruno, by *exposing* the whole alchemical metaphor and alchemical

---

85 For a fuller hermetic and esoteric discussion of this point, see my *Giza Death Star Deployed* (Kempton, IL: Adventures Unlimited Press, 2003), pp. 88–92.

86 Yates, *The Art of Memory*, p. 217.

87 Ibid., p. 216, italicized emphasis added, boldface emphasis in the original.

88 Joseph P. Farrell, *Babylon's Banksters: The Alchemy of Deep Physics, High Finance, and Ancient Religion* (Port Townsend, WA: Feral House, 2010), pp. 77–104, 159–185, 220–225.

magic of the system and making it *public*, thus constituted an implicit threat against the private money power of Venice and the other Italian city-states and their banking dynasties, and to their possible hidden knowledge of financial cycles being coupled to celestial ones. We shall see in greater detail in the next chapter why this is so.

But we *are* able to make some approximation of why Bruno's magical and hermetic revolution was a threat not only to the religious powers of the day, but also to the financial ones, when we realize that his art of memory was nothing but a magical, alchemical operation on the psyche of man himself,[89] for by reproducing "the divine organization in memory" it is possible to access "the powers of the cosmos, which are in man himself."[90] In other words, the fecundity of the metaphor, creating ever more differentiations, is not only a cosmological one, but as we shall discover in the next chapter, a psychic and *financial* one. It is a process of the production of a surplus of information, without debt. Such a "Platonic" view of the endless productivity of the medium could not help but be challenged by Venice, locked as it was into a closed Aristotelian physics and "financial" system, about which we shall have much more to say in a subsequent chapter.

"Here was a man," says Frances Yates, "who would stop at nothing, who would use every magical procedure however dangerous and forbidden, to achieve that organisation of the psyche from above, through contact with the cosmic powers."[91] Those methods of organization, and the very cosmic powers themselves, were the mathematical, topological forms of the constant creation of information via endless "derivatives" and common surfaces from the primordial No-Thing. The astral wheel of Bruno's memory wheels was thus a kind of astral-magical memory machine, and "the master mind who had the sky and all its movements and influences magically imprinted on memory through magic images was indeed in possession of a 'secret' worth knowing!"[92] Indeed, if—as I outlined in *Babylon's Banksters*—the knowledge of financial activity was coordinated to planetary positions, and if, as I averred there, it is a rather carefully guarded secret, then Bruno, on that basis alone, constituted a threat to the powers-that-were in his day.

Indeed, in his book *On Seals*, Bruno described the very *first* seal on his wheel as "the Field."[93] This "field," as Yates notes, "is the memory, or the phantasy, the ample folds of which are to be worked upon by the art of places

---

89 Yates, *The Art of Memory*, pp. 251–252.
90 Ibid., p. 254.
91 Ibid., p. 212.
92 Yates, *The Art of Memory*, p. 215.
93 For further reflections on the physics nature of this ancient metaphor of the Field, see Farrell and de Hart, *Transhumanism*, chapters 1 and 2.

and images."[94] Once again, the memory, like the physical medium, is a "field of potential information," to employ yet another modern physics metaphor that Bruno seems to have anticipated, and one, moreover, with its own Vedic overtones.[95]

In Bruno's hands, this vast system of memory, magic, and philosophical reflection on the meaning and implications of the topological metaphor was transformed into an extraordinary program of a kind of Hermetic ecumenism, by which he hoped to resolve and supplant the divided Christianity of Europe with a new religion based on the reasonable implications of that metaphor. "By using magical or talismanic images as memory-images, the Magus" aspired to a kind of "universal knowledge, and also powers, obtaining through the magical organisation of the imagination a magically powerful personality, tuned in, as it were, to the powers of the cosmos."[96] Like the revisionist Egyptologist Schwaller de Lubicz centuries later, Bruno even recognized that the hieroglyphs of Egypt were deliberately chosen as analogical, archetypal images of operations or functions in the intelligible world of the psyche, and thus, as magical memory talismans.[97]

If all this sounds rather fanciful, from one perspective, it is. But Bruno's basic philosophy is based upon the notion that the individual mind and soul is not a localized phenomenon within the body, and his memory images and the way he used them are anticipations of something very modern, and with a proven— though little understood—track record: remote viewing. Indeed, within the technique of remote viewing, the viewer first clears his mind, then focuses attention on the "target," drawing an initial "squiggle," an *image or ideogram*, which encapsulates all the information that is subsequently to be opened and elaborated upon by the viewer through controlled mental processes. This "squiggle" or ideogram is thus a kind of psychic "zip file."[98] And like Bruno centuries before, the scientists and participants in these remote viewing programs came to the conclusion that the mind, and its memory, were indeed non-local affairs, and that any individual could indeed access the vast sea of "information in the field" that constitutes the substrate to mind and the medium. It constituted— and please note the financial metaphor—a vast *treasury* of information that could be drawn upon by anyone, anytime, anywhere, provided one knew the proper "magical" techniques. Mind and memory were thus, for Bruno, a kind of metaphysical treasury of intellectual

---

94 Ibid., p. 248.
95 See ibid., ch. 2.
96 Yates, *Giordano Bruno and the Hermetic Tradition*, p. 192. See also p. 198.
97 Ibid., p. 263.
98 See, for example, Paul H. Smith, *Reading the Enemy's Mind: Inside Star Gate, America's Psychic Espionage Program* (Tor Books, 2005), pp. 181–182, 193–219.

money, a medium of the exchange of information, accessible to all. As we shall see in the next chapter, this too constituted a threat to the papacy, with its doctrine of the Treasury of Merit.

It was small wonder then that Bruno, having demoted Yahweh to one of many mutable gods, should have caused the ire of the Vatican. And we have provided hints, in this chapter, of why he should have been so anxiously sought by a Venetian nobleman, who, having learned the Nolan's secrets of magical memory, should also have turned him over to the Inquisition. But why would Bruno have been denounced as an atheist in England, and received as the warmest theist in Germany? How does one explain this apparent contradictory assessment of the man and his memory magic? And why would it take a combination of Vatican bishops and Venetian banksters to bring him down?

To answer this, we must go into fuller detail, exploring in the next chapter the relationship of that topological metaphor of the medium to money and politics, and in the subsequent chapters, the rise of merchant banking in the Italian city-states.

⚂ Two ⚂

THE MIND, THE MEDIUM, AND THE MONEY:

The Ancient Alchemical-Topological Metaphor of the Medium and its Physical and Financial Implications

∴

"The Jews answered him, saying, for a good work we stone thee not; but for blasphemy; and because that though being a man, makest thyself God. Jesus answered them, Is it not written in your law, I said, Ye are gods?"
—Gospel of St. John, 10: 33-34, citing Psalm 82:6

"The perfection of all that we see, come from contraries, through contraries, into contraries, to contraries. And where there is contrariety, there is action and reaction, there is motion, there is diversity, there is number, there is order, there are degrees, there is succession, there is vicissitude."
—Giordano Bruno[1]

GIORDANO BRUNO, LIKE MOST Renaissance "humanists," was really a Hermeticist. That is, like fellow philosophers of the Renaissance such as Pico De Mirandola (1463–1494), Tommaso Campanella (1568–1639), and so many others, Bruno was inspired by the appearance in Italy of a body of works purporting to be compositions of the ancient Egyptian philosopher-priest Hermes Trismegistus, or the "Thrice Great Hermes," a body of works known as the *Corpus Hermetica* or the *Corpus Hermeticum*.

How that body of works came to Italy is itself a part of this story, and accordingly, we will spend some time in its telling, rehearsing the efforts of

---

1   Giordano Bruno, *The Expulsion of the Triumphant Beast*, First Dialogue, First Part, p. 91.

scholars from the Renaissance to our own time to pin down its elusive origins. Similarly, we shall also have to examine its presentation of the ancient metaphor for which Bruno gave his life, by way of a wider examination of that metaphor in other cultures, in order to ascertain just how, and why, the Hermetic construction of that Metaphor, and Bruno's adaptation of it, spelled such a threat to the financial and religious powers of Venice and Rome. As such, this will be a somewhat lengthy and technical chapter, but nonetheless an essential one for the understanding of the deep relationships between the Metaphor, the mind, the physical medium, and money.

A cautionary note, however, is in order. In viewing Bruno's martyrdom as being in part the result of the threat that his system posed for Venetian—and indeed all north Italian—merchant banking and finance, we are, of course, departing from standard academic analyses of the motivations of the powers behind his death, which would view such motivations in strictly religious, theological, and political terms. Yet, it seems an obvious though overlooked thing to do, since Venice so profoundly symbolized the rising financial and banking class of the late Renaissance and early modern period. Therefore, though this analysis is speculative, and perhaps even highly so, it is nonetheless long overdue.

A. The Origins of the Corpus Hermeticum
1. The "Author" of the Corpus Hermeticum

The *Hermetica*, or as they are also known, the *Corpus Hermeticum*, are a body of writings in Greek and Latin that purport to be the works of the ancient Egyptian wisdom-god Thoth, or, as he was known to the Greeks, Hermes Trismegistus, the "Thrice Greatest Hermes." In this one fact there lies quite a tale, as we shall discover in this chapter.

The story begins, in fact, with something of a confusion, for when Alexander the Great's armies swept into Egypt and eventually conquered that country, the conquerors quickly deduced that the Egyptians' Thoth was one and the same as their own Hermes, and thus began that merger "of two deities of highly divergent origin"[2] that was to cause such interpretive confusion throughout the ages. The confusion over the authorship of this mysterious body of work is also reflected in its influence on western philosophical history since its first resurgence during the Renaissance. It has been viewed, for example, as a kind of "proto-revelation" given to Egypt that in many respects closely paralleled that of Christianity, particularly in its apparent

---

2   Florian Ebeling, *The Secret History of Hermes Trismegistus: Hermeticism from Ancient to Modern Times*, trans. from the German by David Lorton (Ithaca, NY: Cornell University Press, 2007), p. 3.

endorsement of a doctrine of a Trinity.[3] Similarly, it has been viewed as a banner beneath which philosophical warfare was waged against the constrictions of the Aristotelian theology of the medieval Catholic Church.[4] Bruno, of course, appealed to it in part to champion the Copernican theory, and indeed, Copernicus himself appealed to the *Hermetica* at the beginning of his own treatise outlining his heliocentric theory.[5] It was appealed to, both in order to promote, and to argue against, the Enlightenment.[6] And of course, it was also appealed to for its profound doctrine of the spirit at one and the same time that alchemists invoked it in their quests to confect the Philosophers' Stone.[7]

The Greeks who conquered Egypt had good reason to identify the Egyptian Thoth with their own Hermes, for Thoth was the quintessential "wisdom god," or if one prefers, the god who imparted the high sciences of divination, that is to say, astrology and astronomy, magic, and medicine.[8] Similarly, the Greek Hermes was a wisdom god "who crossed the border between gods and men, between this world and the next"[9] in a manner that recalls how mankind, in Bruno's adaptation of Hermeticism, was viewed as a common surface or boundary condition between the worlds. In a manner recalling Marduk's invisibility suit from the Babylonian epic the *Enuma Elish*, Hermes had a "Hades helmet" that rendered him invisible.[10] And of course, the Greek Hermes was the inventor of oratory and letters. For our purposes, it is also significant that the Greek Hermes was also the patron of trade, finance, and commerce, and thus had a cult among merchants.[11] In the milieu of post-Alexandrian Egypt, then, the two Gods—Thoth and Hermes—became fused, as Alexander's Macedonians and Greeks, sweeping across the ancient world, quickly concluded that the various pantheons of the cultures they conquered were all identical in essence, differing only in their outward cultural form and nomenclature. This led, of course, to a conflation of the functions of the two gods as they amalgamated into the figure of "Hermes Trismegistus," the "Thrice Greatest Hermes."[12] He was the god who lived among men and taught them philosophy and theology, eventually inspiring—so the tradition

---

3   Ibid., p. 2.
4   Ibid.
5   Lynn Picknett and Clive Prince, *The Forbidden Universe: The Occult Origins of Science and the Search for the Mind of God* (New York: Skyhorse Publishing, 2011), pp. 31–32.
6   Ebeling, *The Secret History of Hermes Trismegistus*, p. 2.
7   Ibid.
8   Ibid., p. 4.
9   Ibid., p. 5.
10   For Marduk's invisibility suit, see my *The Giza Death Star Destroyed* (Kempton, IL: Adventures Unlimited Press, 2005), pp. 42–43. For Hermes' Hades Helmet, see Ebeling, *The Secret History of Hermes Trismegistus*, p. 5.
11   Ebeling, *The Secret History of Hermes Trismegistus*, p. 5.
12   Ibid., p. 6.

ran—the philosophers Democritus, Plato, and Pythagoras. In other words, the Hermetic tradition claimed that it was Egypt, and not Greece, that was the origin of philosophy and the basis for science.

It was precisely this conflation that led, very early on, to confusion over the "author" of the *Hermetica*, for as early as the third century B.C. the Egyptian priest Manetho stated that there were in fact *two* Hermes, the ancient one, Thoth himself, who existed prior to the Deluge and who attempted to preserve antediluvian knowledge, and a subsequent Hermes, who, existing after the Flood, translated the works of the first Hermes into Greek.[13] This highlights the problem, for the ancient practice assigned less importance to "authorship" than identifying a series of concepts as belonging to a particular tradition and to its originator. Thus, anonymous authors could compose treatises embodying Hermetic doctrines, and because of this, would attribute "authorship" of such a treatise to "Hermes" as an act of honoring the inspiration behind the treatise. Thus could a body of literature grow and be attributed to "Hermes Trismegistus." With this in mind, we now need to briefly examine the actual composition of the body of works known as the *Hermetica*.

It will have been noted that the claim of Hermeticism goes back to an *antediluvian knowledge*, that is, that the Hermetic texts contained an ancient wisdom, a primordial theology or *prisca theologia*, and this was to play a crucial role in the wide dissemination and influence of the *Hermetica* up until the late Renaissance. For example, Herodotus records that Pythagoras sojourned in Egypt, and, returning to Greece, taught the Greeks philosophy and the mysteries.[14] By the ninth century, the Muslim scholar Albuzar (787–886) noted that the first Hermes, whom the Egyptians identified as Thoth, was the grandson of Adam, and reckoned by the Hebrews to be Enoch, and whom the Muslims, following a tradition in the Koran, took to be the ancient prophet Idris. He, according to Albuzar, erected cities and pyramids in Egypt and warned of the impending Flood, taking the precaution to inscribe all his knowledge on the walls of the temple at Akhmin.[15] Like Manetho, Albuzar maintained that the second Hermes lived after the Flood, and it was he, according to Albuzar, who instructed Pythagoras.[16]

2. The Works in the Corpus Hermeticum

From the foregoing discussion, we may conclude that, without exception, the writings of the *Hermetica* of Hermes Trismegistus are all pseudepigrapha,

---

13   Ibid., p. 7.
14   Ibid., p. 28.
15   Ibid., p. 45.
16   Ibid.

"for their alleged author did not write them."[17] But this also affords us a convenient definition of what *constitutes* the *Corpus Hermeticum*, a definition moreover that is in keeping with ancient conceptions that attribute "authorship" to the assumed origin of the provenance of concepts embodied in a text. Thus, by *Hermetica* we mean simply "all texts that refer explicitly to Hermes Trismegistus as their author" or which "are implicitly ascribed to him."[18] Even the great Neoplatonic philosopher Iamblichus (ca. 245–345) admitted that the Hermetic books were not in fact written by Hermes Trismegistus but were rather "translations from the Egyptian by Greek speaking philosophers"[19] who traced the *origin* of their ideas back to Hermes.[20] As most researchers are also aware, the *Corpus Hermeticum* is divided roughly into two distinct classes of texts, one having to deal with matters of philosophy and cosmology, and the other with "practical" matters concerning magic, astrology, divination, and, of course, the alchemical Philosophers' Stone. We shall in this chapter concentrate almost exclusively on the philosophical texts.

When using this definition, the philosophical component of the *Corpus Hermeticum* may be understood to be a collection of roughly seventeen texts,[21] which were first circulated *as* a collection in the fourteenth century.[22] Most of these texts are titled *Libellus* or *Asclepius*, followed by a number designating the specific treatise in each series. We shall have occasion to examine some of these texts more directly later in this chapter.

3. The Medicis, Ferrara-Florence, and Ficino

While some texts of the *Hermetica* were certainly known to early Church fathers and writers such as Clement of Alexandria (ca. 150–215)—who returned a favorable verdict on them[23]—or Augustine of Hippo (354–430) who did *not*[24]—it was during the Renaissance that they truly exploded into significance, when Western Europe recovered original Greek manuscripts of some of the texts, and in this lies yet another intriguing story.

---

17 Ibid., p. 7.
18 Ibid.
19 Ibid., p. 8.
20 Ibid., p. 9.
21 Walter Scott, trans., *Hermetica: The Ancient Greek and Latin Writings Which Contain Religious or Philosophic Teachings Ascribed to Hermes Trismegistus*, Volume I, *Introduction, Texts and Translations* (Montana: Kessinger Publishing Company, n.d.), p. 17.
22 Ibid. Of course in the modern era further Hermetic texts have been discovered at the Nag Hammadi library and have only relatively recently been translated. As these texts were not known during the Middle Ages or Renaissance, and therefore to Bruno or his accusers, we confine our observations in this chapter to texts that were known during those periods.
23 Ebeling, *The Secret History of Hermes Trismegistus*, pp. 39–40.
24 Ibid., pp. 42–43.

The story begins with a grand event, the reunion Council of Ferrara-Florence, held between 1438 and 1445 to reunify the Greek and Latin churches that had split in 1054.[25] It involves a rather obscure Italian scholar named Ficino, and the very famous Italian banking family he worked for, the Medicis. Florian Ebeling comments on this constellation of relationships, and its significance, as follows:

> A widely believed legend is that Hermeticism, having vanished in the Dark Ages along with the ancient world, remained hidden under the mantle of Christian dogmatism until it was rediscovered in the Renaissance. In 1439 the cover was lifted when Cosimo de Medici relocated the great Council from Ferrara to Florence. *The Greek scholars in attendance, including Bessarion and Plethon, so impressed the Florentine intellectuals, especially Cosimo, with their knowledge of Greek antiquity, that they decided to create a home in Florence for the ancient spirit, particularly Platonism.* Some years later the head of the Medici family chose Marsilio Ficino to render Plato's writings from Greek into Latin. *Then, in 1460 or thereabouts, one of Cosimo's agents sent the texts of the Corpus Hermeticum to Florence.* So while Ficino was still in the process of translating Plato, Cosimo unexpectedly asked him to render the texts of Hermes Trismetistus. Ficino completed the first translation in 1463, a year before Cosimo's death, and with that began the renaissance of Hermeticism, which shaped the intellectual history of the early modern period into the seventeenth century.[26]

Note what we have here:

1) A prominent Florentine banking family—the Medicis—are sponsors of the reunion Council of Ferrara-Florence;
2) Prominent Byzantine humanists, Bessarion and Plethon, are among the Greek delegation in attendance;
3) After the Council, the Medicis somehow acquire the texts of the *Corpus Hermeticum*; and finally,
4) Cosimo de Medici has Ficino immediately drop translation of Plato to concentrate on translating the *Hermetica*.

---

25 The author is well aware that the break between Cardinal Humbert and Patriarch Michael Kerularis in 1054 only finalized an earlier break between Rome and Constantinople that had occurred in 1014.

26 Ebeling, *The Secret History of Hermes Trismegistus,* p. 59, emphasis added.

Why would a banking family such as the Medicis be interested in Platonism, and more importantly, the *Corpus Hermeticum*? And how did these texts *actually* make their way to them?

Once again, we may be looking at the possibility of hidden agendas in play during the episode, for the Byzantine humanists Bessarion and Plethon would likely have had some knowledge of the Hermetic texts, and with the Medicis sponsoring a kind of revival of Plato's academy in Florence, it would have been natural for them to negotiate privately with these humanists for acquisition of the Hermetic texts.[27] As we shall discover in chapter eight, there is other evidence that the West's relationship with the Byzantine Empire was for more than just Christian or political purposes, and there is more evidence that some famous events of history may have been cover stories for the acquisition of hidden or lost knowledge. We shall address the question of why a prominent banking family should have been interested in such texts later in this chapter.

In any case, Ficino's translation activities for the Medicis included important translations of the Neoplatonists Plotinus, Porphyry, and Iamblichus, in addition to the *Hermetica*,[28] and thus played a significant role in launching the Renaissance, as the new philosophical orientation not only challenged the Aristotelianism of the Church, but also provided, as we saw in chapter one, the philosophical basis for the rise of modern science.

In this respect, it is important to understand why Hermeticism so quickly captured the imagination of Renaissance intellectuals and magicians like Bruno. Ficino, in his construction of the genealogy of Hermes Trismegistus, followed the tradition that the individual was a real person, and found so many numerous parallels between Hermes and Moses that the idea could be entertained that the vast body of texts came from ancient times, and that the two figures might be identical.[29] Indeed, in the Renaissance view, Moses was trained in all the arts and sciences of the Egyptians, including alchemy,[30] and thus the ancient texts, including the *Hermetica*, were viewed as encoded information embodying lost high knowledge, the *prisca theologia* of high antiquity.[31] In one text, the *Aurora Philosophorum* or "Dawn of the Philosophers" (1577), the idea was ventured that this knowledge was passed down by Adam's sons, and that it survived the Deluge in Egypt, subsequently being passed by Moses to the ancient Hebrews.[32] Persia and Babylon, likewise, were

---

27 I am grateful to my friend Mr. Daniel A. Jones for pointing out this intriguing possibility.
28 Ebeling, *The Secret History of Hermes Trismegistus*, p. 60.
29 Ibid., p. 63.
30 Ibid., p. 73.
31 Ibid.
32 Ibid., p. 78.

viewed as Hermetic societies founded on the ancient wisdom,[33] and even the Greek mythological figure of Prometheus was understood by Ficino to be a "physicist."[34]

Succinctly put, the widespread tendency of the Renaissance was to take the Hermetic texts at their word, and thus to ascribe the origins of their doctrines to the knowledge and science of High Antiquity. The doctrines consequently spread rapidly.

For example, Giovanni Pico della Mirandola (1463–1494), coming under the protection of Lorenzo de Medici (1449–1492),[35] in 1489 boldly published a series of nine hundred theses, ten of which referred to doctrines gleaned directly from the *Hermetica*. Six of these give strong hints as to why a family heavily engaged in banking activity would seek to extend its protection to the Hermeticist Pico:

1. Wherever there is life, there is soul. Wherever there is soul, there is mind.
2. Everything moved is corporeal, everything moving incorporeal.
3. The soul is in the body, the mind is in the soul, the Word is in the mind, and the Father of these is God.
4. God exists around all and through all things. The mind exists around the soul, the soul around the air, the air around matter.
5. Nothing in the world is devoid of life.
6. Nothing in the universe can suffer death or destruction. Corollary: Life is everywhere, providence is everywhere, immortality is everywhere.[36]

Given this list and its contents, it is easy to see why a powerful banking dynasty like the Medicis would be interested in promoting Hermeticism generally, and protecting Pico particularly. If one pursues the logical implications of these doctrines to their ultimate conclusions, as did Bruno, the necessity for Catholicism, or, for that matter, Protestantism, and their priestly or clerical elites and sacramental systems disappears. It is, in other words, a covert way of challenging the power of the Roman Church, and gaining significant "maneuvering room" for the emerging financial-political classes of northern Italy.

But why, then, would Bruno, clearly an avowed Hermeticist, incur the

---

33   Ibid., p. 79.
34   Ibid., p. 61.
35   Ibid., p. 65.
36   S.A. Farmer, *Syncretism in the West: Pico's 900 Theses (1486)*, Medieval and Renaissance Texts & Studies 167 (Tempe, Arizona: 1998), pp. 340–343, cited in Ebeling, *The Secret History of Hermes Trismegistus*, p. 66.

wrath of the other great banking power of northern Italy: Venice? As we shall see, the answer lies in these very same doctrines. But before we can turn to a consideration of this question, we must first understand why Hermeticism so abruptly declined a few years after Bruno's martyrdom for the system.

4. Isaac Casaubon and the End of Hermes Trismegistus

It was a Franco-Swiss philologist, Isaac de Casaubon (1559–1614), who spelled the end of the *Corpus Hermeticum* as a set of texts purportedly stemming from High Antiquity. Born in Geneva to French Protestant refugees, Casaubon eventually made his way to England, where he published the work that ended the career of Hermeticism, *De Rebus Sacris et Ecclesiasticis*, or "Of Things Holy and Ecclesiastical," in the year of his death, 1614.

Just what did Casaubon do that was so destructive to the claims of the *Hermetica*?

Casaubon began by noting that there were parallelisms between passages of the *Hermetica* and the canonical Gospels of Christianity.

> For example, he compared the passage, "If you do not first hate your body, my son (Tat), you cannot love yourself" … to the passage in John 12:25, "Those who love their life lose it; and those who hate their life in this world will keep it for eternal life."[37]

Additionally, Casaubon observed that the style of the Greek texts was not what one should expect of pre-Christian writers, noting that many words in the Greek *Hermetica* appeared only after the time of Christ.[38] Additionally, Casaubon pointed out that the Platonic influences clearly evident in the texts meant that they could hardly have stemmed from a period earlier than Plato.[39] Hermes Trismegistus was a pseudepigraphal "imposter" who merely stole words of Scripture in order to convince pagans of the truth of Christian doctrine.[40] Furthermore, the fact that no pre-Christian ancient author ever mentioned, or quoted, from the *Hermetica* was another strong argument against its authenticity.[41] The net result of Casaubon's work, in effect, redated the entire *Corpus Hermeticum* to the early centuries of the Christian era.[42]

---

37 Ebeling, *The Secret History of Hermes Trismegistus*, pp. 91–92.
38 Ibid., p. 92.
39 Ibid.
40 Ibid.
41 Picknett and Prince, *The Forbidden Universe*, p. 102.
42 Ibid., p. 175.

With this redating came the shattering of Hermeticism's own "legitimization legends," ushering in the "horrible age" of Hermeticism, as it again went underground in the seventeenth and eighteenth centuries,[43] surviving in the doctrines of secret societies and fraternities. But it was no longer possible to view it as a primeval source of knowledge.[44]

Consequently, it is fair to judge Casaubon's work as signaling not only the end of Hermeticism as a body of knowledge claiming a descent from High Antiquity, but as the watershed work that spelled the end of the Renaissance, since the two were so closely intertwined. Frances A. Yates, once again, squarely addresses this point and all of its implications:

> Some discoveries of basic importance for the history of thought seem to pass relatively unnoticed. No one speaks of the "pre-Casaubon era" or of the "post-Casaubon era" and yet the dating by Isaac Casaubon in 1614 of the Hermetic writings as not the work of a very ancient Egyptian priest but written in post-Christian times, is a watershed separating the Renaissance world from the modern world. It shattered at one blow the build-up of Renaissance Neoplatonism with its basis in the *prisci theologi* of whom Hermes Trismegistus was the chief ... It shattered the position of an extremist Hermeticist, such as Giordano Bruno had been, whose whole platform of a return to a better "Egyptian" pre-Judaic and pre-Christian philosophy and magical religion was exploded by the discovery that the writings of the holy ancient Egyptian must be dated, not only long after Moses but also long after Christ.[45]

But it was not Casaubon, but Bruno and the *Hermetica*, that were to have the last laugh, as we shall now see.

5. Epilogue: Modern Scholarship and the "End" of Isaac Casaubon

In his argument that texts of the *Hermetica* seemed to parallel statements in the canonical Christian Gospels, Casaubon was, of course, arguing for the priority of the latter over the former. But he did not consider the possibility that the Gospels themselves, and in particular that most "Hermetic" of the Gospels, that of John, may have had Hermetic origins and influences, a possibility that modern scholarship has once again opened up.

The problem with Casaubon's analysis, as modern scholarship sees it, is that it makes short shrift of the ancient conception of "authorship," and

---

43 Ebeling, *The Secret History of Hermes Trismegistus*, p. 113.
44 Ibid., p. 114.
45 Frances A. Yates, *Giordano Bruno and the Hermetic Tradition*, p. 398.

indeed, short shrift of the *concepts* embodied in the texts, concepts that do ultimately stem from ancient Egypt. Even Thoth, whom as we saw previously formed the partial basis for the character of Hermes Trismegistus, was revered in Egypt, originally as "twice great," as early as the second millennium B.C.[46] This was quickly expanded to "thrice great," which of course "finally became 'Trismegistus' in the Greek language."[47] And the modern discovery of many Hermetic texts in the Nag Hammadi library in 1945 opened up once again the question of just how much Hermeticism was really Greek, or Egyptian, in origin.[48] In this respect, as Ebeling observes, the mention of Egyptian places and names in the *Hermetica* is "so striking that we cannot dismiss them as mere 'decor,' especially as parallels can be found in ancient Egyptian texts."[49]

Nor is this all.

With the discovery of the Nag Hammadi texts in 1945, with their rich content of Gnostic and Hermetic texts, "the intellectual origins and context of Hermeticism" must be seen "in ever closer relationship to traditional Egyptian thought"[50] according to the modern scholar Garth Fowden. One of the texts of the Nag Hammadi library, *The Ogdoad Reveals the Ennead*, makes it clear that Hermeticism viewed the relationship between the master and the disciple as a component of a long tradition and succession,[51] implying an origin earlier than Casaubon's dating, indeed an origin that ties the concepts to Egypt. It is this idea of a succession, of a *tradition* of concepts, that gave rise to Hermeticism's understanding of its texts as "sacred," but not in the sense of a special revelation.[52] As we have already noted, with this idea of a succession, or tradition, "authorship" to the ancient mind meant primarily the ascription of concepts to their ultimate purported origin, in this case, to Hermes Trismegistus, that is, to ancient Egypt.[53]

The result of all these modern scholarly efforts is that "Egyptian thinking was indisputably a major influence on the *Hermetica*."[54] The mere fact that many texts of the *Hermetica* were written in Greek simply stems from the result of the Greek conquest of Egypt, such that any linkage of them to the Christian texts as Casaubon argued was not direct, but indirect, since both traditions stem from "the same blend of theological and philosophical specu-

---

46 Ebeling, *The Secret History of Hermes Trismegistus*, p. 30.
47 Ibid.
48 Ibid.
49 Ibid.
50 Garth Fowden, *The Egyptian Hermes: A Historical Approach to the Late Pagan Mind* (Princeton University Press, 1993), p. xxiii.
51 Fowden, *The Egyptian Hermes*, p. 157.
52 For this point, see Fowden, op. cit., p. 158.
53 Ibid., p. 1.
54 Picknett and Prince, *The Forbidden Universe*, p. 104.

lation, drawn from various cultures, including the Hellenic, Iranian, Judaic
—and of course, the Egyptian—which were being explored at the time."[55]
The dialogue form of the texts, which superficially resemble the philosophical dialogues of the Greeks, themselves disclose an ultimately Egyptian provenance, for rather than being dialogues between various philosophers, they
are dialogues between master and disciple, as is the case in standard Egyptian
wisdom literature.[56]

The result of these modern findings would have pleased Bruno, and dis-
pleased Casaubon, for

> ... now we're back where we started. As was believed before Casau-
> bon put the feline among the feathered creatures, the Hermetic books
> may have contained traditions, not to say secrets, from the old Egypt,
> the Egypt untainted by the trendy Hellenic glamour of its occupiers.[57]

There is also one final, and very significant, point that indicates an Egyptian
origin of the concepts of the *Hermetica.*

This occurs in the Hermetic text known as the *Asclepius,* and here it is best
to cite Fowden on this point:

> in answer to Aslcepius' enquiry where these gods are at the mo-
> ment, Trismegistus replies (at *Ascl.* 27): 'In a very great city, in the
> mountain of Libya (*in monte Libyco*),' by which is meant the edge of
> the desert plateau to the west of the Nile valley. A subsequent refer-
> ence (*Ascl.* 37) to the temple and tomb of Asclepius (Imhotep) *in
> monte Libyae* establishes that the allusion at *Ascl. 27* is to the ancient
> and holy Memphite necropolis, which lay on the desert *jabal* to the
> west of Memphis itself.[58]

This suggestive coupling of "gods" with "mountains," as readers of my
book *The Cosmic War: Interplanetary Warfare, Modern Physics, and Ancient
Texts* will recognize, resembles the formula "mountains ≈ gods ≈ planets ≈
pyramids," which also occurs in many other ancient texts,[59] and is hardly

55   Ibid., p. 177.
56   Ibid., p. 179.
57   Picknett and Prince, *The Forbidden Universe,* p. 177. For the nature of the Egyptian influence on
     the "technical" *Hermetica,* i.e., on the texts having specifically to do with the mechanics of magic
     and astrology, see Fowden, *The Egyptian Hermes,* p. 68.
58   Fowden, *The Egyptian Hermes,* pp. 40.
59   Joseph P. Farrell, *The Cosmic War: Interplanetary Warfare, Modern Physics, and Ancient Texts*
     (Kempton, IL: Adventures Unlimited Press, 2007), pp. 81–83, 135, 232–233. The association
     between "mountains, music, physics, and the gods" is also found within the Pythagorean-Platon-

Hellenic or Platonic in any sense.

B. The Ancient Topological Metaphor of the Medium

We are now at last in a position to examine the concepts of the *Hermetica* and how they *expressed* the ancient Metaphor of the physical medium directly, and to see why, initially, banking dynasties such as the Medicis would champion Hermeticism, and why, eventually, the banking colossus of Venice would see in a rigorous Hermeticist like Giordano Bruno an explicit threat to its power.

One might say that the essence of Hermeticism is that it brings the process of reasoning by analogy to a very high pitch,[60] indeed, to such a high pitch that it only falls just short of doing so by means of a formal calculus of analogies. To understand why this is so, it is now time to explore the "Ancient Topological Metaphor of the physical Medium" in some depth, a metaphor which we alluded to in the first chapter. While I have written extensively of this metaphor elsewhere, here its implications are reviewed from yet a new perspective, that of finance.

1. Topological Preliminaries

Let us begin with a simple thought experiment from mathematician George Spencer-Brown, and the cryptic remarks that open his masterpiece *Laws of Form*:

> Draw a distinction.
> Call it the first distinction.
> Call the space in which it is drawn the space severed or cloven by the distinction.
> Call the parts of the space shaped by the severance or cleft the sides of the distinction or, alternatively, the spaces, states, or contents distinguished by the distinction.
> Let any mark, token, or sign be taken in any way with or with regard to the distinction as a signal.
> Call the use of any signal its intent.[61]

---

ic tradition. See Joseph P. Farrell, with Scott D. de Hart, *The Grid of the Gods: The Aftermath of the Cosmic War and the Physics of the Pyramid Peoples* (Kempton, IL: Adventures Unlimited Press, 2011), pp. 229–254, and particularly pp. 244–251.

60 For an interesting observation on this point concerning Goethe's Hermeticism as an analogical process, see Ebeling, *The Secret History of Hermes Trismegistus*, p. 129.

61 George Spencer-Brown, *Laws of Form: The New Edition of This Classic with the First-Ever Proof of Riemann's Hypothesis* (Leipzig: Bohmeier Verlag, 1999), p. 3.

Now let us imagine that we envision an indescribable "No-thing," as we envisioned in the first chapter, utterly devoid of any distinguishing features whatsoever, infinitely "extended" in every "direction." We might envision it as the empty space in this box, except of course, our box has no neat lines denoting its "edges":

We have, in other words, an infinitely extended "No-thing" which, as we noted in the first chapter, has a perfect mathematical symbol, the empty hyper-set, symbolized by ∅, to describe it, or as Spencer-Brown calls it, a mark or "signal" of intention.

Now, within this space, we draw the simplest distinction: we *cleave* this space:

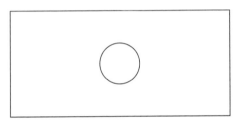

Remembering that our "box" really has no "edges," what we really have is this:

In other words, we have two "spaces," all that inside the circle, and all outside of it, or, in other words, we have what Spencer-Brown calls a "cloven space." Note that the circle is a circumscription, a "writing around" or "peri-graphing," which would be functionally symbolized by the paragraph symbol, ¶, as a symbol of the function of "drawing a distinction" or "cleaving the space."

Note two important things here: (1) we are dealing both with a "space" in the intellectual or conceptual sense, and (2) with a space in the real physics sense, at one and the same time. Additionally, because our original "box" is infinite, the circle or cloven space within it itself has no limits, save that there is a boundary or "side" as Spencer-Brown calls it, a *surface* as the topologists would say, between it and the space outside it. So we may assign symbols or marks to each of the *three* things now distinguished:

1) the space outside the circle we will designate as the "interior" of space 1, with the interior denoted by the topological "o" superscript above the signal or symbol $\varnothing$:

$$\varnothing_1^o$$

2) and similarly the space inside the circle as space 2, another "interior":

$$\varnothing_2^o$$

3) and the common surface of the two, denoted by the partial derivative symbol ∂:

$$\partial\varnothing_{1,2}$$

Notice that what we now have, as a result of performing *one* act of distinction, are three "distinguished nothings." We have created a metaphor of a "one-three," a kind of primordial trinity. Notably, because our original $\varnothing$ was dimensionless or infinite, we cannot assign any real dimensionality to any of the entities thus distinguished either.[62] Notice the all-important point that the signature of $\varnothing$ will always remain in the formal description of the regions or surfaces *no matter how many times the process is repeated. It remains in **all** contexts*, and is thus a basis for analogical connections between all entities subsequently generated by repetitions of this process. One might view this as a kind of "formally explicit calculus of inter-contextual analysis," or, in short, analogical calculus.

Now let us use this very abstract "topological metaphor" to examine its expression in various ancient cultures.

---

62 I presented a very different way of analyzing or "imagining" this primordial cleaving in the appendix to chapter nine in my *Giza Death Star Destroyed*.

2. In the Vedas

Without a doubt, the earliest expression of this metaphor exists in the Vedic traditions of ancient India. For example, in the *Padama Purana*, it says this:

> In the beginning of creation the Great Vishnu, desirous of creating the whole world, became threefold: Creator, Preserver, Destroyer. In order to create this world, the Supreme Spirit produced from the right side of his body himself as Brahma then, in order to preserve the world, he produced from his left side Vishnu; and in order to destroy the world he produced from the middle of his body the eternal Shiva. Some worship Brahma, others Vishnu, other Shiva; but Vishnu, one yet threefold, creates, preserves, and destroys; therefore let the pious make do difference between the three.[63]

There are several significant things going on in this passage.

Firstly, note the metaphor once again is of Vishnu self-differentiating into three entities: Brahma, Vishnu, and Shiva.

But secondly, notice that the *persons* of Vishnu, Brahma, and Shiva are associated *with the functions they perform*

Brahma *creates;*
Vishnu *preserves;* and
Shiva *destroys.*

This association of *persons with functions* is one of the most crucial for our purposes, for it has enormous implications for the development of the doctrine of the corporate person in medieval Western Europe. For example, one finds a distant echo of this association in the "doctrine of appropriations" in the trinitarian formulations of St. Augustine of Hippo. There, the *persons* are once again associated with the *functions* they most "appropriately" perform:

The Father is principally the *Creator;*
The Son is principally the *Redeemer* (note the language of transaction); and
The Holy Spirit is principally the *Sanctifier.*

This association of persons with functions inevitably devolves into the temp-

---

63　W.J. Wilkins, *Hindu Mythology* (New Delhi: Heritage Publishers, 1991), p. 116, citing the *Padma Purana*, cited in Farrell and de Hart, *The Grid of the Gods*, p. 71.

tation to *reduce* persons to functions, or sets of functions, to *define* them as such. This, as we shall see, is precisely the essential step in the elaboration of the doctrine of corporate personhood.

However, there is much more to unpack from this significant passage. Note that Vishnu is also called, at the beginning of this process, the Supreme Spirit, that infinite No-Thing-ness that we have symbolized by the empty hyper-set, $\emptyset$. Once he has self-differentiated, he becomes Brahma, Vishnu, and Shiva, yet by the topological symbolism we have employed to explore the metaphor, at the end of this process we have two interiors, Brahma and Shiva, $\emptyset_1$ and $\emptyset_2$ respectively, joined by a common surface, Vishnu, $\partial\emptyset_{1,2}$. Why is Vishnu the common surface? Because in his *functional description as preserver*, he unites the oppositions of Brahma (creator) and Shiva (destroyer). Thus, something important has happened: Vishnu is revealed as having contained, at the beginning of the process prior to his self-differentiation, all functions. In short, Vishnu symbolizes Bruno's *coincidenta oppositorum*, the coincidence of opposites. Vishnu becomes, as it were, the binding relationship in his person of the other two persons, Brahma and Shiva.

Notice another significant thing that has happened here. At the beginning of this process, it is difficult to state whether Vishnu, as the Supreme Spirit, is a *thing* or a *person*, or to put it in more categorical terms, *nature* or *person*. But at the end of the process, the original $\emptyset$ has differentiated itself *into* persons described or associated with different functions:

$$\emptyset_1 = \text{Brahma}$$
$$\emptyset_2 = \text{Shiva}$$
$$\partial\emptyset_{1,2} = \text{Vishnu}$$

In other words, in the Vedic version of the metaphor, the differentiation *also results in the creation of these categories: nature, functions, and persons*, with the signature of $\emptyset$ that remains in each of the above symbolizations denoting the fact that they all share the same common underlying nature, $\emptyset$. To put this same point somewhat differently, in the initial stage of $\emptyset$ prior to differentiation, one cannot say whether Vishnu, as the Supreme Spirit, is merely a kind of impersonal nature or a person. Indeed, in the unfolding of the metaphor, it is both at the same time. This will have important implications as we shall see. Also bear in mind Vishnu's role here as a common surface or relationship between the other two will be quite crucial when we turn to a consideration of its use as a metaphor of *money*, as we shall see below.[64]

---

64   For a different presentation of this metaphor, see Farrell and de Hart, *The Grid of the Gods*, pp. 70–79. It is to be noted that Shiva also partakes of the characteristics of the *conjunctio oppositorum* in that Shiva is depicted as an androgyne.

a. The Vedic Version of the Metaphor, and Sacrifice

We now approach the Vedic version of this ancient metaphor from a completely different point of view, and in doing so, we also approach the connection of the metaphor to the notions of sacrifice and debt. If one looks at the Vedic version as outlined previously, it is possible to view Vishnu—as the Supreme Spirit who differentiates himself—as *dismembering himself*, that is to say, as "sacrificing" himself in order to bring about creation.[65] As differentiations proceed from Vishnu, Brahma, and Shiva, creating ever more and more gods and differentiations, thus the whole process of continuous differentiation is also the process of continuous dismemberment and sacrifice.

This is, in fact, what one school of Vedic thought did, for it is this sacrifice which is the founding act of creation:

> It is the Sacrifice which is "the center of the Earth," for through the Sacrifice "the gods performed it ... and through it all these powers reach the center ... of heaven where the first performers ... , the gods, are." The different images of perception, either as confused or non-differentiated ... or differentiated ... all end up in the Sacrifice—through decapitation, dismemberment, interaction, or as the sensorium synthesis.[66]

In other words, the metaphor here, as always, has a "both/and" character, being now a metaphor of overflowing fecundity and plenitude, and of the *absence* of debt, and now a metaphor of the *indebtedness of creation* to the "sacrifice" and "dismemberment" which brought it about, leading, as the above quotation illustrates, to two very different ways for the creature to approach the gods, or God, namely, either through the intellectual ascent of the "sensorium synthesis" or through *sacrifice*: "This returning to the original infinite space . . . is no longer the return to inaction, but rather the result of action, an action leading to that illumined instant-moment of light . . . where the 'Father and Mother meet ... '"[67] that is, where the oppositions once again coincide, here, in the coincidence of androgyny.

But Hinduism, during the Brahmist phase, also pursued not only the implication of the principle of *the fecundity of the metaphor* and of a return or union with God or the gods through the intellectual sensorium synthesis,

---

65   Antonio T. de Nicholás, *Meditations through the Rig Veda: Four-Dimensional Man,* New Edition (New York: Authors Choice Press, 2003), p. 147.

66   Ibid., p. 148, citing the *Rig Veda,* 1.164.35 and 1.164.50.

67   de Nicolás, *Meditations through the Rig Veda,* p. 153.

but also construed the metaphor in its sense of the generation of the infinite indebtedness of creation to the gods and their sacrifice. It is quite crucial to note that this notion of sacrifice, of *indebtedness*, does *not* follow logically from the metaphor when understood in its bare, topological nakedness, i.e., when understood in the most sophisticated mathematical fashion, but only does so when the metaphor degenerates from a mathematical expression to a *religious* one. In other words, while there is no *logical* connection between "differentiation" and "sacrifice," the two became equated and identified once the metaphor was stated in religious and metaphysical "financial" language. Once so construed, however, it forms the ultimate basis for the long association of the temples of high finance with the temples of religion, and every effort is bent to prevent the exploration of the metaphor in terms of its inherent principle of fecundity and plenitude.

This is quite the crucial point, for if, as I have argued elsewhere, the societies of the Indus Valley, Egypt, Mesopotamia, China, and so on, are the *legacies* of an ancient Very High Civilization from High Antiquity, possessed of advanced science and technologies, then the degeneration of the metaphor from a topological one to a religio-financial one represents, in one sense, not merely a change in the *terms* by which the metaphor is expressed and symbolized, but a profound misunderstanding of the metaphor in its original mathematical intent. To put it even more succinctly, the likelihood is that the earliest sense of the metaphor was based *solely* on the principle of fecundity and plenitude, not of sacrifice and indebtedness.

This has two implications. As can be seen, the very *nature* of the metaphor is analogical, since the signature of $\varnothing$ remains *across all distinct contexts*. Consequently, one may approach the reascent to "the gods" via the practice of the analogical imagination, and even of sympathetic, or better put, "analogical" magic, to gain influence and power over "the gods," as we saw with Bruno. On the other hand, in the twisted version of the metaphor, one may also seek to gain control or influence over the gods—to "appease" the gods— through the practice of bloody sacrifice. As we shall see when we return to a consideration of the *Hermetic* expression of this metaphor, and to a consideration of Bruno's employment of it, this point has profound implications.

Consequently, the metaphor became *twisted* into a language—and into the actual practice—of sacrifice and indebtedness, and once it did, it began to empower a priestly elite authorized to perform sacrifices, or, alternatively, magical rituals. Significantly, the earliest Vedic literature, dating from 1500 to 1200 BC, "evince a concern with debt—which is treated as synonymous with guilt and sin."[68] For these texts, stemming from the Brahman period, human

---

68   David Graeber, *Debt,* p. 56.

existence "is itself a form of debt."[69] For example, in the *Satapatha Brahmana* 3.6.2.16, this understanding of the metaphor is stated explicitly:

> A man, being born, is a debt; by his own self he is born to Death, and only when he sacrifices does he redeem himself from death.[70]

The consequences of this view are enormous, according to French economic theorist Bruno Théret:

> At the origin of money we have a "relation of representation" of death as an invisible world, before and beyond life—a representation that is the product of the symbolic function proper to the human species and which envisages birth as an original debt incurred by all men, a debt owing to the cosmic powers from which humanity emerged.
>
> Payment of this debt, which can however never be settled on earth—because its full reimbursement is out of reach—takes the form of sacrifices which, by replenishing the credit of the living, make it possible to prolong life and even in certain cases to achieve eternity by joining the Gods. But this initial belief-claim is also associated with the emergence of sovereign powers whose legitimacy resides in their ability to represent the entire original cosmos. And it is these powers that invented money as a means of settling debts—a means whose abstraction makes it possible to resolve the sacrificial paradox by which putting to death becomes the permanent means of protecting life.[71]

But this can only be true, as we have seen, if one misconstrues the metaphor from its deepest mathematical sense—emphasizing the principle of plenitude and the creation of information via ever more differentiations—to the metaphor of indebtedness and sacrifice. For as we shall now discover, the metaphor, in its explicit Hermetic version, contains some very significant clues that suggest profound and deep reasons why Bruno was such a threat to the religious and financial powers of his day.

---

69 Ibid.

70 *Satapatha Brahmana* 3.6.2.16, cited in Graeber, p. 56.

71 Bruno Théret, "The Socio-Cultural Dimensions of the Currency: Implications for the Transition to the Euro," *Journal of Consumer Policy* (1999), pp. 60–61, cited in Graeber, p. 58. In view of the contemporary financial meltdown in Europe, and the pressing of "austerity measures" on the peoples of Europe by private central bankers, it should be asked why a major economic theorist of the euro is writing about the association of religion, sacrifice, and unpayable debt.

3. The Metaphor in the Hermetic Tradition

There is a passage in the *Hermetica* that succinctly embodies the metaphor, and which does so in linguistic terms that unite theology, philosophy, and cosmology very tightly:

> Of what magnitude must be that space in which the Kosmos is moved? And of what nature? Must not that Space be far greater, that it may be able to contain the continuous motion of the Kosmos, and that the thing moved may not be cramped for want of room, and cease to move?—*Ascl.* Great indeed must be that Space, Trismegistus.—*Herm.* And of what nature must it be Aslcepius? Must it not be of opposite nature to Kosmos? And of opposite nature to the body is the incorporeal . . . Space is an object of thought, but not in the same sense that God is, for God is an object of thought primarily to Himself, but Space is an object of thought to us, not to itself.[72]

Notice once again that we have the presence of a primordial Trinity, only this time it is not that of Vishnu, Brahma, and Shiva, nor even the Christian Father, Son, and Holy Spirit, or the Neoplatonic One, Intellect, and World Soul, but God, Space, and Kosmos (Θεος, Τοπος, Κοσμος). Note also that, with the exception of the term God, the other two enumerated entities are *things*, not *persons*.

But like the Vedic version of the metaphor, each of these three entities are distinguished by a dialectic of opposition based on three elemental functions, each of which in turn implies its own functional opposite:

f_1: self-knowledge ⇔ $-f_1$: ignorance
f_2: rest (στασις) ⇔ $-f_2$: motion (κινησις)
f_3: incorporeality ⇔ $-f_3$: corporeality.

As I have pointed out in previous books, each of these three entities—God, Space, and Kosmos—may thus be described as a set of functions or their opposites:[73]

---

72 *Libellus: 1-6b, Hermetica*, trans. Walter Scott, Vol. 1, pp. 135, 137.
73 See Farrell and de Hart, *The Grid of the Gods*, pp. 75–76, and my *The Philosophers' Stone: Alchemy and the Secret Research for Exotic Matter* (Port Townsend: Feral House 2009), pp. 45–46, and *The Giza Death Star Destroyed*, pp. 239–241.

God (θεος) $\{f_1, f_2, f_3\}$	*Kosmos* (Κοσμος) $\{-f_1, -f_2, -f_3\}$	*Space* (Τοπος) $\{-f_1, f_2, f_3\}$
f_1: *knowledge* f_2: *unmoved* f_3: *incorporeal*	$-f_1$: *ignorance* $-f_2$: *in motion* $-f_3$: *corporeal*	$-f_1$: *ignorance* f_2: *unmoved* f_3: *incorporeal*

In this version of the metaphor, it is space that becomes the common surface of the other two entities, since it comprises *functional elements*—as noted in the table above—of the other two entities. So, once again, we have our familiar three topological entities:

1) The "bracketed" region of nothing, or $\varnothing_1$, Hermes' "Kosmos";
2) The *rest* of the nothing, or $\varnothing_2$, Hermes' "God"; and,
3) The "surface" that the two regions share, or $\partial\varnothing_{1,2}$, Hermes' "Space."

But this is not all there is to the Hermetic version of the metaphor.

In the *Libellus II*, there occurs a short, but very significant, exchange between Hermes and his disciple Asclepius:

> *Hermes:* Now what was it that we said of that Space in which the universe is moved? We said, Asclepius, that it is incorporeal.
> *Asclepius:* What then is that incorporeal thing?
> *Hermes:* **It is mind**, entire and wholly self-encompassing, free from the erratic movement of things corporeal … [74]

In other words, in the Hermetic version of the metaphor, there is a direct interface between mind and space, or mind and the physical medium.

But there is more.

The *Hermetica* state quite explicitly that its understanding of the metaphor is almost exclusively based on the principle of fecundity, of plenitude; there is in such passages almost a complete absence of any language of the notion of sacrifice and primordial debt:

> Matter, though it is manifestly ungenerated, yet has in itself from the first the power of generating; *for an original fecundity is inherent in the properties of matter,* which possesses in itself the power of conceiving

---

74 *Libellus II, Hermetica,* trans. Walter Scott, p. 141, boldface emphasis added.

things and giving birth to them. Matter then is generative by itself, without the help of anything else ...

... Thus the space in which is contained the universe with all things that are therein is manifestly ungenerated ... For the existence of all things that are would have been impossible, if space had not existed as an antecedent condition of their being.[75]

Observe that matter and space are both conceived in almost the same terms, as an ingenerate but creative principle, almost as if the *Hermetica* was anticipating modern physics theories of the energy of vacuum space, the zero point energy. And this matter-space, as we have seen, is also *Mind*.

The *Hermetica* make one last association to this complex of Space-Matter-Mind, and that is man himself, who, as the boundary condition or common surface of soul and matter, is the microcosm of the whole creative process at large in the Universe, which as we saw in chapter one is viewed as a "great man," and more besides:

... (That) is why man, unlike all other living creatures upon the earth, is twofold. He is mortal by reason of his body; he is immortal by reason *of the Man of eternal substance.*[76]

Thus this Man of eternal substance is, so to speak, not only the "common surface" of Space-Mind and Matter, but is also a co-creator with God of the entire creation,[77] and thus, *as a co-creator with God, is thus also to some extent God and therefore not indebted to some external power.* For those who are aware of it, this is but another expression of what modern physics would call the Participatory and Final Anthropic Principles, which may be formulated as the following two statements of principle respectively:

1) "Observers are necessary to bring the Universe into being."[78]
2) "Intelligent information-processing must come into existence in the Universe, and, once it comes into existence, it will never die out."[79]

As Bruno put it, Yahweh "represents each one of us." Hermeticism, by embodying the metaphor in metaphysical categories most closely approximating

---

75 *Asclepius II, Hermetica,* trans. Walter Scott, p. 313, emphasis added.
76 *Libellus I, Hermetica,* trans. Walter Scott, p. 123, emphasis added. See also *Asclepius I* in ibid, where it is stated that God "made man as an incorporeal and eternal being ... "
77 Ibid., p. 121.
78 John D. Barrow and Frank J. Tipler, *The Anthropic Cosmological Principle* (Oxford: Oxford University Press, 2009), p. 22.
79 Ibid., p. 23.

the topological properties of the metaphor, thus knows no version of debt or sacrifice—or priestly elites empowered to perform them—and thus, if translated into financial and monetary terms, it is supremely a metaphor of debt-free production and creativity, of debt-free money.

Pause now and consider carefully the threat that Hermeticism posed, particularly in the rigorous form that Bruno advocated it, both to the Papacy and to Venice, that is, to the religious and financial powers:

1) On the one hand, by claiming to stem from Hermes Trismegistus, a provenance more ancient than Moses, the *Hermetica* was also claiming to be based on a hidden tradition of knowledge older than the Yahwist revelation on which the power of the Papacy rested.

2) On the other hand, by framing the metaphor in terms devoid of sacrifice and debt, and in which man himself is both eternal and a co-creator with God, Hermeticism struck another blow at the emerging debt-money banking systems that had begun to emerge in northern Italy in the late Middle Ages, and also at the very sacramental-sacrificial system of the Roman Church.[80]

As the scholar and anthropologist David Graeber puts this point, theories of primordial debt, or versions of the Metaphor which stress the sacrifice-debt interpretation of creation, "always end up becoming ways of justifying—or laying claim to—structures of authority."[81] Indeed, in the primordial topological version, the metaphor is not one of debt at all:

Even if it is possible to imagine ourselves as standing in a position of absolute debt to the cosmos, or to humanity, the next question becomes: Who exactly has a right to speak for the cosmos, or humanity, to tell us how that debt must be repaid?[82]

That, indeed, is the rub, for in the Hermetic version of the Metaphor, every human being is a manifestation of that "eternal Man," and thus no one individual or institution is in a privileged position to speak for it.

---

80   See also Ebeling, *The Secret History of Hermes Trismegistus*, p. 86.
81   Graeber, *Debt*, p. 69.
82   Ibid., p. 68.

4. *Giordano Bruno and Other Renaissance Thinkers*

We return then to a deeper consideration of Giordano Bruno and his place within this vast constellation of concepts of God, space, the medium, Mind, and money. It may safely be said that the problem of the relationship of an infinite space and an infinite deity was the key question engaging not only late medieval theology and philosophy, but science as well.[83] As philosophers and theologians alike noted, both God and Space were described by similar terms, such as "One, Simple, Immobile, Eternal Complete, Independent, Existing in Itself, Subsisting by itself, Incorruptible, Necessary, Immense, Uncreated, Uncircumscribed, Incomprehensible, Omnipresent, Incorporeal, All-penetrating, All-embracing, Being by its Essence, Actual Being, Pure Act," and so on.[84] Because of this fact, many Hermeticists came to identify Space, Mind, and God. The fact that much western medieval theology and philosophy proceeded within a basic Aristotelian framework of a closed system made this question even more crucial once the Platonic, Neoplatonic, and Hermetic traditions reemerged in the fifteenth century.

Bruno, following his own Renaissance version of modern physics' "multi-universe" theories, derived the idea that God created all possible worlds from the Hermetic tradition's interpretation of the principle of plenitude of the Metaphor.[85] Bruno, in short, *rigorously applied* the plenitude principle.[86]

Following the Hermetic principles surveyed above, Bruno deduced fifteen properties of space, among which there is one that is both a direct blow at Aristotle, and at the Church's teaching that God alone is pre-existent and eternal:

> Space is neither a substance nor an accident because things are not made from it nor is it in things. Rather, space is that in which things are locally. It is a nature that exists "before the things located in it, with the things located in it, and after the things located in it."[87]

By removing space from Aristotle's categories of substance and accident,[88] Bruno is in effect saying that space—whose identity with Mind, and with the principle of fecundity we have already noted in the *Hermetica*—is that primordial "No-thing" from which all else is derived.[89]

---

83   Edward Grant, *Much Ado About Nothing: Theories of Space and Vacuum from the Middle Ages to the Scientific Revolution* (Cambridge: Cambridge University Press, 2008), p. 182.

84   Ibid., p. 227.

85   Ibid., p. 184.

86   Ibid., p. 185.

87   Ibid., p. 187, citing Giordano Bruno, *De Immenso* (Wittenberg, 1588).

88   Ibid.

89   Ibid., pp. 188–189.

Moreover, this space is for Bruno's contemporary and compatriot and fellow Hermeticist, Tommaso Campanella (1568–1639), a space with specific mathematical properties (as one would expect from the influence of Hermeticism upon him, and with Hermeticism's strongly topological flavoring of the Metaphor). It was this mathematical property that allowed it to be linked directly to Mind and mental processes.[90] It was, literally, for so many Hermeticists of the day—Campanella included—a potency for the forms of the mind.[91]

For Bruno, Space became a kind of ultra-fine matter from which everything else was created, whereas for another contemporary and Italian Renaissance Hermeticist, Francesco Patrizi (1529–1597), Space was filled with light, thus making it appear that between the two men—Bruno and Patrizi—yet another modern physics conception, the wave-particle duality, was anticipated during the Renaissance.

Given all this, it is clear that Bruno—and others—were explicitly dealing philosophical death-blows to the closed religio-philosophical system of the medieval Church.

C. The Religious, Political, and Financial Implications of the Hermetic Version of the Metaphor

We are at last in a position to understand the full political, religious, and financial ramifications of the metaphor, and in stating these ramifications, one may easily perceive why a rigorous Hermeticist like Bruno posed such a threat to the religious, political, and financial powers of Venice and the Vatican:

1. Political and Religious Implications of the Coincidenta Oppositorum

It has already been noted that Bruno was accused of being an atheist in Britain, but yet was warmly welcomed (for a time at least) in Lutheran Germany, implying his views carried some theistic weight in that country. The reason for this lies in the peculiarity of the Metaphor itself, which, as we have seen, implies the conjunction of opposites,[92] a point which, as we saw in Chapter One, Bruno stated quite clearly. And one of the most difficult aspects of this conjunction is that the Metaphor may be construed in both an atheistic and theistic sense.

---

90 Ibid., p. 195.
91 Ibid., p. 196.
92 See the *Libellus X, Hermetica*, trans. Walter Scott, pp. 193, 195.

a. *The Atheistic and Theistic Interpretations*

If one looks closely at the Metaphor in its topological expression, it constitutes a kind of "First Event" or "Primordial Happening." This implies both an atheistic and theistic understanding:

> … for if analyzed carefully, it is both an act that is supremely irrational and random on the one hand, and supremely rational and non-random on the other, and in that, various people at various times have construed it now in an atheistic sense, and in a theistic sense, and that is the point: it can, and to a certain extent, must be construed as both. Let us look at the "irrational and random" side of it first.
>
> Since it is the First Event, it is *truly random and irrational* as no subsequent events deriving from it can be; there is no prior explanation for it, there are no temporal or physical or metaphysical categories that can be applied to it. In the metaphor of "differentiated nothings deriving from a primordial nothing," one may simply replace the word "nothing" as a translation of $\varnothing$ with the word "randomness," to see that every subsequent event becomes suffused with a condition of randomness, since the signature of that First Randomness, $\varnothing$, always remains as a part of its formal topological description. We are bold to suggest that it is for this precise reason that many scientists and physicists view the world in "atheistic" terms, as a series of random events and the ability of systems to "self-organize," for that is one implication of the metaphor. It is truly random, in other words, because there are no other Events with which it may be compared and statistically modeled; it is the Event from which all events stem.
>
> But, at the same time once again, one cannot imagine any such First Event as occurring without an act of Consciousness to draw the distinction or cleavage in the original space to begin with; one, after all, *imagines* it, and that is a supreme act of a reasoning consciousness. The First Event, therefore, is also a *supremely non-random and rational* event at one and the same time as it is a *supremely random and irrational* one. To put this point in terms that would be understood by an ancient metaphysician, *being is becoming.* This stresses yet another "both/and" characteristic of the Metaphor, for that Primordial Happening stands both inside of, and outside of, time. It stands inside of time in the sense that, in its mathematical description, a change in the state of the system has occurred between $\varnothing$ and the three resultant versions of $\varnothing$ that arise after it is cloven: $\varnothing_A, \varnothing_B,$ and $\partial\varnothing_{A,B}.$ Yet, that first primordial "trinity" stands outside of time as well, since

the First Event leading to their rise occurs *in* the primordial Nothing or ∅ to begin with, and in that ∅, the absence of distinctions means that there is an absence of time.[93]

By adhering rigorously to the Hermetic version of the Metaphor, Bruno was therefore bound to be interpreted by his contemporaries as either a theist, or, as he was accused in England, an atheist, when in fact by the Hermetic nature of the case he was both.

But there is another implication, one that lies hidden in the Hermetic association of God, Space, Mind, and "the eternal Man" acting as the common surface of all, and it is one that hovers over the whole Hermetic enterprise, suffusing itself throughout the implications of Bruno's writings, and that is the *moral* conjunction of the opposites of good and evil. By maintaining that "Yahweh represents or symbolizes us," Bruno was in fact saying that humanity and human intentions, for good or ill, had a kind of group-multiplier effect on the Medium, on God, and hence, that the way to banish ultimate evil was literally by the expulsion of vices—murders, lusts, greed—the expulsion of the Triumphant Beast from within each individual person. That is to say, for the rigorous Hermeticisim of Bruno, the problem of theodicy, of good and evil, lay within man himself, and so did its solution.

b. *The Impersonal and Personal Interpretations*

This same both/and quality of the Metaphor also leads to a second implication, namely, that in its original stage, prior to differentiation, it may be construed in both an *impersonal* and in a *personal* sense, as we saw with the Vedic version. Here too, Bruno criticized the Yahwist revelation, "with its emphasis on a personal God" as destroying "the concept of the Deity as immanent principle, embodied in the natural religion of the Egyptians."[94] Yet, Bruno could, and did, speak of his immanent Deity in very personal terms. Again, in this Bruno was adhering rigorously to the both/and dialectical nature of the Hermetic version of the Metaphor.

2. *Financial Implications*

While we have already noted that the Hermetic version of the Metaphor speaks seldom, if at all, of the idea of sacrifice and debt, but is based on the

---

93   Farrell and de Hart, *Yahweh the Two-Faced God: Theology, Terrorism, and Topology* (Periprometheus Press, 2012), pp. 21–22.

94   Arthur D. Imerti, "The Heretical Premises of *Lo Spaccio*," in Giordano Bruno, *The Expulsion of the Triumphant Beast*, trans. Arthur D. Imerti, p, 42.

pure "topology" of the creation of information in the principle of plenitude, it is worth noting here once again that the *financial* implication is that money becomes a kind of alchemy of creativity and production, a measure of it. Debt, and with it, empowered debt-elites, do not enter the picture. While we must inevitably address this question of money, debt, sacrifice, and the Metaphor in more depth in the coming pages, it is worth noting that, just as in the *Hermetica*, one likewise searches in vain in Bruno for the notion that man owes a debt to God or the universe. Small wonder, then, that Venice was complicit in his holocaust. Bruno's philosophical-Hermetic magic was indeed threatening to the whole financial religious system as it had emerged in the High Middle Ages and existed in his own day.

It is therefore to Venice, the other side in this grisly transaction, that we now turn.

⚞ Three ⚟

SERENISSIMA REPUBLICA, PART ONE:

A Brief History of Shady Dealings
from the Foggy Swamp

∴

"Venice called itself the Serenissima Republica (Serene Republic), but it was no republic in any sense comprehensible to an American … (Its) sinister institutions do provide an unmatched continuity of the most hideous oligarchical rule for fifteen centuries and more … Venice can best be thought of as a kind of conveyor belt, transporting the Babylonian contagions of decadent antiquity smack dab into the world of modern states."
—*Webster Griffin Tarpley*[1]

"The essence of Venice is oligarchism, usury, slavery, and the cult of Aristotle."
—*Webster Griffin Tarpley*[2]

AS THE READER WILL HAVE guessed from reading the above epigraphs, researcher Webster Griffin Tarpley has few, if any, good things to say about the Most Serene Republic of Venice. For him, the Venetian system of merchant banking, mercenary military, and empire is a kind of quintessential icon or font of all the evils associated with predatory banking oligarchies and the inevitable empires and wars they spawn. But surely, one might argue, he is overstating his case? Surely the idea of a fifteen-centuries-long oligarchical

---

1   Webster Griffin Tarpley, "The Venetian Conspiracy," *Against Oligarchy*, http://tarpley.net/online-books/against-oligarchy/the-venetian -conspiracy/, p. 1.
2   Tarpley, "The Role of the Venetian Oligarchy in Reformation, Counter-Reformation, Enlightenment, and the Thirty Years' War," *Against Oligarchy*, http://tarpley.net/online-books/against-oligarchy/the-venetian -conspiracy/, p. 1.

conspiracy going back to Babylon is stretching the case? Surely Tarpley over-stresses the role of Venice and ignores the role of the other Italian city-states and their own merchant bankers? After all, one need only think of Genoa or Padua, and particularly of Florence, home to the Bardi, Peruzzi, and Medici banking and merchant families. More to the point, surely it taxes the imagination to assume that mighty Venice would bend every effort to bring the errant Hermeticist Bruno to heel and ruin?

Well might Tarpley have complained of Venice, however, for understanding the structure of its tangled history in European politics, much less the relationship of that history to its political and financial institutions, and *then* to couple all that to Giordano Bruno, Hermeticism, hidden mathematical metaphors and their scientific and financial implications, and to weave it all into a complex architecture of conspiracy, is like entering a haunted fun house, with progressively more abnormal rooms full of moldering dust and cobwebbed library shelves of ancient manuscripts, where staircases lead to bricked-up walls, where doorways open upon sudden plunges into chasms, where trapdoors are sprung over spiked pits, where the ceilings in rooms are either awkwardly low or dizzyingly high, where one's own voice echoes in the musty gloom.

One might be tempted to argue Tarpley's case on the basis of heraldry, pointing out that Venice's standard was a red flag, boldly emblazoned with a winged lion, and pointing out its similarity to the winged lions of Babylon and Assyria:

The Flag of the Venetian Republic. Note the Babylonian Winged Lion.

Winged Lion with Human Head, from Assyrian King Ashurbanipal's Palace

It is easy to identify the winged lion as the emblem of St. Mark, the patron of Venice, and indeed, the Venetian Republic spared no effort to acquire St. Mark's relics from Alexandria, Egypt.[3] But one can make something of a *deeper* historical case that the connection is indeed Mesopotamian in its ultimate roots, an argument in which the strange appearance of winged Mesopotamian lions on Venice's official flag makes contextual sense.

A. The Euphrates Flowed Into the Tiber: The Pre-History of Venice

I first told this story in the predecessor volume in this series, *Babylon's Banksters: The Alchemy of Deep Physics, High Finance, and Ancient Religion,*[4] but for those who do not know it, a review is in order here.

It all concerns research that was done by an American professor of economic history at Johns Hopkins University at the turn of the last century, a professor named Tenney Frank. His work, *An Economic History of Rome*, as I noted in that book, "became such a standard in the field that it became the basis for entries in the *Cambridge Ancient History* and the *Oxford History of Rome.*"[5] What Professor Frank discovered is as startling now as it was in his own day, for what he found was that "during the period between the Republic

---

3   For this episode, see John Julian Norwich, *A History of Venice* (New York: Vintage Books, 1989), pp. 29-30.

4   Farrell, *Babylon's Banksters,* pp. 267–274.

5   Ibid., p. 268.

and the final emergence of the empire," the population of Roman Italy was by and large "not Roman or Latin at all, but—in a word and without much exaggeration—Babylonian."[6]

Frank came to this conclusion by noting a widespread use of both Greek proper names and surnames on various inscriptions and documents, such that between 300 BC and 300 AD the Roman population underwent such a drastic change that it was no longer Latin at all.[7]

But the Greek names were themselves confusing, for as we saw in the previous chapter, Alexander the Great's conquest of the ancient world from Persia to Egypt spread the Greek language as a *lingua franca* across many diverse cultures.[8] So who were these people?

As I noted in *Babylon's Banksters*, Professor Frank's way of answering this question was "to take Rome's classical authors and satirists at their word, and from this an important and very significant fact emerges."[9] Just what did Rome's classical authors and satirists say? Frank notes that the satirist Juvenal complained "that the Tiber had captured the waters of the Syrian Orantes."[10] He goes on to state:

> When Tacitus informs us that in Nero's day a great many of Rome's senators and knights were descendants of slaves and that the native stock had dwindled to surprisingly small proportions, we are not sure whether we are not to take it as an exaggerated thrust by an indignant Roman of the old stock ... To discover some new light upon these fundamental questions of Roman history, I have tried to gather such fragmentary data as the corpus of inscriptions might afford. The evidence is never decisive in its purport, and it is always, by the very nature of the material, partial in its scope, but at any rate it may help us to interpret our literary sources to some extent. *It has at least convinced me that Juvenal and Tacitus were not exaggerating.* It is probably that when these men wrote a very small percentage of the free plebeians on the streets of Rome could prove unmixed Italian descent. *By far the larger part, perhaps ninety percent, had Oriental blood in their veins.*[11]

---

6   Ibid.
7   Ibid.
8   Ibid., p. 269.
9   Ibid., p. 270.
10   Tenney Frank, *The American Historical Review*, Vol. 21, July 21, 1916, p. 689, cited in Farrell, *Babylon's Banksters*, p. 268.
11   Ibid., pp. 689–690, emphasis added, cited in *Babylon's Banksters*, p. 270.

As I put it in *Babylon's Banksters,*

> One has only to read a bit between the lines to see what Professor
> Frank is implying, for Juvenal, let it be recalled, had complained of
> the Syrian "Orantes" river "flowing into the Tiber," a metaphor for
> people of Chaldean—i.e., *Babylonian*—extraction having "flowed"
> into the bloodlines of the ancient Roman stock: "These dregs call
> themselves Greeks," he complains, "but how small a portion is from
> Greece; the River Orantes has long flowed into the Tiber."
>
> The basic historical outlines are now clear, for as the Roman
> conquests spread into the eastern Mediterranean and eventually
> conquered the old Seleucid Empire—i.e., the portion of Alexander's
> empire based in Mesopotamia with its capital at Babylon - many of
> these people made their way back to the Italian peninsula as slaves,
> and, following the relatively lenient Roman custom of manumission
> of slaves upon the death of their owner, these later became the free-
> men and the backbone of the Roman economy in the very lap of the
> Empire itself.[12]

The implications are enormous, for not only did these slaves bring with them
their religion and culture—a point that would explain the increasing "orien-
talization" of the Roman imperium—but they also brought with them "their
'Babylonian' business and banking practices."[13] And of course, when Attila
the Hun ravaged the peninsula and threatened even Rome itself, many of
these mercantile families fled to northern Italy. It is here that we find, then,
the connection between ancient Babylon's "bullion brokers," Rome, and the
later Italian city-states, with their banking oligarchies.[14]

There is another odd connection between Venice and ancient Mesopotamia. Researcher Webster Griffin Tarpley, whom we cited in the epigraphs to this
chapter, remarked that "Early on, Venice became the location of a Benedictine
monastery on the island of St. George Major. St. George is not a Christian saint,
but rather a disguise for Apollo, Perseus, and Marduk, idols of the oligarchy."[15]
To see the connection to ancient Mesopotamia and Marduk, one need only recall that the iconographic portrayal of St. George is typically that of him seated
on a horse, spearing a fearsome dragon. With that in mind, contemplate the
following images that I first depicted in *Genes, Giants, Monsters, and Men:*

---

12 Farrell, *Babylon's Banksters,* p. 270, citing Juvenal, *Satires,* III:62.
13 Farrell, *Babylon's Banksters,* p. 271.
14 Ibid., p. 272.
15 Tarpley, "Venice's War Against Western Civilization," *Against Oligarchy,* http://tarpley.net/
online-books/against-oligarchy/venices-war-against-western-civilization/, p. 2.

Assyrian King Ashurbanipal Slaying the Lion

Ninurta's Thunderbolt Slaying the Dragon

Tarpley's point is that the symbolism of St. George, like the symbolism of Venice's winged lion, originates with Babylonia.[16]

So with this context in mind, let us look more closely at Venice, for it will afford the port of entry into a wider consideration of Italian banking during the late Middle Ages and Renaissance.

B. A Brief History of Venice

Obviously, any attempt to recount the history of the Most Serene Republic of Venice in a mere chapter is doomed to failure. One can only highlight certain important features of that history for their importance to our story here. Those features have a great deal to do with how hidden knowledge possibly came to late Medieval and Renaissance Italy, and as we shall see, with the execution of Bruno. Additionally, in our cursory exposition of the mechanisms of the Venetian state in this and subsequent chapters, we shall also discover how and why Bruno was such a potential threat to the Venetian state and economy.

1. Foggy Beginnings in a Swamp

Venice's beginnings are literally shrouded in the fog of the swampy lagoon in which the city was raised. During the barbarian invasions of the Western Roman Empire, many families fled northward on the Italian peninsula, some to settle the towns on the lagoon that would eventually become Venice.[17] Why would such an inhospitable swamp be chosen for the base of new settlements? Here Venetian tradition differs somewhat from reality, for the reality is that the lagoon simply afforded a defensive position. The lagoon, in short, was founded on fear.[18] In any case, after Alaric sacked Rome in 410, Venetian tradition held that the city was founded exactly at noon of Friday, March 25, in the year 411.[19]

Without land for agriculture, with no visible means of support, no access to commodities of any kind, this location meant that the population of the lagoon turned almost immediately to the sea, and to trade, as the foundation for their commonwealth.[20] The financial security and empire of Venice that

---

16 As I point out in my *The Cosmic War*, p. 328, the symbolism also has ancient Egyptian roots as well.
17 Tarpley notes: "Already between 300 and 400 AD there are traces of families whose names will later become infamous: Candiano, Faliero, Dandolo. Legend has it that the big influx of refugees came during the raids of Attila the Hun in 452 A.D." (See Tarpley, "The Venetian Conspiracy.")
18 Norwich, *A History of Venice*, p. 4.
19 Ibid., p. 5.
20 Ibid., p. 7.

emerged from this circumstance might be said to be the world's "first virtual economy,"[21] based on a fragile balance of trade in bullion, slaves, both finished and unfinished commodities, and spices. And because of this peculiar circumstance, Venice "lived in perpetual fear that, if its trade routes were severed, the whole magnificent edifice might simply collapse."[22] Thus any threat, whether geopolitical, military, or a cosmological system, was inevitably perceived by the Venetians as a threat to their whole way of life. Indeed, the necessity of trade made Venice, in a certain sense, the first truly modern secular state, with trade conducted on an "amoral" basis free of religious or dogmatic considerations. Venice assumed the right "to buy and sell anything to anyone,"[23] an attitude that would eventually lead to a backlash. Even Byzantium would complain, in the ninth century, of Venice's sale of war materials consisting in part of metals, and slaves for the Cairo Sultan's army.[24]

2. The Influence of the East Roman, or Byzantine, Empire

A visitor to Venice, whether in ancient times or modern ones, would be struck by the fact that, almost entirely alone of all major Western European cities, Venice has a uniquely *Byzantine* look and feel to it, demonstrated especially by the domed church of San Marco with its Greek style-iconography and pageantry. It is this Byzantine influence that forms a second crucial component of the matrix of the Venetian Empire, and its "oriental" or eastward orientation. The Venetian Empire in fact begins with the re-conquest of the Western provinces—the Italian peninsula particularly—under the Roman Emperor in Constantinople, Justinian I (reigned 527–565) and his military genius, the general Belisarius.[25] Venice, for its part, aided in this re-conquest with ships to blockade the provincial capital of Ravenna, and shortly afterward, Venetian ambassadors went to Constantinople and returned with the first of many agreements between Venice and the Empire that accorded the city military protection, but more importantly, unique trading privileges throughout the East Roman Empire.[26] Venice was, as a result of these arrangements, for all intents and purposes an autonomous self-governing city within the Empire, uniquely positioned to dominate the Adriatic Sea and, as will be seen, eventually the rich trading routes flowing from China and India through the Middle East and into the Eastern Mediterranean.

---

21 Roger Crowley, *City of Fortune: How Venice Ruled the Seas* (New York: Random House), p. xxix.
22 Ibid.
23 Ibid., p. 16.
24 Ibid.
25 See Norwich, *A History of Venice*, p. 8.
26 Ibid., p. 9.

Indeed, Venice and Byzantium possessed a "special relationship" rather similar to that of Great Britain and the United States, with the status and power between the two changing, as the Byzantine Empire gradually declined through the centuries, and the power of Venice grew. Yet the special relationship always remained, and was even symbolized when one of the early Doges (Dukes) of Venice was granted "the imperial title of *Hypatos,* or Consul ... "[27] By the early ninth century, Venice, while still nominally a province of the Eastern Empire, was for all intentions and purposes entirely autonomous and self-governing, a situation that the Eastern Empire was fully willing to accept, since Venetian trade benefitted it.

For the Venetians, it was equally important to obtain recognition of that status from the Empire of Charlemagne. This came through the peculiar circumstance of a palace coup in Constantinople, when in 811 the two Empires signed a treaty in which the Eastern Empire recognized the Western Emperor's title, and the Western Empire formally renounced any claims over the territory of Venice.[28] The benefits to Venice of this treaty were huge, for it allowed her to "enjoy all the advantages, partly political but above all cultural and commercial, of being a Byzantine province, without any real diminution of her independence."[29] It was this Byzantine connection, solidified and recognized by both the Holy Roman Empire of the West and the East Roman Empire of Constantinople, which allowed Venice to maintain its Byzantine ties, and thus to remain "virtually untouched by the feudal system"[30] that would emerge in the rest of Medieval Western Europe. This tie was further solidified in a cultural and spiritual fashion when Venetian traders literally stole the body of St. Mark from Muslim Egypt and returned it to Venice, where he would become the patron of the city. Venice was now, literally, an "apostolic see" by dint of its possession of the relics of an early disciple and apostle, a fact that would more often than not induce Venice to a course of spiritual independence in defiance of the papacy, as we shall see.[31]

a. The "Golden Bull" of 1082

The next major step in the "Byzantinization" of Venice and the cementing of the "special relationship" between it and the East Roman Empire came with the so-called Golden Bull of 1082. After the "terrible day" of the Battle of Manzikert on August 26, 1071 and the decisive defeat of the Byzantine

---

27 Ibid., p. 15.
28 Ibid., p. 24.
29 Norwich, *A History of Venice*, p. 24.
30 Ibid., p. 25.
31 Ibid., pp. 29–30.

armies by the Turks, the Empire entered its long and inevitable period of decline, with Venice increasingly being called upon to lend its growing naval and military power to the defense of the Empire and indeed Constantinople itself. In the 1080s, Venice aided Constantinople in its defense against a Norman attempt to take the city. For their reward, the Byzantine Emperor "affixed his golden seal (the *bulla aurea*) to a document that would change the sea forever."[32] In this document, Venice's merchants were granted the right to trade throughout the Empire, exempt from taxation.

> A large number of cities and ports were specified by name: Athens and Salonika, Thebes and Antioch and Ephesus, the islands of Chios and Euboea, key harbors along the coasts of southern Greece such as Modon and Coron—invaluable staging posts for Venetian galleys— but above all, Constantinople itself.
>
> Here, Venice was given a prize site down by the Golden Horn. It included three quays, a church and bakery, shops and warehouses for storing goods. Though nominal subjects of the emperor, the Venetians had effectively acquired their own colony, with all the necessary infrastructure, in the heart of the richest city on earth, under extremely favorable conditions... . Quietly echoing the solemn convoluted lines of the Byzantine decree was the sweetest Greek word a Venetian might ever want to hear: *monopoly.* Venice's jostling rivals in maritime trade—Genoa, Pisa, and Amalfi—were now put at such disadvantage that their presence in Constantinople was almost futile.
>
> The Golden Bull of 1082 was the golden key that opened up the treasure-house of eastern trade for Venice.[33]

The Venetian colony in Constantinople grew to approximately twelve thousand people rather quickly, and, as Roger Crowley notes, slowly, "decade by decade, the trade of Byzantium imperceptibly passed into their hands."[34] Venice had become the lifeblood of the Byzantine Empire. This, more than anything else, was the document that catapulted the Venetian Empire into such economic and military dominance.

---

32 Crowley, *City of Fortune,* p. 16.
33 Ibid., pp. 16–17.
34 Ibid., p. 17.

b. The Fourth Crusade and the Venetian Sacking of Constantinople
(1) The Sequence

This was the circumstance, then, behind what must surely be one of the most despicable betrayals in history: the Venetian role in the Fourth Crusade (1202–1204), and its sacking of Constantinople, in April 1204. This misadventure is one of the most sordid in Western history and some time must be given to it, in order to appreciate Venice's role, and the possible hidden implications that emerge when one adds a bit of speculation into the mixture.

We may begin this part of the story by observing that the East Romans[35] grew to regret the implications of the Golden Bull of 1082, as Venice quickly became synonymous with the trade of the Empire itself. For Venice's part, it was a matter of a careful diplomatic balancing act between the East Romans and the Crusades "on the one hand and their enemy, the Fatimid dynasty in Egypt, on the other."[36] Matters were not helped, at least as far as the East Romans were concerned, by the fact that Venice continued to trade war material, including slaves, with the Fatimids, the mortal enemy of Byzantium. The one weapon that Byzantium did have against the Venetians remained the imperial control of trading privileges. This was exercised against the growing power of Venice in typically byzantine fashion, by "playing the Republic off against its commercial rivals, Pisa and Genoa,"[37] for by 1111 Pisa had been given similar imperial trading privileges in Constantinople, and in 1156, Genoa—Venice's great maritime rival—was granted privileges. Both Pisa and Genoa, like Venice in the original Golden Bull of 1082, were granted "tax breaks, a commercial quarter, and landing stages" in the imperial capital.[38]

Even that was not enough to stem the tide of Venetian influence, so in 1171, Emperor Manuel I "took the whole Venetian population in his empire hostage and detained it for years. The crisis took two decades to resolve and left a bitter legacy of mutual mistrust."[39] Then, in 1198, Pope Innocent III called for a Fourth Crusade against the Islamic world. And with that, the stage was set for the episode that set Byzantium and Venice on a collision course.

When the call was issued, both Genoa and Pisa were at war with each other, leaving Venice alone with the material and maritime resources able to transport an army to the Middle East. The pope, in his call for the Crusade, had forbidden trade with the Islamic world, and this, of course, Venice could

---

35 I refer to them as such because the subjects of the Empire, though predominantly Greeks or Greek-speaking, called themselves "Romans" as a matter of their "national and cultural identity." They did not call themselves "Byzantines" and as such, to do so now would be an inaccuracy.
36 Crowley, *City of Fortune*, p. 17.
37 Ibid., p. 18.
38 Ibid.
39 Ibid., p. 19.

not abide. Hence, it sent legates to Rome to negotiate a lifting of the ban. Innocent III, needing Venetian galleys to transport the Crusade army, relented and lifted the ban, but placed a carefully worded prohibition on any trade of war material to the Middle East.[40]

Against that backdrop, six French knights arrived in Venice during the first week of Lent in 1201 to negotiate with the Venetian Doge, Enrico Dandolo, the terms of Venetian involvement in the Crusade. Dandolo, at this point, was over ninety years old and blind, and hence was known as "the blind Doge."[41]

Here we must digress, for no one knows exactly how Doge Dandolo became blind in the first place. He always maintained that it had occurred from a blow to his head.[42] But others were not so sure that he was even blind at all, for "his eyes were attested to be indeed still bright and clear," and, as we shall see, Dandolo played a crucial role in leading the Venetian military and naval effort.[43] Others merely maintained that the old Doge carefully concealed his blindness. But in any case, Dandolo became symbolic of the cunning and byzantine methods that many came—justifiably—to attribute to the Most Serene Republic.

After carefully scrutinizing the knights' testimonial letters and concluding that they were authentic, the Blind Doge entered formal negotiations, and terms were quickly concluded. The Venetians' terms were generous, and, upon careful examination, duplicitous:

> We will build horse transports to carry 4,500 horses and 9,000 squires; and 4,500 knights and 20,000 foot soldiers will be embarked on ships; and our terms will include provisions for both men and horses for nine months. This is the minimum we will provide, conditional on payment of four marks per horse and two per man. And all the terms we are setting out for you will be valid for a year from the day of departure from the port of Venice to serve God and Christendom, *wherever that may take us.* The sum of money specified above totals 94,000 marks. And we will additionally supply fifty armed galleys, free of charge, for as long as our alliance lasts, with the condition that we receive half of all the conquests that we make, either by way of territory or money, either by land or at sea. Now take counsel

40 Crowley, *City of Fortune*, pp. 21–22.
41 Ibid., pp. 22–23.
42 Ibid., p. 24.
43 Ibid. Norwich maintains that Enrico Dandolo's relative Andrea Dandolo, a historian, stated that Enrico's blindness came from his antagonism of the Roman Emperor Manuel I during the hostage crisis, and that, as was Byzantine legal custom, Dandolo was blinded on the Emperor's command. (See Norwich, *A History of Venice*, p. 124.)

among yourselves as to whether you are willing and able to go ahead with this.[44]

Note the phrase "wherever that may take us," for the knights quickly assented to the terms and the contract of alliance was concluded. Little did they or Pope Innocent III know that the contract's *lack* of any mention of Egypt was deliberate, for as the contract was being sealed, Venetian ambassadors were in Cairo negotiating a trade agreement with the Viceroy of the Sultan, giving him "a categorical assurance that Venice had no intention of being party to any attack on Egyptian territory."[45]

That left a landing in the Eastern Mediterranean town of Acre as the only viable option, unless of course the Venetian objective was something else entirely, as suggested by the phrase "wherever that may take us." As we shall see the events unfold, this may indeed be a possibility, for while Venice was secretly negotiating assurances with Cairo, at the very same time it had negotiated a secret agreement with the knights themselves that the destination was not to be the Holy Land, but Egypt![46] What was the driving force behind this agenda? It is worth noting that a mere one hundred years earlier, the Venetian Doge Ordelafo Falier (1101–1118) "had raised to the status of a patriotic duty the demand that merchant ships returning from the East *should bring back antiquities*, marbles, and carvings for the decoration of the newly rebuilt Church of Saint Mark."[47] This raises the possibility that *other types* of "antiquities" were actually being sought, such as manuscripts and *ancient maps*, an invaluable source of knowledge to a maritime power such as Venice. As we shall see later in this chapter, and again in chapter nine, this possibility becomes more likely as each episode is considered. That Egypt may have been, at least as far as the *knights* were concerned, the ultimate strategic objective made military sense, for Saladin's incomparable victories over the Crusaders in the Holy Land had been accomplished by drawing on the vast resources of Egypt and the supply lines from Alexandria and Cairo.

As far as the knights were concerned, the expedition was to cut the supply lines to the Holy Land, leaving it to fall into the Crusading army's lap like an over-ripened fruit. But note that as far as *Venice* was concerned, the secret double-dealings between the Egyptian Viceroy and the French knights had left them in de facto control of the objectives, since they commanded the fleet that was to transport the army. Venice had created conditions of maximum diplomatic and military flexibility, which could be exploited to the fullest for

---

44 Crowley, *City of Fortune*, pp. 25–26, emphasis added.
45 Norwich, *A History of Venice*, p. 128.
46 Crowley, *City of Fortune*, p. 31.
47 Ibid., p. 30, emphasis added.

its own benefit. Indeed, if they chose to land the expedition in Egypt, Venice stood to gain by stealing the Genoese and Pisan dominance of Egyptian trade out from underneath them.

And already, the Venetians had profited from the contract of alliance, known as the Treaty of Venice, for the knights had to borrow the first two thousand marks of down payment from Venetian banks on the Rialto to finance the expedition.[48]

In any case, the fleet was to be ready to receive the crusading army by Saint John's Day, June 24, in 1202.[49]

All the construction of this vast fleet, with its siege engines, ropes, galleys, sails and so on was conducted in large part by the Venetian State Arsenal, established in 1104 a kind of assembly line of the implements of military and maritime power.[50] When the date for the assembly and embarkation of the army came, the army had barely begun to assemble, stragglers were coming in small numbers, and the size of the army was far below that for which Venice and the knights had contracted. Other portions of the army simply departed for the East from other ports altogether. By July, the army was still assembling in Venice, but its numbers were still far below that for which the alliance was negotiated. As time wore on, tensions increased between the army and the Venetians, and still the army had not sailed for the East.

At this juncture, Dandolo negotiated a deferment of payment from the army in return for the army's embarkation and a share in its conquests.[51] And the very first of these targets that Dandolo had in mind was the port city of Zara, on the Dalmatian coast of the Adriatic, long a thorn in Venice's eyes, and, most importantly, a Christian city. Pope Innocent III, learning of Dandolo's intentions, threatened the entire city of Venice with excommunication should it attack Zara.[52] In spite of this threat, Zara was attacked, and the Lion of St. Mark once again flew from its ramparts, virtually guaranteeing that the entire Adriatic sea was now a Venetian lake. But the papal excommunication came anyway.

By the time Zara had fallen, it was too late to continue the Crusade during winter. And here, once again, fate—and Venetian diplomatic treachery—intervened. On January 1, 1203, King Philip of Swabia sent ambassadors to the Crusading army and to Doge Dandolo, who was travelling with them. Philip's brother-in-law was an East Roman nobleman and prince, Alexius Angelus, whose uncle, Isaac, had been deposed from the imperial throne in

---

48 Ibid., p. 34.
49 Ibid., p. 29.
50 Ibid., pp. 35–36.
51 Ibid., p. 41.
52 Ibid., p. 48.

Constantinople by its current Emperor, Alexius III. It is quite crucial to note that this political backdrop was clearly known to Dandolo and the Venetian diplomatic corps long before the expedition finally set sail. And we have already seen the example of Venetian duplicity with respect to the Egyptians and to the French knights. So this opens up the possibility that the embassy from Philip, and Philip's and Alexius Angelus' intentions, were known prior to the expedition ever having embarked.

The Germans offered the Crusaders and Dandolo a new deal: in return for Venetian support in restoring Alexius' "inheritance," i.e. the imperial throne of Constantinople, Alexius in return would place the entire Eastern Church—which had severed communion with the papacy and the Church of the West some three hundred years before—under Roman obedience. The deal was sweetened with a promise to pay the Venetians 200,000 silver marks, and to pledge East Roman military assistance in Egypt for a year.[53] Dandolo, in the meantime, had completely razed Zara's fortifications and palaces, leaving only the churches standing, "determined that the rebellious city should be incapable of further defiance."[54]

Meanwhile, Pope Innocent III thundered excommunications against the Venetians in the expedition. Unfortunately, his letters were simply suppressed by the bishops accompanying the army,[55] doubtless at the instigation of Dandolo.

In any case, the expedition, now determined upon Constantinople as its target, arrived in the imperial city on June 23, 1203. While the details are too lengthy to go into here,[56] it is to be noted that the Blind Doge himself played a leading role in the assault, thus again raising the question of whether or not he was truly blind. In any case, the result of the sack of Constantinople by the Fourth Crusade was predictable: a Latin hierarchy was installed in Constantinople, and a Latin Emperor, virtually a puppet of Venice, was also installed.

---

53 Ibid., pp. 53–54. It should be noted that Crowley states, "It is uncertain if Dandolo knew in advance of the plan to divert the Crusade to Constantinople; it is likely that he appraised it with a very cool eye," (p. 55). I find this highly unlikely, since a trading empire such as Venice would certainly have had up-to-date intelligence on the circumstances in Egypt, Constantinople, and Germany, with which it carried on a lucrative trade in silver bullion and other commodities. In my opinion Dandolo skillfully negotiated the original contract to allow Venice maximum flexibility, including the ability to change the strategic objectives of the Crusade. He could hardly have been oblivious to the circumstances of Alexius Angelus and his imperial claims, and given the prior bitterness between Byzantium and Venice over the Venetian hostage crisis, and Byzantium's subsequent allowance of rivals Pisa's and Genoa's trading privileges, I think it is highly likely that this entered into Venetian planning from the outset. The attack against Zara would therefore have been an inevitable lure to the Germans to send the embassy, making it appear that Alexius, and not Venice, had initiated the events that followed.

54 Ibid., p. 57.

55 Ibid., p. 56.

56 For the story of the Fourth Crusade's sack of Constantinople, see the eminently readable account in Crowley, pp. 60–92.

But most importantly, Venice obtained a virtual lock-out of rivals Pisa and Genoa from Constantinople and a restoration of its monopoly trading privileges. Given that Venice had negotiated duplicitously both with Egypt and with the French knights, and that the Crusade ended up in Constantinople with Venice exercising a virtual stranglehold on the Empire, it is possible that this was the Blind Doge's intentions from the outset.

But there was something else Venice may have gained, and here the facts end, and the speculations begin …

(2) The Speculation

At one time, at the height of its extent from the Emperors Justinian I to Heraclius I (610–641), the East Roman or Byzantine Empire extended from Tunisia in North Africa through Egypt, into Mesopotamia, Anatolia, the southern Balkan peninsula, and of course Dalmatia, Venezia, and southern Italy. As such, it had access to the rich library resources of Egypt and whatever may have remained of the treasures of the lost library of Alexandria, including whatever was left of ancient high maritime knowledge and maps. As we shall discover in chapter nine, there is indeed evidence that such maritime knowledge, and other lost knowledge from Egypt, made its way into the imperial archives of Constantinople. The imperial city was not only a vast storehouse of actual treasures,[57] but a treasure house of *information.*

Let us now make an assumption, involving the following components:

1) That there was in High Antiquity a maritime knowledge of the world commensurate with our own, and this knowledge included the existence of the North and South American (and Antarctic) continents that were only (re) discovered during the voyages of exploration in the fifteenth century;
2) That this knowledge was retained on charts and maps copied, with varying degrees of accuracy, through the ages;
3) That this knowledge was retained in various repositories, including the Library of Alexandria;
4) That some of this knowledge survived the destructive fires that swept that Library; and finally,
5) That some of this knowledge made it to the imperial archives of the East Roman Empire.

---

57   Ibid., pp. 64, 103.

As will be discovered in chapter nine, there is some evidence that all these components of our assumption are true.

Now we make one final assumption. We assume that at some point Venice may have encountered the existence of this knowledge, perhaps during the sack of Constantinople, and the re-establishment of its monopoly over the trade through the imperial city. What would Venice have *done* with such knowledge, if it had possessed it? I contend that it would have *suppressed* that knowledge, for the simple fact that its geopolitical situation in the northwest of the Adriatic Sea would not have easily allowed it access through the Straits of Gibraltar, having to run the gauntlet of Genoese, Pisan, and later Spanish dominance of the Western Mediterranean. The opening of trade routes that by-passed the Eastern Mediterranean and overland routes to the Far East, much less of a whole "New World," would have been a threat to that trading Empire, one which, given its geopolitical situation, Venice would have wanted to suppress, and to deny to potential competitors. Indeed, as we shall see in chapter nine, there is a Genoese connection to this whole train of thought ... a famous one in fact.

c. The Fall of Constantinople (1453), and the Beginning of the Decline

For the moment, however, we must return to our historical survey.

When Constantinople finally fell to the Turks and Sultan Mehmet II in 1453, it was inevitable that many Greeks fled to the most Byzantine city in the west, bringing what remained of the library and treasures of the Imperial City with them[58] and thus contributing to the rise of the Renaissance in Italy in the fifteenth century. But we are getting ahead of ourselves, for the Fall of Constantinople to the Turks also meant that Venice became the frontline state of Christendom.[59] As the Ottoman Empire slowly and gradually grew in military and naval power, Venice's colonies and bases in the eastern Mediterranean were slowly chipped away, forcing the Republic to turn to an expansion of territory on the Italian mainland. Additionally, the opening of the route to the Far East around the horn of Africa by Portugal, and the discovery of the New World by Genoese adventurer Christopher Columbus for Spain, spelled the end of Venice's virtual trading monopoly with the East. Indeed, Tarpley notes that the discovery of the New World meant that "At the deepest level, some patricians realized that the lagoon city could now be crushed like an egg-shell, and was not a suitable base for world domination. As after 1200 there had been talk of moving the capital, perhaps to Constantinople, so now

---

58 Norwich, *A History of Venice*, p. 340.
59 Crowley, *City of Fortune*, p. 317.

plans began to hatch that would facilitate a metastasis of the Venetian cancer towards the Atlantic world."[60] We shall have more to say about that metastasis later in this and subsequent chapters.

3. The Reformation, Counter-Reformation, and Venice

The other signal event, after the discovery of the New World and its subsequent colonization in the 16th century, was the Protestant Reformation and Catholic Counter-Reformation, and we shall spend some time with it, because again both Venice and Giordano Bruno are curiously implicated.

To see exactly *how* Bruno and Venice are implicated, it is important to recall from the previous chapter that Bruno's basic cosmological view was Hermetic and Neoplatonic in nature, reliant upon that ancient Topological Metaphor of the Medium. The Venetian oligarchy, conversely, pursued a basic cosmological view of materialism, rooted in "the cult of Aristotle."[61] Indeed, as Webster Tarpley notes, the Venetians were the first Western Europeans to read Aristotle in the original Greek.[62]

Into the midst of this ferment stepped Martin Luther, with his doctrine of justification by faith alone. But there is a hidden Venetian influence on Luther. Gasparo Cardinal Contarini—and pay attention to that last name for we will encounter it again in the next chapter in an extraordinary way—wrote an amazing passage during the crisis of the League of Cambrai (which we shall discuss in the next section):

> I began with my whole spirit to turn to this greatest good which I saw, for love of me, on the cross, with his arms open, and his breast opened up right to his heart. This I, the wretch who had not had enough courage for the atonement of my iniquities to leave the world and do penance, turned to him; and since I asked him to let me share in the satisfaction which he, without any sins of his own, had made for us, he was quick to accept me and to cause his Father completely *to cancel the debt I had contracted, which I myself was incapable of satisfying.*[63]

This is, of course, an appeal to the doctrine of Anselm of Canterbury, who formulated the doctrine of the Atonement in terms of *debt*. According to this doctrine, mankind, having offended the infinitely righteous God, owed

---

60 Tarpley, "The Role of the Venetian Oligarchy," pp. 2–3.
61 Ibid., p. 1
62 Ibid.
63 Ibid., p. 4, citing Jedin, "Ein 'Thurmerlebnis' des jungen Contarini," p. 117, and Dermot Fenlon, "Heresy and Obedience in Tridentine Italy," p. 8.

an infinite debt to Him, but since mankind was only finite, could never pay it. Yet, since mankind owed the debt, *only* mankind could be the responsible party for paying it. Anselm's solution to this dilemma was to state that this was the reason for the Incarnation. The infinite Son of God became man, and re-paid the debt, thus "balancing the books," a doctrine that effectively reduced God and salvation to a ledger transaction.[64] It is highly significant that, once again, we find the pattern we first encountered in *Babylon's Banksters* being repeated, namely the association of the temple with finance, this time through the direct importation into religion of the language of debt redemption and sacrifice. And it is equally significant that a Venetian Cardinal is adopting this language. As Tarpley notes, "the parallels to Luther are evident, even though Contarini still allows hope and a little love a role in salvation, in addition to faith. Later, in a letter of 1523, after Contarini had seen Luther, he would go beyond this and wholly embrace the Lutheran position."[65]

Note what we have: a Roman Catholic Cardinal embracing the Lutheran position at the height of the beginning crisis of the Reformation. This is, as we shall see shortly, not the only time Venetian agents are playing both sides of the religious issue, for we find at the same time, in Henry VIII's England, Thomas Cromwell, who had replaced Cardinal Wolsey as Henry's chief advisor. "Cromwell," Tarpley notes, "had reportedly been a mercenary soldier in Italy during the wars of the early 1500s, and, according to (Cardinal) Pole, was at one time the clerk or bookkeeper to a Venetian merchant. One version has Cromwell working for 20 years for a Venetian branch office in Antwerp."[66] Concurrently with all of this, Pope Paul III directed Cardinal Contarini—the same man who had embraced a basically Lutheran position— "to chair a commission that would develop ways to reform the church. Contarini was joined by Caraffa, Sadoletol Pole, Giberti, Cortese of San Giorgio Maggiore,[67] plus prelates from Salerno and Brindisi—an overwhelmingly Venetian commission."[68] In other words, Venice had taken control of the Catholic Counter-Reformation.

One effect of this commission and the Catholic reforming Council of Trent was the creation of the notorious "Index" of books which were prohib-ited for Catholics to read. Needless to say, the "Aristotelian" bias of the Index quickly became evident, as Neoplatonic and *Hermetic* books were prohibited. It was, as Tarpley observed, "a barometer of who now held power in Rome.

---

64 See Farrell and de Hart, *The Grid of the Gods*, pp. 201–217.
65 Tarpley, "The Role of the Venetian Oligarchy," p. 4.
66 Ibid., p. 8.
67 San Giorgio Maggiore, the Benedictine monastery dedicated to St. George in the Venetian lagoon.
68 Ibid., p. 9.

By 1565, there were no fewer than seven Venetian cardinals."[69] Here lies the ultimate reason for Bruno's denunciation by Mocenigo, for Bruno, of course, was a Hermeticist, and his cosmology challenged the whole broadly Aristotelian materialism that Venice was trying to promote.

But Venice's promotion of both sides of the emerging religious conflict during the sixteenth century was deliberate. Then, as now, the world was entering a new era of the rapid dissemination of information made possible by the movable type printing press. Then, as now, this threatened the power of oligarchical financial elites, particularly that of Venice, and then, as now, that elite moved quickly to inject its influence into the information stream by acquiring the technology of the printing press, and quickly promoting the publication of works of *both* sides in the religious controversy. Tarpley observes that "What gave Luther and the rest of the Protestant reformers real clout was a publicity and diffusion of their ideas that owed much to the Venetian publishing establishment. The Venetian presses quickly turned out 40,000 copies of the writings of Luther, Calvin, Melancthon, and the heresiarch Juan Valdes, especially popular in Italy."[70] Meanwhile, the same Gasparo Cardinal Contarini who had adopted the views of Martin Luther had cultivated a relationship with Ignatius Loyola, the founder of the Jesuits, and the implacable *foe* of Protestantism. Contarini intervened directly with the Pope to influence the papal approval of the Jesuit order.[71]

Why would Venice have played both sides against the middle, backing both Protestant and Catholic causes? As noted previously, the discovery of the New World spelled the end of the Venetian trade and financial empire. The strategic decision was therefore taken to quite literally transfer the headquarters of their financial oligarchy northward, under the cover of deliberately exacerbated religious tensions in Europe.[72] It was a goal of Venetian policy to foment a general religious war in Europe to facilitate the transfer of the vast family oligarchical fortunes northward,[73] a war that eventually became the Thirty Years' War (1618–1648).

In the sixteenth century, however, it was Gasparo Cardinal Contarini who was at the center of networks reaching deep into both Catholic and Protestant Europe, dispatching his agent Francesco Zorzi to England to act as Henry VIII's "sex councilor" in his divorce from Catherine of Aragon. Contarini's networks also protected John Calvin and Luther[74] while Contarini was

---

69 Ibid, p. 11.
70 Tarpley, "The Venetian Conspiracy," p. 16.
71 Ibid., p. 17.
72 Tarpley, "The Role of the Venetian Oligarchy," p. 9.
73 Ibid., p. 14.
74 Tarpley, "Venice's War Against Western Civilization," p. 4.

involved in helping to midwife the Jesuit order into existence! Venice's influence in Lutheran Germany and Bohemia, moreover, was the Count Heinrich
Mathias "of Thurn-Valsassina (1567–1633). This is the senior branch of the
family, originally from Venetian territory, which is otherwise known as della
Torre, Torre e Tasso, and later as Thurn und Taxis."[75] This, as we shall discover
in coming chapters, is not the only link between the oligarchical families of
the northern Italian city-states and the prominent and powerful noble houses
of Saxony, Hanover, the Netherlands, and England.

Bruno, of course, stepped into this picture in the late sixteenth century
with his journeys—suspiciously—to Calvin's Geneva, Catholic Paris, Anglican England, and Lutheran Germany, before being tempted back to Venice
by the perfidious Mocenigo. Bruno, in other words, may have been a Venetian
agent in his travels.

There is some evidence for this. Tarpley notes that

> After 1582, the oligarchical Venetian government institutions were
> controlled by the Giovani, a cabal of patricians who had emerged
> from a salon of strategic discussions called Ridotto Morosini. The par-
> ticipants included Morosini, Nicolo Contarini [!], Leonardo Dona,
> Antonio Querini, the Servite monks Paolo Sarpi, and Fulganzio
> Micanzio, Galileo Galilei, and sometimes Griodano Bruno.[76]

Indeed, Tarpley states explicitly that Venice sent Bruno, and later one of his
disciples, to Paris.[77]

Here we must pause and speculate for a moment about why Venice
would then have been so complicit in Bruno's execution. As we have noted in
previous chapters, Bruno's whole cosmological and memory system posed a
threat to the basic worldview of Venice. It was something the Venetian oligarchy both had to control and monopolize for its own purposes, as evident in
Mocenigo's efforts to get Bruno to teach him his memory system, and also to
prevent spreading to its potential rivals.

But now we have an *additional* possible motivation behind Venice's role in
Bruno's arrest, for Bruno, it will be recalled, had disclosed to Zuane Mocenigo
his intentions to found a secret society precisely to spread his Hermetic
teachings, an act that would have spelled an end to the Venetian oligarchy's
attempt to monopolize the system. Additionally, according to Tarpley Bruno
was a part of the strategic discussions in Venice, which may indeed have
disclosed to him Venetian intentions to foment a religious crisis. On that

---

75 Tarpley, "The Role of the Venetian Oligarchy," p. 16.
76 Ibid., p. 11.
77 Tarpley, "Venice's War Against Western Civilization," p. 14.

score alone, Bruno may have been able to expose the whole enterprise, and thus had to be eliminated.

By the end of the sixteenth century and the beginning of the seventeenth, shortly after Bruno's execution by the Inquisition, Venice had done something else, and here we must cite Tarpley extensively:

> Venice was extremely liquid at this time, with about 14 million ducats in coins in reserve around 1600.[78] At about the same time, incredibly, the Venetian regime had completed the process of paying off its entire public debt, leaving the state with no outstanding obligations of any type. This overall highly liquid situation is a sure sign that flights of capital are underway, in the direction of the countries singled out by the Giovani as future partners or victims: France, England, and the Netherlands.
>
> The Genoese around the St. George's Bank received virtually the entire world's circulating gold stocks. The two cities teamed up starting around 1579 at the Piacenza Fair, a prototype of a clearing house for European banks, which soon had a turnover of 20 million ducats a year. This fair was a precursor of the post-Versailles Bank for International Settlements.
>
> In 1603, Venice and Genoa assumed direction of the finances of Stuart England, and imparted their characteristic method into the British East India Company. It is also this tandem that was present at the creation of the great Amsterdam Bank, the financial hinge of the seventeenth century, and of the Dutch East India Company. Venice and Genoa were also the midwives for the great financial power growing up in Geneva, which specialized in controlling the French public debt and in fostering the delphic spirits of the Enlightenment.[79]

In other words, during the religious upheavals of the sixteenth and seventeenth centuries (which Venice certainly helped exacerbate, as we have seen, by publishing Protestant works while simultaneously promoting the creation of the Jesuit order and playing an influential role in the Catholic Counter-Reformation), Venice was quietly creating new corporate fronts in Amsterdam and England, and transferring the bulk of the oligarchical family fortunes from the swamp in the Venetian lagoon to the swamp from which Amsterdam grew.

But why, in addition to its strategic conclusion that the seat of their oligarchical empire had to be transferred northward and toward the Atlantic

---

78 1600, it will be recalled, was the year of Bruno's execution.
79 Tarpley, "The Venetian Conspiracy," p. 18.

because of the discovery of the New World, did Venice sense such urgency to transfer its base of operations? The answer is in what was, literally, the first real general European War, the War of the League of Cambrai ...

4. The War of the League of Cambrai (1508–1516): The True First General European War

By 1508, Europe had had it with the byzantine methods, intrigues, and double dealings of the oligarchs and bankers of the Most Serene Republic of Venice. It was, literally a war of Europe—represented by the Papacy, France, Spain, and the Hapsburg Empire in Austria—against Venice.[80] The formation of this powerful alliance was the brainchild of Julius Cardinal della Rovere, who, upon his election to the Papacy, took the name of Julius II. Julius determined to put an end to Venetian ecclesiastical independence after typically Venetian affronts to the papacy:

> Determined to assert his jurisdiction, 'even'—as he put it—'if it costs me the tiara itself', he now summoned all his diplomatic strength towards his primary objective, not just the isolation but the humiliation of Venice, her deliberate reduction to a level whence she could never recover her old authority and prosperity. A new stream of emissaries was dispatched from Rome—to France and Spain, to (Hapsburg Emperor) Maximilian, to Milan, to Hungary and the Netherlands. All bore the same proposal, for a joint expedition by western Christendom against the Venetian Republic, and the consequent dismemberment of her Empire.[81]

The carrots Pope Julius II dangled in front of each of the European powers were significant. The Austrian Hapsburg Empire would receive Verona, Vicienza, and Padua. France would obtain the territories of Bergamo, Brescia, Crema, Cremona "and all those territories that Venice had acquired by the Treaty of Blois nine years before."[82] In southern Italy, Brindisi and Otranto would go back to the House of Aragon and Hungary would receive the Dalmatian coast. There would, as John Julian Norwich quipped, "Be something for everyone."[83] Julius's geopolitical reasoning was simple: in the south, Spanish Naples was the strong state, in the north, French-dominated Milan.

---

80   For the background to the formation of the League, see Norwich, *A History of Venice*, pp. 390–392.
81   Ibid., p. 394.
82   Ibid.
83   Ibid.

But the rest of Italy had to be dominated by the Papacy, and that meant the Venetian Empire had to go.[84]

We can get a measure of European loss of patience with the Most Serene Republic by a glance at the actual formal preamble to the Treaty that created the League of Cambrai, for it was formed, as it explicitly states,

> … to put an end to the losses, the injuries, the violations, the damages which the Venetians have inflicted, not only on the Apostolic See but on the Holy Roman Empire, on the House of Austria, on the Dukes of Milan, on the Kings of Naples and on divers other princes, occupying and tyrannically usurping their goods, their possessions, their cities and castles, as if they had deliberately conspired to do ill to all around them.
>
> Thus we have found it not only will-advised and honourable, but even necessary, to summon all people to take their just revenge and so to extinguish, like a great fire, the insatiable rapacity of the Venetians and their thirst for power.[85]

France quickly marched, and inflicted a crushing defeat on Venetian forces at the Battle of Agnadello.[86] Emperor Maximilian quickly mobilized a large army and also began to move—slowly— against Venice.

With the advent of the Portuguese trade routes around Africa and the rise of the Ottoman Empire in the Middle East, the impending loss of her territories on the Italian mainland spelled disaster for Venice, for her Empire no longer depended solely on sea trade.[87]

Venice had to fight against overwhelming odds, and though it retook Padua from the French and subsequently successfully defended it against French and Imperial forces,[88] causing the League to begin to unravel with the help of quiet Venetian diplomacy,[89] the mere threat of Maximilian's huge armies pressing from the north, and papal armies from the south, forced Venice to contemplate the unthinkable: an alliance with the Ottoman Empire.[90] "To the princes of the West, had they known of it, such an appeal could only have appeared as an additional proof of Venetian faithlessness."[91] Unfortunately for the Venetians, the Sultan did not respond to their proposals, forcing Venice to accept Pope Julius II's terms:

---

84 Ibid., p. 395.
85 Ibid.
86 Ibid., p. 399.
87 Ibid., pp. 400–401.
88 Ibid., pp. 404–405.
89 Ibid., pp. 405–406.
90 Ibid., p. 407.
91 Ibid.

They proved savage: Venice must subject herself totally to the Holy See. Gone would be her traditional right to appoint bishops and clergy within her boundaries, to try them in her courts, to tax them without papal consent. Gone, too, would be her jurisdiction over subjects of the papal states in her territory. The Pope was to receive full compensation for all his expenses in recovering his territories and for all the revenues which he had lost while those territories were in Venetian hands. The Adriatic Sea was henceforth to be open to all, free of the customs dues which Venice had been accustomed to demand from foreign shipping.[92]

With the Venetian surrender, Julius II had effectively dissolved his own league, viewing France now as the chief enemy in the north, and effectively siding with Venice.[93] The League had for all intents and purposes fallen apart.[94]

Finally, to make a very long and complicated story short, when the Venetian and Papal alliance against the French in northern Italy proved to be of no benefit to Venice when Julius essentially cut them out of any share of the spoils, Venice, in typical fashion, changed sides once again and allied with France.[95] Julius' treachery was not helped by his threat against Venice to revive the League of Cambrai.

> Thus, in scarcely more than four years, the three principal protagonists in the war of the League of Cambrai had gone through every possible permutation in the pattern of alliances. First France and the Papacy were allied against Venice, then Venice and the Papacy ranged themselves against France; now Venice and France combined against the Papacy—and indeed, all comers.[96]

One sees here the Venetian behavior and *Realpolitik* that had led to the formation of the League in the first place, with the city-state performing classic balance-of-power diplomacy and playing its chief rivals off against each other. But for Venice and its financial oligarchs, the lessons of the League, and the discovery of the New World shortly before, were clear: the oligarchs had to move headquarters.

---

92 Ibid., p. 408.
93 Ibid., p. 409.
94 Ibid., p. 414.
95 Ibid, p. 425.
96 Ibid., pp. 425–426.

5. The End of the Most Serene Republic:
Napoleon Bonaparte and His Peculiar Demands

The end of the Most Serene Republic of Venice came, of course, from revolutionary France, and a general named Napoleon Bonaparte. Since the beginning of the French Revolution, Venetian intelligence had been warning the Republic of the danger that the revolutionaries posed,[97] in their stated objective to export the revolution to all of Europe. Venice was a particular target because, as we shall discover in the next chapter, her constitution, while republican, was hardly the embodiment of the egalitarian principles of the French Revolution. Quite the contrary, it was an elitist constitution,[98] a republic by the oligarchy and for the oligarchy. By the time of Napoleon's northern Italian campaign against Austria and the arrival of French armies on Venice's doorstep, the rot had long set in, and the real financial power had long since been transferred northward.

Bonaparte's demands, as the French ships began to unload artillery on the outer islands of the lagoon, say it all: the oligarchy must dissolve the Republic and abdicate, replacing the constitution with a democracy.[99] Napoleon also demanded, "The credit of the mint and the national bank (were) to be guaranteed by the state."[100] In effect, Bonaparte had said that the oligarchy must abdicate not only their political power, but their financial monopoly over the credit and currency of the Venetian state.

But as we have seen, almost two centuries before the arrival of Napoleon the oligarchs had liquidated the public debt and assembled a huge reserve of liquid capital for their flight capital program northwards, a long-range strategic consideration that in its outlines resembles the similar flight capital plan of the Nazis toward the end of World War II. By the time Napoleon forced the dissolution of the Republic, the spoils had fled.

But what was the secret of Venetian oligarchical longevity? Indeed, who *were* the oligarchs? This is where the story gets even darker …

---

97 Ibid., p. 606.
98 Ibid.
99 Ibid., p. 627.
100 Ibid., p. 630.

⚜ Four ⚜

SERENISSIMA REPUBLICA, PART TWO:

The Venetian Oligarchy: Its Methods, Agendas, Tactics, and Obsessions

∴

"If oligarchical methods are allowed to dominate human affairs, they always create a breakdown crisis of civilization, with economic depression, war, famine, plague, and pestilence. Examples of this are the fourteenth century Black Plague crisis and the Thirty Years War (1618–1648), both of which were created by Venetian intelligence."
—*Webster Griffin Tarpley*[1]

IF ONE LOOKS at a list of the Doges, or Dukes, of Venice, certain features begin to emerge. Consider the following partial and very incomplete list:

Domenico Contarini 1043–1071
Vitale Falier 1084–1096
Vitale Michiel I 1096–1101
Ordelafo Falier 1101–1118
Domenico Morosini 1148–1156
Enrico Dandolo 1191–1205
Marin Morosini 1249–1253
Acopo Contarini 1275–1280
Giovanni Dandolo 1280–1289

---

1   Webster Griffin Tarpley, "Venice's War Against Western Civilization," *Against Oligarchy,* http://tarpley.net/online-books/against-oligarchy /venices-war-against-western-civilization, p. 1.

Pietro Gradenigo 1289–1311
Francesco Dandolo 1329–1339
Bartolomeo Gradenigo 1339–1342
Andrea Dandolo 1343–1354
Marin Falier 1354–1355
Viocanni Gradenigo 1355–1356
Marco Corner 1365–1368
Andrea Contarini 1368–1382
Michele Morosini 1382
Tommaso Mocenigo 1414–1423
Pietro Mocenigo 1474–1476
Giovanni Mocenigo 1478–1485
Marco Barbarigo 1485–1486
Agostino Barbarigo 1486–1501
Leonadro Loredan 1501–1521
Antonio Grimani 1521–1523
Francesco Venier 1554–1556
Lorenzo Priuli 1556–1559
Girolamo Priuli 1559–1567
Pietro Loredan 1567–1570
Alvise Mocenigo I 1570–1577
Sebastiano Venier 1577–1578
Marino Grimani 1595–1605
Antonio Priuli 1618–1623
Francesco Contarini 1623–1624
Nicolo Contarini 1630–1631
Carlo Contarini 1655–1656
Domenico Contarini 1659–1675
Alivese Contarini 1676–1684
Francesco Morosini 1688–1694
Alvise Mocenigo II 1700–1709
Alvise Mocenigo III 1722–1732
Pietro Grimani 1741–1752
Francesco Loredan 1752–1761
Alvise Mocenigo IV 1763–1778[2]

Note the recurrence of several family names (and these are but a few)—the Contarinis, the Priulis, the Loredans, the *Mocenigos*. In other words,

---

2   Norwich, *A History of Venice*, pp. 641–642.

Venice is in the hands of an oligarchy.[3] Zuane Mocenigo, the man who turned Giordano Bruno over to the Venetian Inquisition after the latter refused to impart his secrets of memory, belonged to one of these families, the Mocenigos. The oligarchy, in other words, was possibly after the secrets of *power* of the Metaphor, and it is easy to see why. Such memory secrets would allow the banking-oligarchy to keep books literally in their heads—secret books perhaps—while maintaining the public ledgers for government inspection. Even if this were not the case, such memory abilities would give any banking family an immense advantage over its rivals. Indeed, as we shall discover later, keeping "secret account books" was a hallmark of the north Italian city-state oligarchies.

Something else needs to be pointed out, and that is the tremendous continuity of these families over a large span of time. When placed into the wider context of the migrations of those families northward after the fall of the Western Roman Empire, a picture emerges that allows one to speculate. In *Babylon's Banksters* I pointed out the deep connection between the ancient temple, astrology and astronomy, and the bullion brokers and banking classes of ancient times.[4] We now make two assumptions:

1) That the continuity of oligarchical families represented in the list of the Doges of Venice represents a *much deeper* continuity of those families stretching back to Mesopotamia; and,

2) That this continuity in turn also *continued the possible hidden knowledge of the connection of economic cycles with the astronomical-astrological knowledge of the ancient temples,* albeit in probably weakened form.

When these assumptions are made, it becomes much easier to see why Bruno would have represented a threat to the Venetian banking oligarchies, for he was literally exposing secrets that they would not wish to see exposed. Additionally, given Bruno's legendary memory prowess, it may have been evident to those oligarchical families that their own knowledge or systems were incomplete, and hence his secrets had to be pried from him, which would explain the Mocenigo family's interest. It would also explain why Mocenigo, in his testimony to the Inquisition, also mentioned that Bruno had talked about founding a secret society, for it would be in their interest not to see such knowledge spread in an underground stream, beyond their control.

---

3   Ibid., p. 66.
4   Farrell, *Babylon's Banksters*, pp. 159-184.

A. The "Structure" and Methods of the Venetian Republic:
The Major Families, Players, and Implications

1. The Methods of Empire

In the previous chapter's brief summary of Venetian history, we noted several byzantine methods that Venice employed to maintain the power and position of its oligarchical ruling elite families:

1) *The use of balance-of-power diplomacy,* playing off powerful rivals against each other through the fomenting of endless conflict which benefitted Venetian traders. For example, the sale of war material and slaves to the ostensible enemies of Christendom, the Fatimid Muslims and Ottoman Turks,[5] while simultaneously cultivating alliances and trading privileges with Byzantium, or, alternatively, in its shifting alliances during the crisis of the War of the League of Cambrai;

2) *The exacerbation of the Protestant-Catholic religious divisions of Europe during the Reformation, chiefly by the acquisition of the new technology of the printing press,* which was used to disseminate both Catholic and Protestant religious writings;

3) *The possible recruitment of Hermeticists* such as Giordano Bruno to learn the secrets of Hermetic arts, to spread Venetian influence through the same, and to suppress their wider public dissemination;

4) *The possible suppression of hidden knowledge* of the New World gained from archives in Constantinople, which knowledge would have ended the Venetian oligarchy's power;

5) *The willingness to transfer the seat of oligarchical power to other centers as the situation demanded,* such as the consideration, at one point, to transfer the capital to Constantinople, and later, after the discovery of the New World, to bases on the Atlantic coast allowing it access to the new global trade;

6) *The creation of **naval and military bases**, rather than colonies per se, to protect Venetian trade and allow the swift projection of military force when necessity occasioned it;*[6]

---

5   See Crowley, *City of Fortune: How Venice Ruled the Seas,* p. 162

6   Crowley, *City of Fortune,* p. 118. Crowley aptly writes, "Venice came in time to call its overseas empire the Stato da Mar, the 'Territory of the Sea.' With two exceptions, it never comprised the occupation of substantial blocks of land—the population of Venice was far too small for that—rather it was a loose network of ports and bases, similar in structure to the way stations of the British Empire. Venice created its own Gibraltars, Maltas, and Adens, and like the British Empire it depended on sea power to hold these possessions together."

7) *The use of diplomacy with "short, sharp applications of military force,"*[7] as we saw in the previous chapter with the Venetian sacking of Zara and Constantinople during the Fourth Crusade.

We must now probe more deeply into the structures and methods of the Venetian oligarchical power, for in doing so, other secrets of the maintenance of such power are laid bare.

2. The Three Pillars of Venetian Power

In the previous chapter we noted that Venice had created a state arsenal, an institution that aided in the swift creation of the vast fleet needed to transport the army of the Fourth Crusade. This constitutes one of the main pillars of Venetian power, with the other two represented by the Doge's palace—and hence all the mechanisms of the government, the Senate, the Grand Council, and, as we shall see below, the notoriously infamous "Council of Ten"—and the bankers of the Rialto, with whom we have not yet dealt. But all three of these mechanisms of power—the agencies of government, the institutions of finance, and the implements and agencies of war—were in the hands of the same small group of oligarchical families.[8] The oligarchical families, and their fortunes made through trade and banking, are the real nerve center of Venetian power, and to them we now turn.

3. The Venetian Oligarchical Families

The oligarchical families of Venice are divided into two classes, the Longhi, i.e., the families of ancient provenance that could claim, and prove, their lines of noble status prior to the year 1000, and the Curti, newer families who had acquired wealth and status within the Republic, and which, beginning in 1382, were admitted into the ranks of the nobility and thus became eligible to hold offices of government, including that of Doge. As Webster Tarpley notes, the Longhi included the Dandolo, Michiel, Morosini, Contarini, and Giustinian families.[9] The newer families included the Mocenigo, Loredan,

---

7   Ibid., p. 232.

8   Crowley, *City of Fortune: How Venice Ruled the Seas*, p. 377.

9   Tarpley, "The Venetian Conspiracy," *Against Oligarchy*, http://tarpley.net/online-books/against-oligarchy/the-venetian-conspiracy/, p. 3. It is possible, Tarpley also notes, that the Giustinian family was related to the East Roman Emperor Justinian I the Great. One factor that makes this a possibility is that Justinian came from Dalmatia, long a region under Venetian influence and dominance, and with which Venice maintained trading relationships from the earliest founding of the settlement in the lagoon.

Dona, and Trevisan families, among others.[10]

Within the Venetian state, the principle means of government was the Dogeship and the Grand Council, membership of which was restricted to the male members of these noble families, a body which grew to some 2,000 members by 1500,[11] a fact of great importance, as we shall discover when we turn to a consideration of the establishment of the notorious Council of Ten. In any case, the upper house of this Grand Council was the Pregadi, in effect the Venetian Senate, which oversaw—until the establishment of the Council of Ten—foreign affairs and the appointment of Venetian ambassadors.[12]

The Great Council was, in effect, the apex of the "self-perpetuating oligarchy"[13] that was Venice:

> From the start the Council had been self-electing; thus, inevitably over the years, it had grown more and more into a closed society. In 1293, to give but one instance, it included ten Foscari, eleven Morosini and no less than eighteen Contarini.[14]

By 1298, the oligarchy had succeeded in passing a law in this Council that essentially restricted membership to those families that had previously been represented on it, an action that was called the *Serrata*, literally "the locking," an act which "created, at a stroke, a closed caste in the society of the Republic; a caste with its own inner elite of those who had sat in the Great Council ... "[15] To ensure security against any false claims to nobility that might be advanced to gain a seat on this council, the Republic created the *Libro d'Oro*, the Golden Book, essentially a state census of all who were eligible within Venice for such a seat, in other words, a kind of Venetian *Burke's Peerage*, a registry of all nobility.[16]

This reflects a typical obsession of the Venetian oligarchical families: ethnic purity, a policy of strict segregation between the subject peoples of the empire and the Venetians themselves.[17] We may speculate here that this policy may also have been in part to protect and preserve the knowledge among those families of their ancient Roman imperial, and ultimately Babylonian origins, as outlined at the beginning of the previous chapter. Such knowledge,

---

10   Ibid.

11   Ibid.

12   Tarpley, "The Venetian Conspiracy," http://tarpley.net/online-books/against-oligarchy/the-venetian-conspiracy, p. 4.

13   Norwich, *A History of Venice*, p. 182.

14   Ibid., p. 183.

15   Ibid., pp. 183–184.

16   Ibid., p. 184.

17   Crowley, *City of Fortune*, p. 183. See also p. 240.

if it existed, had to be preserved and also *restricted to* those families. Nor is this a fanciful speculation, since the Venetian oligarchical families obviously *are* obsessed with the preservation of their line.

In this respect, it is worth pausing to note that one of these Venetian noble houses, the House of Guelf-Este (or, to give it its German variant, Welf-Este), ruled over Padua and Verona as virtual Venetian satraps.[18] This house, as we shall see in subsequent chapters, is significant to the story of the transfer of the oligarchy northward into German and, eventually, into England.

4. *The Suppression of Factional Infighting*

It is quite crucial to notice what the Great Council really is: the deliberately created body wherein all major familiar or factional interests were represented and given voice. This is an important clue into the nature of the polity of Venice, namely, that the individual factional or familial interests were deliberately subordinated to the interests of the oligarchical class as a whole, and "by the ironclad delimitation of noble status to those already noble in 1297 and their male descendants, and by continuous terror against the masses and against the nobility itself."[19] In other words, the Great Council represented the mechanism of the *suppression of factional infighting*, and it is this factor that in part constitutes one reason for the profound longevity and stability of the Venetian state.

B. The Council of Ten: Terrorism as a Matter of State Policy

But what of terrorism as a matter of official state policy of the oligarchy? Here we must turn to consider that preeminently and uniquely Venetian symbol and instrument of terror, the Council of Ten—how it came to be created, and what possible influence or precedent the Venetians were drawing upon when they created it.

We have already noted that by 1500 the Great Council had grown to some 2,000 members, all of whom, of course, were members of the Longhi or Curti noble families, thus making it a cumbersome body to deal with a crisis.[20] Even long before 1500, the Great Council was too bulky and ungainly to deal with emergencies, and this fact led to a typically oligarchical response. Rather than adjust the existing bodies of state, a new body was created by the Great Council on July 10, 1310 in response to a local insurrection: the Council

---

18 Norwich, *A History of Venice*, p. 186.
19 Tarpley, "The Venetian Conspiracy," http://tarpley.net/online-books/against-oligarchy/the-venetian-conspiracy, p. 4.
20 Norwich, *A History of Venice*, p. 199.

of Ten.[21] Like all such bodies, it was originally intended as a temporary body to deal with a short-term situation, but its charter kept being renewed until, in 1334, it was made a permanent body.[22]

> Though its corporate powers were immense, they were subject to characteristically Venetian checks and balances to prevent any individual member's using them for his personal ends. Election— by the Great Council, from lists drawn up by itself and the Signoria respectively—was for a single year, and re-election was forbidden until a further year was passed, during which time any alleged abuses would be carefully investigated. Two members of the same family could never sit simultaneously. Furthermore the Council never allowed itself a single head; there were always three—the *Capi dei Dieci*—serving for a month at a time, a month during which they were forbidden to go out into society lest they should be exposed to bribes or baseless rumours. Finally—the most important point of all and perhaps the one most frequently forgotten—the Ten were powerless by themselves. They acted only in concert with the Doge and his six councillors, bring their effective number to seventeen.[23]

From the outset, the Council of Ten served first to coordinate a vast network of spies, both inside of and outside of Venice, extending even to the Mongols.[24] It thus coordinated all counter-intelligence and intelligence *and* police and surveillance operations both inside and outside the Republic and its territories.[25] More importantly, it was authorized to decide matters of policy and state in the name of the Great Council, and thus, its decrees had the force of law of the Great Council itself.[26]

But there was more:

> Venice's superb communications and the almost legendary stability of her government had made her Europe's principal centre of espionage, an international clearing-house for secrets of state. By now all the principal nations of the world were represented there, by embassies, agencies, banks, trading centres or other more clandestine associations, and for many of them the gathering of intelligence was

21 Ibid., p. 197.
22 Ibid.
23 Ibid., p. 198.
24 Tarpley, "The Venetian Conspiracy," p. 9
25 Norwich, *A History of Venice,* pp. 198–199.
26 Ibid., p. 199.

a primary function. For such purposes extra pairs of eyes and ears were always useful; nor did a skilful hand with a knife or a none-too-sensitive conscience invariable come amiss.

It would have been odd if Venice, with an intelligence system of her own far more highly developed than that of any foreign power, had not maintained a close eye on all these covert activities and, where possible, used them for her own ends. Every embassy, every foreign household even, was thoroughly penetrated by Venetian agents, reporting directly back to the Ten details of comings and goings, of letters received and conversations overheard. A special watch was kept on leading courtesans, several of whom were paid by the state to pass on any information that might prove useful, for blackmail or otherwise. There was also an active network of double agents whose task was to feed false or misleading information into foreign systems.[27]

In other words, the Council of Ten combined both foreign policy, internal security, international espionage, *and* a law-making capacity in one body.

The ubiquity of this surveillance system, particularly within the territories of the Republic itself, meant that "the contents of any discussion among oligarchs or citizens was routinely known to the Ten within twenty-four hours or less,"[28] and the Doge's palace was punctuated with numerous mail-slots in the shape of lion's mouths "marked *Per Denontie Segrete* ('For Secret Denunciations') for those who wished to call to the attention of the Ten and their monstrous bureaucracy individuals stealing from the state or otherwise violating the law."[29]

Nor was this all.

The Council of Ten was empowered to issue bills of capital attainder, and could thus, like the Star Chamber later in England, conduct secret trial of individuals so denounced. Any death sentence issued by the Council was without appeal; offenders found guilty were simply rounded up by the Ten's police, "disappeared" from view, and usually executed (by strangulation) the very same day their sentence was passed, their bodies hung by the leg in the Piazetta (Tarot enthusiasts, take note!).[30] Thus, in addition to being a police, intelligence, counter-intelligence, foreign policy, disinformation, espionage clearing-house and law-making body, the Council of Ten was also a secret and supreme court, and executioner. Like all such monstrous creations, the

---

27   Ibid., pp. 521–522.
28   Tarpley, "The Venetian Conspiracy," p. 5.
29   Ibid.
30   Ibid., see also Norwich, *A History of Venice*, p., 526.

Council soon encroached on the powers of other government agencies, either by directly co-opting their powers, or by internal penetration, or both.[31]

There is even some suspicion that the great Italian epic poet Dante Alighieri ran afoul of the Council of Ten:

> Dante visited Venice in 1321, acting in his capacity as diplomatic representative of the nearby city of Ravenna, whose overlord was for a time his protector. He died shortly after leaving Venice. The two explanations of his death converge on murder: one version state(s) that he was denied a boat in which to travel south across the lagoon. He was forced to follow a path through the swamps, caught malaria, and died. Another version says that a boat was available, but that to board it would have meant certain assassination. Venetian records regarding this matter have conveniently disappeared.[32]

We may thus once again speculate that when Bruno announced to Mocenigo his intention to found a secret society based upon Hermetic principles, Mocenigo in turn denounced him to the Ten, which arranged his arrest by the Inquisition, for Venice was implacably opposed to the Neoplatonism and Hermeticism of the Renaissance.[33]

In any case, it is important to recognize the steps of the oligarchy in the establishment of the Council of Ten, for they have become their classic playbook ever since, in states such as England, and in more recent history, the United States of America:

---

31 See Norwich, op. cit., p. 538.

32 Tarpley, "The Venetian Conspiracy," p. 6.

33 Ibid., p. 11. Tarpley notes something quite crucial: "Since the Venetian oligarchy relied for its survival on the secret weapon of political intelligence manipulation, its primary strategic targets were first and foremost dictated by epistemological rather than military criteria. Fleets and armies, even in the hands of a powerful and aggressive enemy state, could well redound to Venetian advantage. The real danger was a hostile power that developed epistemological defenses against manipulation and deceit. In the face of such a threat, Venice did, and does—kill.

"The Italian Renaissance of the fifteenth and sixteenth centuries, perhaps the greatest outpouring of human creativity in history, represented such a threat to the Serene Republic, and in a more concentrated form than it had ever faced before. The threat arose from the epistemological warfare and alliance system of the great Cosimo de' Medici of Florence and his successors. Venice mobilized every resource at its disposal to destroy the Renaissance. After decades of sabotage, going to far as to arrange the ravaging of Italy by foreign armies, Venice succeeded."

This epistemological warfare was, as we saw in Chapter Two, the threat posed to the financial-religious oligarchy of Venice, accustomed as it was to Aristotle, by the Hermetic and Neoplatonic views of the Renaissance that were, in particular, sponsored by the Florentines, and which culminated in Bruno's expression of the ancient metaphor.

1) The normal mechanisms of the government are perceived by the oligarchy to be too cumbersome to respond to a sudden crisis;

2) rather than amend or alter those bodies in such a fashion to be able to respond to such a crisis, new, streamlined agencies or bodies are established to *represent* the original constitutional body, which retains *de jure* authority, and thus protects the larger interests of the oligarchy;

3) this body becomes—in modern parlance—a "continuity of government" agency, vested with plenary powers of arrest, secret trial, ability to rule by decree, and the final clearing house of all intelligence and for the analysis thereof;

4) on the basis of this intelligence, this body also becomes a policy-making body for the state.

Additionally, as we saw in the last chapter, *ad hoc* and "informal discussion groups"—Venetian versions of the Council on Foreign Relations, or Bilderberg groups—can emerge within this overall structure to discuss policy and its execution, such as the Giovani group that once included Bruno. Such groups seek to promote "memes" within the broader culture whose object is to enhance the power and security of the oligarchy.

C. GIAMMARIA ORTES AND THE ORIGIN OF THE CARRYING CAPACITY MYTH, AND OTHER OLIGARCHICAL MEMES

In this respect, we must examine the crucial figure of Giammaria Ortes, whom Webster Tarpley, in a significant and magisterial piece of research exposing the origin of the meme of overpopulation, called "the decadent Venetian kook who originated the myth of 'carrying capacity.'"[34] Carrying capacity is simply the idea that the Earth has a maximum population that it can "carry" or support, an idea that, not surprisingly, originated with Venice's financial oligarchy. This "meme" was the brainchild of one Giammaria Ortes, a "defrocked … monk and libertine, who in 1790, in the last year of his life, published the raving tract 'Reflections on the Population of Nations in Relation to National Economy.'"[35]

Tarpley observes that the essence of Ortes' argument is summarized in a statement he made in his work "Della Economia Nazionale" ("On National Economy"): "National economy is a matter which cannot be improved in

---

34 Tarpley, "Giammaria Ortes: The Decadent Venetian Kook Who Originated the Myth of 'Carrying Capacity,'" http://tarpley.net/online-books/against-oligarchy/giammaria-ortes-the-decadent-venetian-kook-who-originated-the-myth-of-carrying-capacity/

35 Ibid.

any way by any particular action, and all attempts by persons seeking to organize national economy according to a better system, as regards provision or increase of goods, have to end as useless efforts."[36] One notes here a typical oligarchical theme, namely, that any effort to improve economic structure is useless, the implication being that any advocated systems of change need not be pursed.

Ortes followed this up with an argument that readers of *Babylon's Banksters* will readily recognize:

> But that the general wealth cannot be increased for some without an equal deficiency of them for others; that no one can find himself better off without some else being worse off, or without somebody's suffering; that the mass of common goods is determined in every nation by the need, and that it cannot exceed this need by even a hairsbreadth, neither by the charms of a charlatan nor by the work of a philosopher nor even by the work of a sovereign ... [37]

Notice the three implicit assumptions of a *closed* system of economics and finance present in these two quotations:

1) All economies are *closed* systems;
2) all economies are *static* systems, that is to say, no new technological innovations can be envisioned which recreate new mechanisms for wealth creation; and hence,
3) all wealth accumulation is also wealth privation: there can be *no creation* of wealth, all wealth involves *debt*.

Given these assumptions, it is easy to see why the Neoplatonic and Hermetic influences within the Italian Renaissance, with their emphasis on *creation* of information, and the general fecundity of the underlying physical medium, were so adamantly opposed by the financial oligarchy of Venice.

From these implicit assumptions, it is a short step to the derivation of the idea that the Earth has a maximum population carrying capacity:

> Hence, derives for Ortes the fixed and unimprovable level of the wealth of each nation, which will always be the product of its population multiplied by the irreducible minimum amount of work. Or, as Ortes says:

---

36   Ibid., p. 7.
37   Ibid.

"Having posited this truth, I say again, the substances spread throughout a nation and by means of which the nation exists must be determined precisely by the needs of the nation, without any abundance or deficiency; so if we suppose in any nation some number of persons, they will require certain goods in order to survive, and the reason for the production of these goods will only be precisely providing for these persons. Because however these persons can only consume a determined quantity of goods, these goods cannot fall short or be excessive in relation to their need, thanks to the fact that if the goods were not there or were inferior to the needs of all, all those persons would not survive, which is contrary to our supposition, and if the goods were excessive or were superior to the need, then those goods would have been produced and would be kept without sufficient reason, without which nothing is ever done, as we pointed out."[38]

This is a classic definition of a closed system, or, as Tarpley very aptly observes, "Ortes has thus preceded John Von Neumann and others in defining economic reality as a zero-sum game."[39] Ortes is even more explicit in his physics analogy, making comparison between his economic model and a zero-summed vector system:

> *The good therefore,* understood as the possession of goods in excess of what is needed, *can only be expressed between the individual and the commonality as the number zero*, and since there is an inevitable lack of goods for some if these are to be abundant for others, this good can only appear as a mixture of economic good and evil, which tends neither to one nor to the other, *or as the vector sum of forces which, operating with equal energy in different and opposite directions, destroy each other and resolve themselves into nothing.*[40]

Lest the reader miss this important point, we state it explicitly: this is one of the first times in history that the connection between physics and finance has been articulated, and notably, the relationship between the two is one of a closed, static equilibrium zero-summed model. *Absent entirely is the ancient Metaphor of the medium, and its non-equilibrium model of information creation.*

From this closed system static approach to economic (and physics!) models, and given Ortes' *assumption* of the lack of technological developments that

---

38 Ibid., p. 8.
39 Ibid.
40 Ibid., emphasis added.

can *open* the system back up, and his implied assumption *of fixed unchangeable rates of production flowing from it,*[41] it is a short step to the conclusion that, inevitably, the Earth must reach a point of maximum population growth.[42] That maximum limit Ortes fixed at three billion people, a limit which has obviously long since been exceeded.[43] Not surprisingly, Ortes recommended that policies be implemented for zero population growth, including celibacy, prostitution, castration and "other modes of incontinence used by the barbarous nations."[44]

Hand-in-hand with this zero-population-growth, maximum-carrying-capacity "meme" is the hidden doctrine and allied meme that man has no soul, no consciousness or reasoning capacity.[45] Man becomes reduced to a collection of purely material forces, summing, in Ortes' model, to zero. Small wonder then, that Venice, in the name of its basically Aristotelian materialism, waged a constant ideological warfare with the rest of the Italian Renaissance and its Neoplatonic and Hermetic impulses, for which virtually everything was a manifestation of the cosmically creative powers of intellect, consciousness, and soul.[46] And small wonder, also, that Bruno, who so epitomized those Hermetic impulses, had to be eliminated, not only for his possible knowledge of Venetian intrigue (as was seen in the last chapter), but more importantly, for his mastery of the Hermetic system, and its powers of soul, intellect, and memory. It is this ideological, epistemological, and cosmological commitment *to closed systems of finance and physics* that ultimately lies behind Venice's long-standing hostility to the humanist Renaissance of Medici dominated Florence.[47]

There is one final, all-important clue, connecting all these themes and Giordano Bruno to the Venetian oligarchy represented by the Mocenigo family, one of whose members (as we know well by now) betrayed Bruno to the Inquisition. During the years that Ortes was formulating his views, he was "closely associated" with one of those informal "discussion groups" deliberating on matters of social philosophy that we have earlier seen Galileo and Bruno involved with. This was the *conversazione filosofica e felice,* or "philosophical and happy conversation group."[48] Notably, one of the members of this oligarchical discussion group—a kind of Venetian forerunner to the Council on Foreign Relations or the Royal Institute for International Affairs—was

---

41 Ibid., p. 10.
42 Ibid., pp. 9–10.
43 Ibid., p. 1o.
44 Ibid., p. 11.
45 Tarpley, "Venice's War Against Western Civilization," p. 6.
46 Ibid., p. 3.
47 Tarpley, "The Venetian Conspiracy," p. 1.
48 Tarpley, "Giammaria Ortes," p. 2.

the namesake of the Mocenigo who had first sought to acquire Bruno's art of memory secrets: Alvise Zuanne Mocenigo.[49]

The Venetian oligarchy and its policy and methods were, if nothing else, remarkably consistent.

---

49   Ibid., p. 3.

❧ Five ❧

CONCLUSIONS TO PART ONE

∴

"If any one individual symbolizes the tormented history of the Hermetic tradition it is Giordano Bruno." [1]

*"But Bruno was, in reality, a martyr for **the Hermetic Tradition**."* [2]
—Lynn Picknett and Clive Prince

IT HAS BEEN A LONG JOURNEY from the fires that roasted Giordano Bruno through the soaring heights of his cosmology and arts of memory, through the implications of the ancient Topological Metaphor of the Medium, to the rise of the Republic of Venice and the cunning and brutality of its byzantine institutions, its oligarchy, and its mechanistic, closed-system cosmological views, reflected in its static view of wealth and physics. But we are at last in a position to summarize our results thus far:

---

1 Picknett and Prince, *The Forbidden Universe*, p. 341.
2 Ibid., p. 342.

1) *The motivations for Bruno's murder by Venice and the Papacy are two-fold:*

   a) *Bruno was murdered because there is a possibility he was a Venetian agent.* In support of this possibility, we have in the previous pages noted the following things:

      i) As was pointed out in Chapter One, when Bruno fled the Kingdom of Naples for northern Italy—Padua and Venice—he had already explicitly and openly disavowed Catholic dogmas and practice, such as the deity of Christ and the veneration of relics and images of the saints. It is significant in light of Bruno's *subsequent* denunciation for heresy to the Inquisition by Mocenigo that Bruno was not denounced for clearly heretical views on his *first* visit to Venice. This implies that he was possibly under protection from Venice during his first visit.

      ii) Bruno's subsequent travels to Geneva, Paris, Oxford, London, and Germany took him to the heart of all the religious controversies of the day. Since Venice had made a goal of publishing both Protestant and Catholic works during his lifetime, and since through Venetian efforts the Index of Prohibited Books and the Jesuit Order were established, the possibility arises that Bruno's travels throughout Protestant and Catholic Europe may have been in service of this typically Venetian dual agenda. Additionally, as was noted, Bruno did take part in the many "informal discussion" groups in Venice *prior* to his first departure from that city, discussion groups which included members of the oligarchical Mocenigo family.

      iii) Mocenigo's subsequent contact with Bruno while the latter was in Frankfurt also suggests that Bruno's whereabouts were being closely followed by Venetian spies in the service of the Council of Ten. The very fact of Bruno's contact with that powerful Venetian oligarchical family indicates that Bruno was of extreme interest to the oligarchy.

      iv) Therefore, Bruno's subsequent *acceptance* of Mocenigo's invitation to return to Venice to teach him his art of memory system is no longer a mystery, for Bruno might have assumed the latter's protection was assured, based on his prior contact with that family during his first Venetian sojourn and participation in the discussion group.

      v) Bruno's revelation to Mocenigo that he intended to found a secret society—the Giordanistas—in Europe to promote his Hermetic philosophy as a religion to replace both Protestantism and Catholicism ran counter to the Venetian agenda of fomenting religious conflict between the two camps, and thus, for this reason alone, Bruno would have posed a threat to Venice's agenda. Additionally, this may have been seen as Bruno's betrayal of whatever possible assignment he had been originally given as a possible Venetian agent. The question then arises of why Bruno was not simply strangled in a private execution, as was customary for the methods of the Council of Ten. The answer may be that because of his notoriety, and the possibility that he had *already* founded his secret society, a more public message had to be sent to any possible adherents of that society.

b) *Bruno was murdered for the threat his Hermetic views and system of memory posed to the oligarchical financial elite of Venice and to the religious elite of the Papacy:*

i) As was seen in Chapters One and Two, Bruno's Hermeticism implied that there was an "original theology" or *prisca theologia* stemming from Ancient Egypt that was "more true" than either Judaism or Christianity, and, by implication, Islam. As such, Bruno, like many Renaissance humanists and Hermeticists of his day, viewed Christian doctrine—especially the Resurrection and Trinity—as disguised elements of Egyptian religion. Bruno went further than most during his day and advocated the complete abolition of Christianity, a position that brought him into conflict with the oligarchical powers of Venice and the religious powers of the Papacy. Additionally, Hermeticism claimed, as we saw, to be a continuation of antediluvian knowledge;

ii) By taking this position, Bruno also pointed out that the character of Yahweh was morally contradictory, and one, moreover, that was an anthropomorphic projection of humanity itself. He advocated a return to the God of the Metaphor, to which all men, without the need of special revelation or divinely sanctioned institutional structures such as the Church, could, through the powers of reason, have access. Again, this brought him into direct conflict with the financial and religious powers of his day, and for these reasons, both Venice and the Papacy colluded to have him murdered in a public fashion that would "send a message" to anyone similarly tempted;

iii) Additionally, Bruno's Hermeticism, as we saw, made him—in his own words—a "citizen of the world," a position of political as well as religious "egalitarianism" that conflicted directly with the political and religious institutions of his day, and that anticipated, as we saw, the views of the subsequent Bavarian Illuminati and the revolutionary movements of the late eighteenth and early nineteenth centuries;

iv) As we also discovered, in the implications of the Topological Metaphor of the Physical Medium, and particularly in Bruno's exposition of it, mankind itself is, to a certain extent, the "common surface" of the differentiated "regions" of the medium, with the medium, and therefore man, to that extent becoming symbols of the alchemical Philosophers' Stone, the transmutative, information-creating medium. In Bruno's view, this means that mind or soul is a non-local phenomenon binding all things together and making possible the practice of magic through the bringing of the mind into harmony with universal archetypes based on astrological principles;

v) As we also noted, the Metaphor is a metaphor of *fecundity*, of the *creation of information* that is, in a word, *debt free* and open and available to all. This explicit implication of the Metaphor and the general Neoplatonic and Hermetic impulse of the Italian Renaissance was a clear threat to the closed-systems Aristotelian materialism of Venetian oligarchs, for whom wealth was a zero-sum, debt-encumbered system, as we discovered in the thought of Giammaria Ortes. Lest this point be missed, it is best to restate it in more modern terms: for both Bruno and the Hermeticists, and for the Venetian financial oligarchy, *there is a clear and explicit connection between the types of systems of finance being advocated, and the cosmological and physics systems being advocated.* In this context it will be recalled that Ortes formulated his sociological meme of carrying capacity and zero population growth as not only a zero-sum game but a *zero-summed vector field*, implying a clear physics model. We may therefore view Ortes as being the first modern "econophysicist." By emphasizing the principle of fecundity in the Metaphor, Bruno and other Renaissance humanists were a threat to the entire mercantilist financial system;

vi) In Bruno's version of the Metaphor, as noted, there is a direct connection between memory, mind, astrology, alchemy, and the physical medium. Here we may speculate on another possible reason for the sudden Venetian oligar-chical "about face" with respect to Bruno. In chapter three, we noted that Venetian oligarchical families may have in fact descended from Chaldean slaves brought to Italy from Meso-potamia during the Roman Empire. In *Babylon's Banksters*, I noted that financial and economic cycles appear in some sense to be coordinated to planetary positions, an essentially astrological notion, and that this knowledge of the coupling of financial with physical systems may have been a declined legacy of a high science passed down from High Antiquity, and a closely-held secret of the temple elites of Babylonia. Thus, it is a possibility that such knowledge was passed down precisely in these families to medieval times. With his state-ments to Mocenigo that he intended to found a secret society based on his Hermetic principles, Bruno would have been threatening to end the possible monopoly of this closely held secret by those families, and hence had to be permanently silenced;

vii) This possibility of hidden and suppressed knowledge became evident in our exploration in a different way, for as we have seen, *some* account has to be made for why the Italian Renais-sance so suddenly exploded with knowledge of Neoplatonic and Hermetic texts. We suggested that this occurred through access to the imperial archives of Constantinople, access pos-sibly given to Florence through the participation of Byzantine humanists in the Church reunion Council of Ferrara-Flor-ence, and also possibly through Venice's sacking of Constanti-nople during the Fourth Crusade, which would have provided access to archival information, some of which may ultimately stemmed from the ancient Library of Alexandria. We noted the possibility that this may have included ancient maps clear-ly depicting the New World, and alternate trade routes to the Far East bypassing the Venetian stranglehold and trading mo-nopoly on the Eastern Mediterranean. In such a circumstance, Venice would have chosen to *suppress* not only any Hermetic cosmological knowledge it recovered from Constantinople, but also any geographic and cartographic knowledge. As we shall discover in chapter nine, there is evidence that such car-tographic knowledge did indeed exist, and that it was a closely held secret during the Middle Ages prior to the discovery of the New World by Columbus;

viii) With respect to the Metaphor, we also observed that in the Vedic and Christian trinitarian versions, the Metaphor creates not only an initial triadic structure but also the implicit categories of *persons, functions, and nature*, with persons being closely associated with peculiar functions. This is, as we shall encounter in the next part of this book, the basis for the rise of the doctrine of the corporate person in theology and jurisprudence;

ix) Finally, we noted that the Metaphor is always of a both/and dialectical nature, having both theistic and atheistic interpretations, personal and impersonal interpretations, and that all are necessary to maintain in order for a full understanding of the Metaphor and its implications. We noted also that in its original understanding, the Metaphor is one of fecundity, and not tied to notions of debt and sacrifice.

2) *With respect to Venice itself, we noted the following classic and telltale signs of the operations and methods of oligarchical imperialism and financial mercantilism, each of which, again, is directly threatened by the opposing epistemology of Neoplatonism and Hermeticism:*

a) With respect to Venetian history, we noted that there are three possible ways that it is connected with ancient Mesopotamia, two of these via *symbolism*, and one of them via actual physical descent:

i) The first *symbolic* connection is through the winged lion of St. Mark, Venice's patron saint. The winged lion, as we saw, ultimately derives from Babylonia;

ii) The second *symbolic* connection is more tenuous, via the monastery of San Giorgio Maggiore in the Venetian lagoon. The image of St George on a stead killing a dragon with a spear is similar to Mesopotamian and Egyptian images;

iii) The third, and most important, connection to Babylonia is via the possible descent of Venetian oligarchical families from Mesopotamian slaves brought to Rome. As noted above, it is possible these families preserved the knowledge of the connection between planetary alignments and financial and economic cycles. As also noted, these Venetian oligarchical families took great pains to protect their racial and ethnic purity from "contamination" by subject peoples in their Empire;

b) The Venetian connection to Byzantium and the heavy Byzantine influence on its culture and institutions was also noted, and this influence, we now note, *extended to its methods of intelligence gathering, influence building, and empire building.* These methods included:

i) A consistent policy of mercantilism, evident in the obtaining of special trading privileges and tax exemptions for the Byzantine empire;

ii) Use of obfuscation in military expeditions, as in the possible cover story of the Fourth Crusade being to expel the Muslims from the Holy land, when a certain amount of evidence suggests that Constantinople, at least as far as Venice was concerned, was the original goal of the expedition. Venetian intelligence would, for example, have known of Alexius Angelicus' presence in Germany and of his claims to the Byzantine imperial throne.

iii) Duplicitous secret diplomacy and intrigue was practiced at all times, as, for example, in the aforementioned Fourth Crusade, when Venice was negotiating simultaneously with the French Knights to lead an expedition which *they* thought ultimately targeted Egypt, while concurrently negotiating with the Viceroy in Egypt to guarantee that no attack on Egypt was forthcoming. This, again, is evidence that Venice's goals during the Crusade may have been Constantinople all along. Similarly, as we have noted, Venice promoted both the Catholic and Protestant cause during the Reformation, with a view to fomenting crisis and war in order to begin the transfer of its center of operations from the lagoon northward, to a new strategic base with access to the Atlantic trade;

iv) The Byzantine influence and oligarchical method is also evident in the creation of the notorious Council of Ten, which combined the functions of foreign policy-making, legislation, trial, intelligence and counter-intelligence gathering and analysis, disinformation, assassination, and so on. In this, the Council of Ten resembles the Byzantine Empire's Bureau of Barbarians, which combined similar functions. The fact that this Council was created with explicit controls designed to keep it in the hands of the oligarchical families is testament to its utility to their designs and security. In short, *terrorism* was an official state policy;

v) The oligarchy similarly promoted the idea of the closed system of physics and wealth as a zero-sum game, as we saw with Giammaria Ortes. This becomes a *major identifying factor* in all oligarchical meme-promotion ever since, and it is therefore an identifying marker of the fact that Venetian oligarchical methods have survived to our own day;

vi) Similarly, as we have also noted, the oligarchy would have to *suppress any epistemological, cosmological system or any other knowledge threatening that closed-system approach, and this would have included—and does include—cartographic knowledge.*

vii) The oligarchical method of empire included, as we have also discovered, two important points, namely the willingness to transfer the center of operation if the situation arises, and secondly, the promotion of empire by the maintenance of bases and ports of call that allow for the swift projection of military power and the protection of trading interests. These methods, too, have survived from the collapse of Venice, through the founding and dissolution of the British Empire, and the founding and rise of America as an empire.

With these thoughts in mind, we are now ready to take the plunge into the murky world of medieval finance and banking, the rise of corporations, and the little-known story of the possible real reasons that the New World was discovered. But before we can do all that, we must first look back, once again, to ancient times, and their understanding of money and the Metaphor, as well as a little-known hidden "Hermetic" hand in the promotion of the former, and preservation of the latter ...

II

MONETIZING THE METAPHOR, AND THE PYRAMID OF POWER

"Italian bankers ultimately managed to free themselves from the threat of expropriation by themselves taking over governments, and by doing so, acquiring their own court systems (capable of enforcing contracts) and even more critically, their own armies."

—David Graeber,
Debt: The First 5,000 Years, p. 291.

❧ Six ❧

RETROSPECTIVES ON THE TOPOLOGICAL METAPHOR AND MONEY:

Brahma, Buddha, Babylon, and Greece

∴

"... theories of existential debt always end up becoming ways of justifying—
or laying claim to—structures of authority."
—David Graeber[1]

IN THIS CHAPTER, we will encounter the extraordinarily brilliant and insightful work of two scholars of the subject of money, who approach the subject not from the standpoint of standard economic or numismatic history but from classical literature (Richard Seaford), and anthropology and cultural history (David Graeber). If there were two books that I would recommend to readers for further study, it would be Seaford's *Money and the Early Greek Mind*, and Graeber's *Debt: The First 5,000 Years.*

That said, we shall here seek to place their work within the wider metaphysical and cosmological context of the ancient Topological Metaphor, for in doing so, a very different picture of the relationships between money and cosmological physics emerges. To summarize this relationship as we have encountered it thus far, we would have to say that there is a direct and analogical connection between the way the medieval world of Europe viewed money and the way it viewed the cosmos, as we saw in the case of Giammaria Ortes and Venice. The question now becomes: What was the *order* of concepts? Did the rise of money influence the cosmology? Or was the converse true, did cosmol-

---

1   David Greaber, *Debt: The First 5,000 Years* (Brooklyn: Melville House, 2011), p. 69.

121.

ogy influence the view of money? As we shall see, Seaford argues that money influenced the rise of philosophical cosmology in ancient Greece. But as we shall also discover, there are indications in Seaford's own research that the converse is true, that cosmology not only influenced the view of money, but that there were possibly hidden hands, in the form of secret societies and mystery schools, namely Pythagoreanism, that played a significant role.

But first, we must look even farther back in history to the ancient world before Greece, and to the unusual views of money and cosmology that it maintained.

A. Debt, Sacrifice, and the Metaphor:
1. Primordial Debt Theory: Brahmanism, Babylon, and Buddhism

One of the ancient Brahmanic texts, the *Satapatha Brahmana,* states, "In being born every being is born as debt owed to the gods, the saints, the Fathers and to men."[2] The *Rig Veda* likewise alludes to this primordial debt theory, and its role in Hinduism's view of the material world as a form of illusion, when it states, "Let us drive away the evil effects of bad dreams, just as we pay off debts."[3] As Graeber observes, the earliest Vedic texts, which date from approximately 1500 to 1200 B.C., show a consistent "concern with debt—which is treated as synonymous with guilt and sin."[4] To put it in terms that I first proposed in *The Grid of the Gods*, the metaphor has been transformed, by some process of reasoning, from a Metaphor of fecundity—the "Corn God"—to one of debt, guilt, and sacrifice—"the Blood God".[5] This idea has given rise in modern economic theory to "Primordial Debt Theory," which maintains that this idea of interpreting the Metaphor is not unique to Vedic texts, but is rather a universal phenomenon "essential to the very nature and history of human thought."[6] Needless to say, most of those promoting this idea have some connection to the contemporary financial and banking oligarchies, and one is once again confronted by what Webster Tarpley called the epistemological warfare being waged by financial oligarchies, and the meme they wish to implant that "debt is primordial; there is no escaping it." The implication of this view, as Graeber correctly points out, is that if our lives "are on loan then who would actually wish to repay a debt?" To repay it would mean annihilation. *Nihilism* is, in other words, the inevitable logical consequence of this view.[7]

---

2 Graeber, *Debt*, p. 43, citing the *Satapatha Brahmana,* 1.7.12. 1–6.
3 Ibid., citing the *Rid Veda*, 8.47.17.
4 Ibid., p. 56.
5 Farrell and de Hart, *The Grid of the Gods*, pp. 201–203.
6 Graeber, *Debt*, p. 57.
7 Ibid.

However, as Graeber points out through numerous details scattered throughout his book, there is no historical nor necessary philosophical reason that this is so. In short, such a view is simply untrue.

While the complexities of Graeber's book are far beyond the scope of this book, we may gain some approximation of the importance of "primordial debt theory" for current theorists from the following quotation by one of its major proponents, Bruno Théret, in his significantly-titled article "The Socio-Cultural Dimensions of the Currency: Implications for the Transition to the Euro," written for the *Journal of Consumer Policy* in 1999:

> At the origin of money we have a "relation of representation" *of death as an invisible world*, before and beyond life—a representation that is the product of the symbolic function proper to the human species and which envisages birth as an original debt incurred by all men, a debt owing to the cosmic powers from which humanity emerged.
>
> Payment of this debt, which can however never be settled on earth—because its full reimbursement is out of reach—takes the form of sacrifices which, by replenishing the credit of the living, make it possible to prolong life and even in certain cases to achieve eternity by joining the Gods. *But this initial belief-claim is also associated with the emergence of sovereign powers whose legitimacy resides in their ability to represent the entire original cosmos. And it is these powers that invented money as a means of settling debts*—a means whose abstraction makes it possible to resolve the sacrificial paradox by which putting to death becomes the permanent means of protecting life.[8]

It is precisely here that viewing the Metaphor as *a declined legacy* from a scientifically advanced culture in High Antiquity—that is, viewing the Metaphor *shorn of its metaphysical and religious language, and solely from the standpoint of a formally explicit topological-mathematical-physics metaphor*—reveals its utility, for when viewed *in that way, absolutely **no notion** of debt is implied at all, moral, financial, or otherwise.* Why this is so is readily apparent, for the abstract language of mathematics conveys the concepts without the connotations that normal language inevitably entails.

Additionally, as we have seen, even *in* certain versions of the Metaphor—the Hermetic for example—no notion of debt or of *death* is implied in that stage of initial differentiation, for at that level, the Metaphor is chiefly and uniquely a Metaphor of *life, fecundity, and creation.* By construing it as a

---

8   Bruno Théret, "The Socio-Cultural Dimensions of the Currency: Implications for the Transition to the Euro," *Journal of Consumer Policy,* 22:51-79, cited in Graeber, *Debt,* p. 58, emphasis added.

Metaphor of *debt and sacrifice*, however, Théret does point out one important cultural consequence in human history, namely, the creation of elite powers, institutions, and authority structures that *claimed an exclusive right to represent the Metaphor in its interpretation as debt, and therefore, to create financial and religious systems based upon and powered by the analogically parallel idea of sacrifice and debt.* What Théret is in effect saying is that it is in this twisting that the notion of the divine right of kings arises. Graeber himself notices and comments on precisely this point:

> The ingenious move of course is to fold this back into the state theory of money—since by "sovereign powers" Théret actually means "the state." The first kings were sacred kings who were either gods in their own right or stood as privileged mediators between human beings and the ultimate forces that governed the cosmos. This sets us on a road to the gradual realization that our debt to the gods was always, really, a debt to the society that made us what we are.[9]

Note what has happened: the Metaphor has first been reinterpreted from a metaphor of life, information creation, and fecundity—an *open* system—to a metaphor of death, debt, sacrifice, and monetized debt created by a self-authorized elite—a *closed* system.

Consequently, it comes as no surprise that within the Indo-European family of languages words for "sin" and "guilt" are often etymologically related to words indicating money and debt.[10] The problem with the whole primordial debt theory, at least as far as its contemporary theorists (who are attempting to derive it from Vedic texts) are concerned, is that even here, repayment of such a debt implies that the parties in the transaction are equal—that mankind and God or the Gods are equal.[11] Additionally, if the primordial debt theory were true, then the repayment of debt owed to the Gods and/or state would be in the form of taxation, but ancient societies did not normally tax their citizens.[12] As we shall discover, revenues were raised largely by *tribute* extorted or expropriated from conquered and subjected peoples, which gave rise to what Graeber calls the "military-coinage-slavery" complex. It is the implied equality of God or the Gods and mankind that makes the idea of sacrifice an impossibility, *an illicit interpretation of the Metaphor*, since even sacrifice implies transaction, and *transaction implies the subtle ontological parity of the parties in the exchange.*

---

9   Graeber, *Debt*, p. 58.
10 Ibid., p. 59.
11 Ibid., p. 63.
12 Ibid.

A glance back at the formal mathematical notation of the Metaphor will show why this is so. As we saw in chapter two, the initial differentiation leads to a one-three structure, a triadic or trinitarian structure of the *first derivatives.* There, we explored the Metaphor in terms of mathematician George Spencer-Brown's *Laws of Form*, and ended with two regions joined by a common surface. Let us recall what we said in chapter two:

> Draw a distinction.
> Call it the first distinction.
> Call the space in which it is drawn the space severed or cloven by the distinction.
> Call the parts of the space shaped by the severance or cleft the sides of the distinction or, alternatively, the spaces, states, or contents distinguished by the distinction.
> Let any mark, token, or sign be taken in any way with or with regard to the distinction as a signal.
> Call the use of any signal its intent.[13]

Now let us imagine that we envision an indescribable "No-thing," as we envisioned in the first chapter, utterly devoid of any distinguishing features whatsoever, infinitely "extended" in every "direction." We might envision it as the empty space in this box, except of course, our box has no neat lines denoting its "edges":

We have, in other words, an infinitely extended "No-thing" which, as we noted in the first chapter, has a perfect mathematical symbol, the empty hyper-set, symbolized by $\emptyset$, to describe it, or as Spencer-Brown calls it, a mark or "signal" of intention.

Now, within this space, we draw the simplest distinction: we *cleave* this space:

---

13   George Spencer-Brown, *Laws of Form: The New Edition of This Classic with the First-Ever Proof of Riemann's Hypothesis* (Leipzig: Bohmeier Verlag, 1999), p. 3.

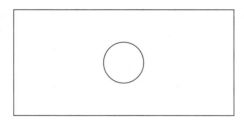

Remembering that our "box" really has no "edges," what we really have is this:

In other words, we have two "spaces," all that inside the circle, and all outside of it, or, in other words, we have what Spencer-Brown calls a "cloven space." Note that the circle is a circumscription, a "writing around" or "peri-graphing," which would be functionally symbolized by the paragraph symbol, ¶, as a symbol of the function of "drawing a distinction" or "cleaving the space."

Note two important things here: (1) we are dealing both with a "space" in the intellectual or conceptual sense, and (2) with a space in the real physics sense, at one and the same time. Additionally, because our original "box" is infinite, the circle or cloven space within it itself has no limits, save that there is a boundary or "side" as Spencer-Brown calls it, a *surface* as the topologists would say, between it and the space outside it. So we may assign symbols or marks to each of the *three* things now distinguished:

1) the space outside the circle we will designate as the "interior" of space 1, with the interior denoted by the topological "o" superscript above the signal or symbol $\varnothing$:

$$\varnothing_1^o$$

2) and similarly the space inside the circle as space 2, another "interior":

$$\varnothing_2^{\circ}$$

3) and the common surface of the two, denoted by the partial derivative symbol ∂:

$$\partial\varnothing_{1,2}$$

Notice that what we now have, as a result of performing *one* act of distinction, are three "distinguished nothings." We have created a metaphor of a "one-three," a kind of primordial trinity. Notably, because our original $\varnothing$ was dimensionless or infinite, we cannot assign any real dimensionality to any of the entities thus distinguished either.[14] Notice the all-important point that the signature of $\varnothing$ will always remain in the formal description of the regions or surfaces *no matter how many times the process is repeated.* *It remains in **all** contexts*, and is thus a basis for analogical connections between all entities subsequently generated by repetitions of this process. One might view this as a kind of "formally explicit calculus of inter-contextual analysis," or, in short, analogical calculus.

If we were to formally notate with the use of the "peri-graphing" symbol ¶ this function, we would write a simple mapping function of this first set of derivatives as follows:

$$\P\varnothing \rightarrow \varnothing_1^{\circ}, \varnothing_2^{\circ}, \partial\varnothing_{1,2}$$

with each of the three resultants on the right side of the mapping representing the two regions, and their common surface, respectively.

If one imagines repeating this process again, say, to the common surface, to divide *it* into two or more surfaces, one would end with what topologists and mathematicians would call a *second* derivative, which is symbolized by the superscripted "2" in the following notations, which would then look something like this:

$$\partial^2\varnothing_{1,2}^{\text{a}}, \partial^2\varnothing_{1,2}^{\text{b}}$$

---

14 I presented a very different way of analyzing or "imagining" this primordial cleaving in the appendix to chapter nine in my *Giza Death Star Destroyed.*

Obviously, this "second derivative" is *not* equivalent nor identical to the original. At some point, where mankind emerges in this process, one might view it as an "nth" derivative, and so on, again, clearly not equivalent or identical to the previous derivatives in the process. The *equating of subsequent derivatives thus implied in the idea of debt and sacrifice is thus a massive misinterpretation of the formal characteristics of the Metaphor*, and hence, as Graeber rightly observes, the selection of simply the Vedic texts to justify "primordial debt theory" ignores other texts which do *not* contain this false equation, and thus prejudices the case and begs the question.[15]

The notation above also hints at why the notion of *debt* would be so easily attached to the Metaphor, for a careful contemplation of its symbolism will disclose that each description of subsequent derivatives from the initial Nothing depends on the *prior* process; each *description* is *dependent* on prior processes, and that purely formal, algorithmic, and ontological dependency can easily be twisted into the idea of indebtedness, whereas the formal description is just that, a *means of discerning between differentiated "No-things" within the overall analogical process, and nothing more.*

Indeed, as Greaber also points out, by the late Brahmanic period and just prior to the appearance of the Buddha—who took the last step in repudiating the whole idea of the Metaphor as debt—the notion was already being circulated that the debt did not even exist because

... one is not in fact separate to begin with,

(a notion that is implied by the constant appearance of the first No-thing, or $\emptyset$, in *all* subsequent derivative expressions)

and hence that the very notion of canceling the debt, and achieving a separate autonomous existence, was ridiculous from the start. Or even that the very presumption of positing oneself as separate from humanity or the cosmos, so much so that one can enter into one-to-one dealings with it, is itself the crime that can be answered only by death. Our guilt is not due to the fact that we cannot repay our debt

---

15   Graeber, *Debt*, pp. 62–63. Graeber implies that the ploy is transparent, since what is being implicitly argued is a *ploy*, namely, to transfer from *religion to central banks* the idea of the payment of infinite debt, which is, as we have seen, a massive misreading of the Metaphor. Graeber notes that there is little to distinguish the older religious reading of this primordial debt and the modern nationalist one: "One might even say that what we really have, in the idea of primordial debt, is the ultimate nationalist myth. Once we owed our lives to the gods that created us, paid interest in the form of animal sacrifice, and ultimately paid back the principal with our lives. Now we owe it to the Nation that formed us, pay interest in the form of taxes, and when it comes time to defend the nation against its enemies, to offer to pay it with our lives." (*Debt*, p. 71.)

to the universe. Our guilt is our presumption in thinking of ourselves as being in any sense an equivalent to Everything Else that Exists or Has Ever Existed, so as to be able to conceive of such a debt in the first place.

Or let us look at the other side of the equation. Even if it is possible to imagine ourselves as standing in a position of absolute debt to the cosmos, or to humanity, the next question becomes: Who exactly has a right to speak for the cosmos, or humanity, to tell us how that debt must be repaid? If there's anything more preposterous than claiming to stand apart from the entire universe so as to enter into negotiations with it, it is claiming to speak for the other side.[16]

This is precisely the claim that the Three Great Yahwist monotheisms make, and two of them do so, let it be remembered, in the name of great sacrificial systems. Moreover, as we shall see, the Papacy in particular claims to speak for it in a unique way, a way that enables it to adjust the cosmic account books. But more of that later.

For the moment, we must consider that primordial No-thing which we have designated by the empty-hyperset $\varnothing$. It will be noted that each and every conceivable derivative adds or grafts more and more information around it, to betoken specific instantiations of it. It thus came—within Vedic India, Ancient Egypt, the rise of philosophical rationalism in Greece, and, of course, in the Neoplatonists and Hermetica that so profoundly influenced the Renaissance humanists—to stand for the primordial substance, the physical medium, or God, Him/It-self. It could, as we shall see below in the Greek philosophers, be modified through a process of "applied alchemical stress," whether that stress was "being heated, cooled, combined, divided, compressed, extended, or set in motion,"[17] give rise to the entire diversified cosmos and each individual thing in it, and it "was also that into which all those forms would eventually dissolve."[18] In this, it was that transmutative "gold" of the Philosophers' Stone of the alchemists.[19]

Eventually, of course, recognition of the basic nature of the Metaphor led Hindu law to drastically proscribe the notion of debt peonage,[20] and to other novel approaches to circumvent the "debt" misreading of the Metaphor. One of these, which arose in Buddhist monasteries in early medieval China, is the notion that, because the Metaphor is indeed a Metaphor of inexhaustible fecundity and creativity, it creates an "inexhaustible treasury" from which one

---

16 Ibid., p. 68.
17 Ibid., p. 245.
18 Ibid.
19 See my *The Philosophers' Stone*, pp. 25–81, 260–267.
20 Graeber, *Debt*, pp. 256–257.

can draw—through the proper Buddhist authorities of course—a spiritual "credit" to cancel one's (or even one's *relatives'*) spiritual debts.[21] This, westerners will recognize, is almost the exact same doctrine as the Papacy's "Treasury of Merit," wherein the infinite sacrifice of Christ abolishes all spiritual debt, and the merits of the saints *add* to that a surplus of "spiritual credits" upon which the Papacy can make "withdrawals" in the form of indulgences that remit or mitigate temporal punishments for sins in purgatory.

There is, as we implied in previous paragraphs, yet another misreading of the Metaphor, one we encountered in the citation from Bruno Théret, namely, that the first No-Thing from which, in the view of the Metaphor, all things derive, is *Death*, i.e., the absolute annihilation of "otherness." Within the Buddhist, and indeed, later Hindu repudiation of the "debt" reading of this Metaphor, the repudiation consists precisely in *nihilism*, in the absolute repudiation of all "otherness," including the individual person or "I" at the center of human beings' consciousness.[22] In this, too, there is a misreading of the both/and quality of the Metaphor, and of its *direction* or vector in time, which is precisely toward diversity, a diversity wherein the signature of the original No-Thing always remains in any formal description of derivatives deriving from it. If one takes that original $\varnothing$ as connoting a substrate of "Self" or Personhood, then the formal notation makes it clear that it is a fecund situation *both* of one "Self" *and* many "Selves," rather than a system of nihilism.

This fecundity, as the Metaphor was explored in terms of its monetary implications, eventually led to the system of state-created fiat paper money—money that was essentially debt-free—in medieval China, where the Bureau of Exchange Medium[23] was created to issue notes in 1023. Obviously the system led to inflation, and periodically the notes would have to be recalled and re-issued.[24] As Graeber observes, there is a harsh lesson here for "Metallists," who are prone to argue that fiat money, when backed by nothing but "state power," eventually collapses, for this period in China, which prevailed until the seventeenth century, is understood to be "the most economically dynamic in Chinese history."[25] The problem, really, with China's period of inflation under this system was that the money supply was inflated beyond the demands of the market, not in the system itself. Even the Buddhist monasteries in China gradually broke from the influence of "metallism," or bullion and coinage, and functioned under a system of extension of virtual credit.[26]

---

21 Ibid., pp. 262–265.
22 Ibid., p. 266.
23 Ibid., p. 270.
24 Ibid.
25 Ibid.
26 Ibid., see p. 235ff.

With these considerations in mind, it is when we turn to ancient Sumeria that things begin to get even more interesting.

2. Sumeria, The Breaking of the Tablets and the Jubilee: Pressing the "Reset/Reboot" Button

Greaber begins his discussion of the system of credit and finance in ancient Sumeria by observing that the name *Ur* itself is a word that means, simultaneously, "liver, spleen, heart, soul, bulk, main body, foundation, loan, obligation, interest, surplus, profit, interest-bearing debt, repayment," and finally "slave-woman."[27] Indeed, that really does not even come close to all the possible uses of the phoneme *ur* within the complex of Mesopotamian languages, but for our purposes it affords a convenient port of entry, notwithstanding some inaccuracies that arise from it.

Indeed, while primordial debt theorists often appeal to the ancient Vedic texts, they appear to be curiously reluctant to do so with respect to Sumer or Babylonia, a fact made more curious because it was precisely in Sumer and Babylon that the practice of lending money at interest apparently began, almost two thousand years before any Vedic text was set down in writing.[28] It is when one looks closely at these societies that the reason for the primordial debt theorists' avoidance of them becomes evident, for what one encounters "is in many ways the exact opposite of what such theorists would have predicted,"[29] namely, that when Sumerian monarchs *did* choose to intervene in the lives of their subjects, they did so not through the imposition of public debts, but *in the cancellation of private ones.*[30]

In order to understand why this practice arose and what it specifically involved, we must return to something I first pointed out in *Babylon's Banksters*, namely, that the earliest form of circulating money in Sumeria and later Babylonia consisted simply of clay tablets recording credit agreements. These clay tablets were

> ... inscribed with some obligation of future payment, that were then sealed inside clay envelopes and marked with the borrower's seal. The creditor would keep the envelope as a surety, and it would be broken open on repayment. In some times or places at least, these *bullae* appear to have become what we would now call negotiable

---

27 Ibid., p. 165.
28 Ibid., p. 64.
29 Ibid.
30 Ibid.

instruments, since the tablet inside did not simply record a promise to pay the original lender, but was designated "to the bearer"—in other words, a tablet recording a debt of five shekels or silver (at prevailing rates of interest) could circulate as the equivalent of a five-shekel promissory note—that is, as money.[31]

Sumeria, in other words, was circulating not only clay tablets as debt-free state-issued money on the surpluses of the state warehouse, but in addition to this, circulated *private* credit instruments—monetized debt—as money.

This circumstance gave rise to the uniquely Sumerian and Babylonian institution of the Jubilee—the public remission and cancellation of all *private* debts—by the sovereign. The circumstances leading to this are rather easy to envision. The security against such debts could be literally anything: livestock, grain, bullion, or even, in many cases, the collateralization of children or other family members' labor to the creditor.[32] While theoretically any of these things could be redeemed upon repayment, in practice this was often difficult, for the more a debtor's assets were collateralized and taken from him, the more difficult repayment of debts became, as cattle or family members were taken to repay interest and principle.[33] Multiply this procedure throughout society at large, and a problem inevitably surfaced, as families—to avoid having to pay such debts when circumstances beyond their control occurred (bad weather leading to bad harvests, for example)—would simply flee their fields and lands, leaving society bereft of production.[34]

As a result of this, and confronted "with the potential for complete social breakdown, Sumerian and later Babylonian kings periodically announced general amnesties ... Such decrees would typically declare all outstanding consumer debt null and void (commercial debts were not affected), return all land to its original owners, and allow debt-peons to return to their families."[35] This soon became a regular institutionalized practice with Sumerian and Babylonian rulers practicing the "ritual of the breaking of the tablets," literally, breaking the clay records of recorded debts.[36] This ritual was often performed in the springtime, where the restoration of order and harmony in human society was understood to mirror the restoration of life in the wider cosmos.

---

31 Ibid, pp. 214–215.
32 Ibid., p. 65.
33 Ibid.
34 Ibid., see the discussion on p. 183 in connection with this point.
35 Ibid., p. 65.
36 Ibid., p. 217. It is interesting to note, with respect to Sumerian and Babylonian attitudes to sex and the Metaphor, that procreative sex was considered merely human, whereas sex as a non-procreative pleasure was considered to be divine. See Graeber, *Debt.*, p. 181.

But then, ca. 600–500 B.C., from the Ganges Valley to China, across Persia, into Mesopotamia, and beyond into Greece, everything began to change with the suspiciously simultaneous and "coincidental" rise of coinage.[37]

3. Bullion, Coins, Militaries, and the "Military-Coinage-Slavery Complex"

Thus far in our brief survey we have encountered two basic solutions to the problem incurred when the Metaphor is misinterpreted to be a Metaphor of Primordial Debt, those two solutions being perpetual debt—with the inevitable need for constant expansion as we shall see momentarily—or a debt jubilee, a practice that arose in ancient Sumeria and Babylonia.[38]

This consideration brings us to that crucial period, ca. 600–500 B.C., that the German philosopher Karl Jaspers called the Axial Age. Jaspers so designated it because it was the era of the great "axiomatic" philosophers and philosophies, the Buddha, Confucius, and, of course, the beginnings of rational philosophical debate in ancient Greece, symbolized by the great secret society founder Pythagoras.[39] Not coincidentally, as we shall now see, this was also the era in which *coinage* arose. This was also, not coincidentally, the period when vast empires—and the wars that invariably accompanied them—arose. As Graeber notes, the reason for the conjunction of the two is very easy to understand, for in wars bullion and coins can be paid to anyone anywhere, and of course, can be stolen as war booty. By contrast, the sorts of virtual credit instruments in ancient Sumeria and Babylonia, with their clay tablets of negotiable credit instruments, or, for that matter, the paper money of China, were essentially instruments that were only good *within* the societies using them and nowhere else. These types of negotiable credit instruments, were "by definition, a record, as well as a relation of trust,"[40] and thus were of little utility in raising, provisioning, and paying the large armies of the great ancient empires.

This led, inevitably, as I noted in *Babylon's Banksters*, to a vicious circle. On the one hand, it created a class of international traders in bullion (and of course, coins), and to slaves to mine the bullion *for* the coins. This created in turn, on the other hand, vast military machines to conquer territory and slaves to mine the bullion to pay the armies![41] Bullion, in the form of coins, thus moved out of the hands of the temple elites during the Axial Age, and

---

37   Ibid., p. 212.
38   See Graeber's remarks, *Debt*, p. 231.
39   Ibid., p. 223.
40   Ibid., p. 213.
41   See Graeber's discussion, *Debt*, pp. 225–226.

into the hands of the masses.[42] This vicious cycle created what Graeber calls the "military-coinage-slavery complex"[43] where the brutal circularity of the system was quickly evident, since money, in the form of bullion and coins, "was needed to pay armies to capture slaves to mine gold to produce money."[44] And this, of course, led to the rise of an international class of people engaged in the production of coins, the mining of bullion, and its adjutant, slavery.

However, there is a hidden working of the Metaphor in all this development, but in order to see what it is and how it occurred, we must turn to the other great non-economic and numismatic examination of the rise of coinage, that of Richard Seaford.

B. Mind, Metaphysics, and Money in Ancient Greece

Along with Graeber's *Debt: The First 5,000 Years*, Richard Seaford's *Money and the Early Greek Mind* is a magisterial examination of the relationship between the rise of coinage in ancient Greece on the one hand, and the rise of rational philosophical cosmological speculation on the other. Coinage, as Seaford notes, does not come from Egypt or Babylonia,[45] for as we have already seen, the principle form of money in Babylonia was negotiable credit instruments inscribed on clay tablets. Thus we are confronted by the odd fact that money, in the form of coinage, coincides with the rise of philosophical cosmology in ancient Greece,[46] a fact that Seaford argues is not coincidental. Here again, we will only be able to briefly summarize Seaford's complex and detailed book, but in doing so I will propose a *different* relationship between the rise of coinage and that of cosmological philosophical speculation than Seaford. However, in order to make that alternative interpretation clear, we shall first have to understand what he has argued.

Seaford begins his study by observing the metaphysical quality of money, that it is "both a thing and a relation."[47] In the latter capacity, it is a command over the labor "of others in general,"[48] or even, one might say, over "Otherness" itself. As such, it is a token or symbol (especially in the modern age of electronic money). But a symbol or token of what?

It is when one considers this question that the metaphysical properties of money come to the fore, and with them, its direct relationship to the Topo-

---

42 Ibid., p. 226.
43 Ibid., p. 229.
44 Ibid., p. 239.
45 Richard Seaford, *Money and the Early Greek Mind* (Cambridge: Cambridge University Press, 2004), p. 126.
46 Ibid., p. xi.
47 Ibid., p. 1.
48 Ibid.

logical Metaphor of the Physical Medium. The fact that money transcends all the goods and services for which it can be exchanged, or in the purchase of which it can manifest itself *as* those goods and services, renders it analogous to that initial No-thing that distinguishes the first step of the Metaphor. And like that initial No-thing, it possesses (to borrow Seaford's apt phrase), "promiscuous exchangeability."[49] Like the initial No-thing of the Metaphor, it possesses a kind of alchemical transmutability or convertibility.[50]

It was largely the Greeks, following the example of the Lydians, who first introduced the widespread use of coinage in the ancient classical world of the West. As we noted in *Babylon's Banksters*, the association of bullion, coinage, and the religious temples was often close and complex, and this is no less true of Greece, where temples often also functioned as temples of money-changing, and coins were often issued by temples bearing images of various deities[51]— further suggesting that the relationship of money to the cosmological Metaphor was very much present in the Greek mind.

1. Coins, and the Metaphor
a. The Stamp

However, when we turn our attention to what coinage actually *is* in the ancient world, and particularly in Greece, the relationship between money and the Metaphor becomes much more explicit. We begin by recalling a fact we first mentioned in *Babylon's Banksters*, and one which is especially true of ancient Greece, namely, that the *intrinsic bullion value of coins was often **less** than the value officially declared and **stamped** on the coins themselves.* The stamp, so to speak, actually created or added value to the instantiation of bullion in the coin itself,[52] such that the *stamp* itself became the measure of value, rather than the process of *weighing* the bullion.[53] This in turn led to the close association of states and temples with the minting of money, and as they came to exercise a kind of "money minting monopoly,"[54] a money-making elite inevitably arose.

But of course, at the same time that all this was happening, philosophical cosmological speculation also arose, leading Xenophanes, for example, to speculate that behind all the diversity of the world, there was an underlying, impersonal "stuff" or substance from which that world derived, and therefore,

---

49   Seaford, *Money and the Early Greek Mind*, p. 2.
50   In this respect, see Seaford's comments on p. 4, regarding Sophocles' observations on money.
51   Ibid., p. 4.
52   Ibid., p. 6.
53   Ibid., p. 126.
54   Ibid., p. 6

all the gods of the Greek mythology were but man-created projections of humanity.[55] One was left, during this period of the simultaneous appearance of pre-Socratic philosophy and coinage, with a kind of idealized monism versus an empirical multiplicity.[56] Coinage gave *order* and rationality to this multiplicity, and especially to the limitless variety of interpersonal human relationships uniting behind the state or sovereign, who brought order to the cosmos and to those relationships.[57] To put it differently, the rise of money in general, and coinage in particular, was to a certain extent inevitable, since it was implied in the physical implications of the metaphor. The problem was, which type of money was it? Money based on the productivity of the state (interpreting the "fecund" version of the Metaphor as an open information-creating system), or money based on a closed system of a finite amount of metal, a zero sum game of debt (interpreting the "closed" or debt version of the Metaphor).

Note what is occurring here, for it will become quite a crucial point in our deeper analysis of the relationship between money, the Metaphor, and the elites behind both, in a moment. For the present, we observe that the creation of money, and philosophical cosmological speculation itself, were both being done by *elites*, and that this introduced a bifurcation into Greek society, in which the common masses continued to practice and to believe in the deities of Greek mythology, while the elites began to believe in the impersonal version of the Metaphor.[58] Seaford notes that

> At the apex of the long-term transactional order the anthropomorphic deities are replaced—at least in the minds of an elite—not so much by the polis as by the metaphysical projection of the impersonal, unitary, abstract, transcendent, seemingly self-sufficient power of money, a process that is first observable in Anaximander in early sixth-century Miletus (probably the very first thoroughly monetized society in history) and that culminates in the metaphysics of Parmenides and Plato.[59]

In other words, the elite was not so much *irreligious* as it was an elite that had adopted a *different* religion than the masses, the "religion behind the religion," the philosophy of the Metaphor.

It is important to pause here and observe what Seaford is really arguing, for he is maintaining essentially that the whole tradition of philosophical cos-

---

55 Ibid., p. 11.
56 Ibid., p. 217.
57 Ibid., p. 222.
58 Ibid., p. 12.
59 Ibid., pp. 14–15.

mology, from the Pre-Socratics up through Plato and Parmenides and right on through to the Neoplatonists, is the *result* of the rise of coinage; money—in the form of coins—led to philosophy and to the construction of the Metaphor, not vice versa.

But this, as we have seen, cannot be true either, because, simply put, the Metaphor certainly existed prior to the appearance of coinage. So what was it about coins in particular that influenced a new burst of philosophical exploration of the Metaphor? We may summarize these influences as follows:

1) The bullion of coinage[60] represented that immortal, changeless, underlying unitary substance of the cosmos, since, for all practical intents and purposes, bullion was immortal, and a unitary substance (such as gold, silver, and so on);[61]

2) As such, the bullion of coinage symbolizes the underlying physical medium, the No-thing of the Metaphor, in its homogeneity and ability to be exchanged—i.e., metaphorically transmuted—into anything else, i.e., goods and services;[62]

3) This homogeneity of coinage also reduces the *users* of coinage to a homogeneous status, since it makes all parties to the transaction equal, and makes them manifestations of the underlying No-thing that coinage represents as well;[63]

4) The division of the bullion of coinage represents the process of differentiations in the Metaphor, as bullion is segregated into individual *coins*, and then *stamped* with a value that exceeds the intrinsic value of the bullion itself. This is a vitally important point, for note how accurately the Metaphor is being reproduced here: the *stamp* of value *adds information and indeed* **constitutes** *the information contained in the coin—its "value"—just as the process of differentiation in the Metaphor distinguishes "types of No-thing" by the information content within each type of "distinguished No-thing."* Additionally, money has value more or less *independent of time and space*, at least in the thinking of the early Greeks.[64] In this respect, as we shall see sub-

---

60 It should be recalled that not all Greek city-states used precious metal bullion in their coinage. Some, like Sparta, used iron.

61 See Seaford's suggestive comments in *Money and the Early Greek Mind*, p. 16.

62 Ibid., p. 150.

63 Ibid., p. 151.

64 Ibid., p. 246. Seaford also states this principle on p. 257 in no uncertain terms: "The oneness of monetary value must, through all its exchanges with a vast variety of goods, retain its identity. It is important for the functioning of money that monetary value be exactly the same not only in different places but also at different times. It is this unprecedented all-pervasive *functional* unchanging oneness, uniting in the minds of its users one place with another and present with future, that enters unconsciously into Parmenidies' conception of the One." (Emphasis in the original.)

sequently in this chapter, money is—in physics terms—a non-local phenomenon, for coinage represents that "common surface" that occurs during exchange, and as such, that common surface is a non-local phenomenon.

It is this distinction between the *information* contained *in* the coin, versus the substance *of* the coin (its bullion), that gives rise, according to Seaford, to the metaphysical categories such as substance and accident, or substance and individual form.[65] Additionally, the initial No-thing of the Metaphor is viewed, in the Hesiodic cosmogony, as an undifferentiated chaos. Information adds *differentiation*, just as with the Metaphor itself;[66]

5) Notably, in Greek thinking of this period, there is no notion of *debt* or *limit* to this system, for just as the No-thing of the Metaphor could differentiate without limit, there was similarly no limit to money.[67] The Greeks, in other words, in spite of the rise of debt and early banking practices, understood the Metaphor to be an *open* system, rather than a *closed* one;

6) In the imposition of *information*—i.e., value—on the stamp on coins, *measure* and *reason, or ratio* (λογος), are imposed on the world of plurality and "Otherness";[68]

7) Thus, *individuality* or *personhood* come to reside—at least for the basic implications of Greek thinking—*in the differentiations themselves* rather than in *the first No-thing*, and individual coins with their stamp of value are a metaphor of this implication. Money itself, and the underlying substance which it represents, are understood to be *impersonal*.[69] In this, as we have seen, the Greeks are opting for the "impersonal/atheistic" interpretation of the Metaphor. Yet, one might also say that since man is the "common surface" or micro-cosm—as we discovered in chapter two—that money comes to represent man, and to that extent, is also a microcosm, a "common surface" binding and transacting human exchange. Hence it could be argued that the Medium, prior to its first tripartite differentia-

---

65 Ibid., p. 136: "The invention and use of the earliest coins demanded the recognition of the combination of, and antithesis between, sign (or form) and substance, an antithesis in which, although the substance must have some intrinsic value, decisive is the sign, which implies a homogeneous ideal substance distinct from the metal in which the sign is expressed." Note very clearly what Seaford has stated here: the *bullion* of the coin is *itself* a symbol, which, along with its stamp of value, *represents or symbolizes the physical medium and its differentiations via the information content of those differentiations.* See also Seaford's comments on p. 149.

66 Ibid., p. 220.

67 Ibid., p. 165.

68 Ibid., p. 231–232.

69 Ibid., pp. 152, 155–156.

tion, and *in* that threefold differentiation, is a kind of "super-Self" or "super-Person";

8) We thus arrive at the most succinct statement of Seaford's thesis: "The presocratic (sic) cosmos is, in its various forms, a projection of human institutions (especially money) onto the cosmos no less than is the Olympus of ordinary believers."[70] Seaford is arguing, then, that money or coinage, in other words, created philosophy, created the Metaphor, and not vice versa.

With these thoughts in mind, we are now in a position to begin making some preliminary observations. Seaford has noted that the rise of coinage was coincident with the rise of philosophical reflection on the Metaphor. In his opinion, the rise of coinage to a certain extent *originated* that reflection, if not indeed the Metaphor itself. In this, he argues, we see both the rise of a *financial* elite, and the rise of an *intellectual or philosophical* elite, whose true "atheistic" views (not believing in the gods, *not* as not believing in the divinity of that primordial substance) are hidden from the masses. As we also saw in our review of Graeber's work in the previous section of this chapter, the Metaphor was twisted in some early—and very modern—thinking, into the Primordial Debt Theory. But if one assumes the *opposite* ordering of the relationship between the Metaphor and money than does Seaford, i.e., if one assumes that the Metaphor gave rise to money, and not vice versa, then an interesting picture emerges, namely, that of debt theory as a "meme" of social dominance promoted by the elites who were created by the rise of coinage.

It is important to understand the both/and nature of the Metaphor in this respect, and how it would inform the motivation of such elites in promoting that meme, for the Metaphor itself would, as noted previously, constitute a new kind of "religion" in polytheistic societies like ancient Greece. By believing in the underlying unchangeable substance, such philosophical elites privately hold a very different doctrine than that publicly promoted in the temples. In this interpretation, their motivation in promoting the meme would be theistic. However, in the view of that underlying substance as *impersonal*, their view in promoting the meme of primordial debt would be *atheistic*, but in either case, the result is the same: a meme would be created that would enhance the power of that philosophical-financial elite.

---

70 Ibid., p. 284.

b. The Idealized Substance and the Coincidence of Opposites

We have just suggested that rather than coinage giving rise to the Metaphor—as Seaford implies—that the reverse is true, the Metaphor gave rise to coinage. In the broadest historical point of view, this is true, for the Vedic texts that contain the Metaphor are, as we have seen, much older than coinage. But before we can make the argument about the Metaphor giving rise to coinage tighter, we must explore other details of the relationship between the two.

We may begin by noting an observation that Seaford makes concerning the relationship of this underlying substance to the primordial elements—earth, air, fire, and water—and to money:

> Just as the circulation of goods (money-goods-money, etc.) is driven by (unsubstantial yet all-underlying) money according to a numerical abstraction (*logos*) that may seem embodied in the money, so cosmic circulation (fire-things-fire etc.) is driven by (insubstantial yet all-underlying) fire according to the *logos*, which appears to be embodied in the fire. *Both money ... and fire have the transcendent power to transform things into their opposite.*[71]

This returns us to a property of that underlying No-thing of the Metaphor that we noted in chapter two in connection with Giordano Bruno: the coincidence of opposites in that medium.

Money thus combines a uniquely *impersonal* characteristic with a uniquely *super-personal* one, in an almost identical fashion to the way the initial No-thing of the Metaphor can be viewed both as supremely impersonal, random, and chaotic, and supremely personal and ordered.[72] In this, once again, it is a faithful reflection of the both/and nature of the dialectic of the Metaphor, and of its conjunction of opposites.

2. The Hidden Elite's Hand: Pythagoreanism

As we have noted, the essence of Seaford's argument is that money, in the form of coinage, created the philosophical and cosmological speculations of rational Greek philosophy during the pre-Socratic period. We have also discovered there are weighty and cogent reasons to support such a view. It is, however, when we turn to a consideration of the possibility of hidden elites *driving* the spread of coinage that this view begins to unravel, and indeed, it

---

71   Ibid., pp. 232–233, emphasis added. See also pp. 170–171, 238, 242, 248.
72   See Seaford's excellent discussion in *Money and the Early Greek Mind* on pp. 224–225.

is Seaford himself who notices it: "In the advanced city-states coined money was used generally, but belief in the impersonal cosmos of the presocratics was almost certainly confined to an elite."[73] One such elite, as Seaford observes, are the Pythagoreans, who, moreover, appear to have had an influential role in the spread of coinage in cities where their secret society was present:

> ... the Pythagoreans of Croton controlled numerous other Greek cities of Southern Italy. This is supported by the evidence of contemporary coinage. The earliest coinage of Southern Italy had... spread very quickly, with several cities sharing a remarkable uniformity both of technique and of weight standard.[74]

The Pythagoreans, as Seaford observes, were especially renowned for three different types of activity: they were, first of all, a secret society dedicated to a particular way of life. Additionally, they were a *political* society in that they sought, and exercised, political power. Finally, they were, as most know, a society dedicated to a philosophy that was orally transmitted, a philosophy whose core doctrine was that "number is all."[75] This doctrine of "number is all" once again dovetails quite neatly into the appearance of coinage, with its stamp of value on a metal. Pythagoreanism, in other words, is the key group reflecting the "mathematicization" of human society and transaction represented by coinage.[76]

However, as I have stated elsewhere, there is significant evidence to suggest that the Pythagoreans have a connection to Mesopotamia and to Babylonia, both in their mathematical speculations and in the cosmological implications they deduced from them.[77] The idea of cosmology and the connection to number, in other words, *predated* the rise of coinage, and the Pythagoreans were definitely connected to both, making it thus possible to view their role influencing the spread of coinage as deliberate. When we couple this implication to what was stated in Part One of this book—that Hermeticism itself appears to have ancient Egyptian roots—then the possibility becomes much more likely that these hidden elites are driving the

---

73 Ibid., p. 12, see also p. 269 for the link between calculation, money, and political and social order.
74 Ibid., p. 268.
75 Ibid., p. 266.
76 Ibid., pp. 266–267.
77 See my *Giza Death Star*, pp. 202–216, and *Grid of the Gods*, with Scott D. de Hart, pp. 229–254. Seaford notes that music—definitely a preoccupation of the Pythagoreans through their discussions of the "Pythagorean comma" (see *Giza Death Star*, pp. 202–216)—is connected in their thinking with the abstract valuation of money. See Seaford, *Money and the Early Greek Mind*, pp. 280–281. This means, to put it as nakedly as possible, that money is a component of their cosmological doctrine, not vice versa.

appearing of coinage very deliberately, as a social and monetary reflection of the Metaphor.

There is one final point to be adduced in this regard. In my book *Genes, Giants, Monsters, and Men*, I outlined how ancient megalithic sites appeared to have been constructed—millennia before the rise of ancient classical civilizations and therefore millennia prior to the appearance of *any* kind of money, clay tablets, coinage, or otherwise—around uniform standards of measure that were astronomically and geodetically based, and that their appearance was possibly due to the influence of hidden elites,[78] a thesis I explored further in *The Grid of the Gods* with co-author Scott D. de Hart.[79] As I noted in *Genes, Giants, Monsters, and Men*, such a uniform standard of weights and measures could only *be* uniform if they were based on astronomical and geodetic observation; moreover, uniformity of such weights and measures is a prerequisite for commerce on a large scale.

It would appear then that the Metaphor is driving the elites, and that they in turn are driving not only vast construction projects, but the appearance of money, in any form.

C. The Tally: Money as the Common Surface of the Metaphor

Before taking leave of this retrospective, it is worth pausing to consider one final detail. We have noted that coinage, in its use of metals with a stamp of abstract value, embodies in an almost perfect analogy the ancient Topological Metaphor of the Physical Medium, both with respect to the "eternity" of the substance of the bullion in coins themselves, and in the abstract "common surface" of a non-local character that they represent as a stable form of exchange and transmutability across specific times and places. It is worth observing, then, that there is yet another form of money that emerged in ancient times, and continued even throughout the Middle Ages, and that is the notion of the "tally," a physical object such as a stick—or broken clay tablet—whose two halves symbolized a transaction between two parties. Here, Graeber comments very aptly: "A tally does away with the need for witnesses; *if the two surfaces agree then everyone knows that the agreement between the contracting parties exists as well.*"[80]

However, as a closer examination of this notion reveals, the two parts of the tally are conjoined, not upon *two* surfaces, but upon *one abstract common surface which joins the two parts, no matter how far apart the two parts are from*

---

78   *Genes, Giants, Monsters, and Men: The Surviving Elites of the Cosmic War and Their Hidden Agenda* (Port Townsend, WA: Feral House, 2011), pp. 31–65.
79   Farrell and de Hart, *The Grid of the Gods*, pp. 63–126.
80   Graeber, *Debt*, p. 302.

each other. In this, too, the common surface becomes a non-local phenomenon.
The apparently crude mechanism of the tally is thus in fact a very sophisticated embodiment of the whole notion of money and the Metaphor's common surface as a non-local phenomenon.

Philosophical speculation therefore did not appear as the *result* of coinage, but as is more likely, the reverse: coinage appeared as the *result* of the Metaphor, as hidden elites contemplated its implications for the ordering of society and commerce. However, as this chapter has also suggested, the appearance of coinage *did* raise the issue of impersonal *substance and transaction* versus the notion of the *persons* conducting them.

In order to contemplate that relationship more fully, we must now return to the Middle Ages, to the rise of modern banking and that most important conception squatting in the middle of it all, the rise of the doctrine of corporate personhood.

❧ Seven ❧

LAW, LANGUAGE, AND LIABILITY:

The *Persona Ficta* of the Corporate Person
in Theology and Finance

∴

*"Quite often, in fact, we find bankers accused of buying counterfeit coins as well
as stolen valuables such as gems and silver belts. As we have seen ... sometimes
they themselves were discovered to be partners in the production and distribution
of counterfeit coins, or they were found to have ordered the wholesale clipping
and filing of mint coins, even though culling was a criminal activity."*
—Reinhold C. Mueller[1]

THERE IS A JOKE GOING AROUND in the wake of the vast fraud committed by the banking and securities communities over the past few years:
"I'll believe that corporations are persons," says our anonymous interlocutor,
"when the state of Texas executes one of them." In some versions of the joke,
the names of the corporations—J.P. Morgan-Chase, Goldman Sachs, and a
host of others—top the list of those on "corporate death row." Of course, in
the audience there is always a lawyer or two who objects that the whole *purpose* of corporations is to limit personal liability for the misdeeds of a corporation or its officers.

But it was not always so, and indeed, the original basis of the doctrine
of the corporate person is theological, and the whole *point* of the theological
version of the doctrine was precisely to make sure that an individual could

---

1   Reinhold C. Mueller, *The Venetian Money Market: Banks, Panics, and the Public Debt, 1200–
     1600* (Baltimore: Johns Hopkins University Press, 1997), p. 70.

be morally culpable for someone *else's* misdeeds. So how did we get from the theological doctrine to the current state of affairs? How did we start with a doctrine whose whole purpose was to hold humanity corporately responsible and morally culpable for an individual's misdeed, and arrive at the present, when the corporate person can, and has, gotten away with fraud on a massive scale, while many corporate officers presiding over the fiasco have actually given themselves bonuses for their "performance"?

A. The Theological Part of the Story

The theological part of this story begins with a mistranslation made by St. Jerome in the Latin *Vulgate*, and with how St. Augustine of Hippo Regius, on the basis of that mistranslation, formulated the Western Church's doctrine of "Original Sin."

But first, some caveats.

The first caveat is this: to attempt to survey the vast amount of literature that has been written about the doctrine of corporate personhood as an adjunct of the Western Church's doctrine of original sin in a few mere pages in a chapter is an impossibility. Whole tomes have been written about the subject, and all that can be accomplished here is to show the basic theological concepts, their roots, interconnections, and a few of the sweeping implications of that doctrine for the formation of Western culture, jurisprudence, and finance.

The second caveat flows from those previously mentioned roots, interconnections, and implications, for the doctrine as the *Western* Church came to hold it—in one form or another, and in varying degrees of "severity"—was precisely a *western* doctrine, unique to the medieval Latin Church, and therefore in its conceptual roots unique to the Protestant churches that broke from it. *It was not, and is not, the doctrine of the Eastern Orthodox churches*, which do not even refer to the doctrine as "original sin" but as "the ancestral sin." As we shall discover in this short excursus, the western doctrine is intimately related to the notion of the "infinite debt" that mankind supposedly owes God, and to the Western Church's interpretation of the sacrifice of Christ as a kind of "infinite sacrifice" balancing the divine account books.

1. The Central Verse and Crux Interpretum
a. The Greek and the King James

The easiest way to approach this complex subject in our theologically illiterate culture is by examining just one verse in the New Testament, a verse that is, so to speak, the foundation for the doctrine of original sin. That verse is Romans 5:12. In our exposition of this verse, it is important for the reader to remember that we are *compacting* centuries of analysis and theological interpretation, and thus, the reader will have to learn a bit of theology, and a little Greek and Latin, along the way. We cite the verse here in the translation of the Authorized (King James) Version, for reasons that will become apparent shortly:

> Wherefore, as by one man sin entered into the world, and death by sin; and so *death* passed upon all men, for that all have sinned.

Before we proceed with complex analysis, it should be noted that the verse does *not* say that "sin nature" or even "guilt" passed upon all men, but that *death* did.

Now let us begin to look at this verse, and particularly the last clause of the verse—"for that all have sinned"—very closely. In the original Greek, this reads εφ ω παντες ημαρτον, and the two words that concern us here are εφ ω (or "eph ho," to transliterate it), which the King James translators have very carefully (as we shall see) translated "for that." The interesting thing about this expression—εφ ω—is that it is capable of three different interpretations all at the same time (after all, this is Greek!). These two little Greek words are, in the first instance, an idiomatic expression, meaning simply "because." Thus, the first meaning of the verse in the Greek is this:

> Wherefore, as by one man sin entered into the world, and death by sin; and so *death* passed upon all men, because all have sinned.

However, it is when we consider the meaning of the two Greek words εφ ω—*eph ho*—*separately* that the meaning becomes more specific. The second of these words, ω, or *ho*, is a *masculine singular reflexive pronoun*, referring, obviously, to a masculine singular antecedent in the previous parts of the sentence. The first word, εφ, or *eph*, is a preposition, which in this grammatical construction means "for that reason" or "because of which." Notably, by adopting the translation "for that," the King James translators were being scrupulously faithful in trying to preserve not only the *first* meaning—"because"—but also the other two possible meanings— "because of which" or "for that reason".

So the question at this point becomes "what is the antecedent of the masculine singular pronoun ω, or *ho*?"

In the previous parts of the verse, there are only two possibilities in the Greek, the "one *man*" (ο ανθρωπος) and death (ο θανατος).

If one takes the first antecedent, the "one *man*," then the meaning of the verse becomes this:

> Wherefore, as by one man sin entered into the world, and death by
> sin; and so *death* passed upon all men, because of the one man all
> have sinned.

But there is a problem with this reading, and many Greek church fathers saw
it immediately. The problem is that in such constructions, the normal rules
of grammatical exegesis infer that reflexive pronouns refer, not to the *farthest*
antecedent, but to the *nearest*, which in this case, is not the "one man," but
death. Thus, the more specific reading of the verse is this:

> Wherefore, as by one man sin entered into the world, and death
> by sin; and so *death* passed upon all men, because of death all have
> sinned.

What this means is that on the *first* reading of the verse—"so death passed
upon all men, because all have sinned"—is that death is a punishment for
individual personal sin, whereas on the *third* reading of the verse—"so death
passed upon all men, (and) because of death, all have sinned"—it is *death*,
i.e., physical and spiritual corruption, that is passed from Adam and Eve to
their descendants, but *not the moral culpability* for their sin. In other words, it
is the *consequence* of their action—death—that is passed on, *but not the moral
responsibility* for someone *else's* misdeed. Indeed, it is largely the first and the
third reading that the Greek church fathers favored, and hence, there is *no*
notion within Eastern Orthodoxy that one inherits a moral culpability for
Adam and Eve, or a "sin nature" as is often stated in the western version of
the doctrine.

This close reading of the verse had enormous consequences for how the
Eastern Church interprets other texts relating to this issue, and also had enormous consequences for legal and cultural developments in the East, not the
least of which was that within Orthodox cultures it is not the Crucifixion of
Christ that is the central liturgical event, but the Resurrection of Christ that
is the central liturgical and cultural event. The reason is simple: the basic
problem of mankind, on this view, is not so much a *moral* one (and hence,
not a problem of infinite debt), but, so to speak, a *physical* one that only God
Incarnate, through the conquest of death, can repair.[2]

Note something very important here, for it will be crucial to understanding how the *Western* doctrine is in fact a doctrine of inherited guilt or moral

---

2   I am well aware that the meaning of "death" for the Greek fathers implied both a physical *and spiri-
     tual* corruption, but am stressing the "physical" aspect of it for western audiences unaccustomed to
     thinking of such issues in other than moralistic and thus purely spiritual terms, in order to show
     that there is no notion of an inherited moral, or "legal," culpability or guilt for someone else's sin.

culpability *based on the doctrine of corporate personhood*. In the Greek, death is indeed a *natural* consequence, that is to say, it inheres in the common human nature passed on from parent to child, and thus, in the Orthodox Christian view, from Adam and Eve to the rest of humanity. But in the Orthodox view *sin* remains a *personal* choice, and hence, the moral culpability is only ascribed to the individual *person* committing the act. Thus, a very clear distinction is drawn between *person* and *nature*, a distinction that, as we shall now see, dissolves in the Western version of the doctrine.[3]

b. The Latin Vulgate and All Other English Translations

It is when we turn to the Latin Vulgate translation of St. Jerome that we see the origins of the western doctrine that will become codified by St. Augustine of Hippo Regius, for here, there is clearly an implied doctrine of a "corporate person." In the Vulgate, Romans 5:12 reads this way:

> Wherefore, as by one man sin entered into the world, and death by sin; and so *death* passed upon all men, in whom all have sinned.

The Latin of the last phrase is quite clear, emphatic, and insistent: *en quo omnes peccaverunt*, opting to translate only the *second* possible meaning of the Greek εφ ω παντες ημαρτον, a reading that, as we saw, was not favored by the Greek fathers nor really even consonant with normal rules of grammar.

Now we must "parse" this reading somewhat, again compacting massive amounts of theological writings of the period, and massive amounts of analysis. Our guide here will be the two crucial categories of *person* and *nature*, and the third metaphysical category so essential to theological dogmatics, the category of *natural operation*. We may get a glimmer of what each of these categories are designed to do, by noting the questions they are designed to answer:

1) *Person* answers the question *who is doing something?*
2) *Natural operation* answers the question *what is it that they are doing?* and
3) *Nature* answers the question *what are they that they are doing these things?*

We can gain an appreciation of the second and third questions from the old adage "if it looks like a duck, walks like a duck, and quacks like a duck, all natural operations of ducks, it's a duck, i.e., possesses the common nature of

---

3   It should also be noted that the King James *alone* of all English translations achieves a translation rending most of the subtleties of the underlying Greek text, whereas other translations opt to translate only one meaning, and the simplest one at that.

duckdom." We get close to an understanding of the difference between person and nature here by noting that ordinary language maintains it. We say "I *am* a person (person)" but "I *have* a soul" (nature), and thus, the rational faculties of human nature and soul *are distinct from the person itself.* As we shall see, it is customary for those in the West's culture to make the mistake of identifying *person* with *soul* and thus to reduce person to the soul's rational and volitional faculties, for reasons we shall get to shortly, reasons closely allied to the doctrine of an inherited moral culpability, the corporate person, and the peculiarly and uniquely western doctrine of "original sin" as distinct from the Eastern doctrine of *ancestral* sin.

It is these three categories of metaphysical distinctions—person, natural operations, and nature—and the three questions associated with them that form the basis of trinitarian theology, the doctrine of the Incarnation, and theological anthropology. It is worth pausing to take a short look at the first two, before passing on to a consideration of what happens to these three categories when viewed in the context of the implied doctrine of inherited guilt and the theological anthropology of the Western reading of Romans 5:12. It is important to note that our sole purpose here is *not* to defend the truthfulness or falsity of these doctrines, but merely to elucidate the general method of *thinking behind them.*

With respect to the database or dataset of the first two fields— trinitarian theology and the Incarnation—the texts of the canonical New Testament became, of course, the basis on which the questions were posed. For example, if in the New Testament the fathers saw Christ uttering phrases with the words "I am"—the name of God in the Old Testament—and performing miracles or forgiving sins, and if the Holy Spirit could be blasphemed against, then the clear implication was that the "Whos" that were "doing these things" had the same common "divine" nature. Hence, three *persons* doing *common operations* of a common underlying *nature.*

With respect to Christ, the same order of asking questions in terms of the categories led to a different result. There, *one* person was performing *two entirely different sets* of natural operations: "divine" ones like healing the sick, forgiving sins, and so on, and human ones like walking, talking, and so on. This led to the famous Chalcedonian definition in 451 that he was *one Person* in *two* natures. In both the trinitarian and christological instances, it is important to note that the distinction of the three categories has been maintained.

Now let us return to the Western version of Romans 5:12 and parse what is going on in terms of the *categories* of person, natural operation, and nature, to see what has happened. First, let us recall the reading of the Vulgate itself:

Wherefore, as by one man sin entered into the world, and death by sin; and so *death* passed upon all men, in whom all have sinned.

Note now the implied steps of the metaphysical "logic" here:

1) The *person* of Adam—the "one man" of the verse—sins;
2) Sin is a *personal use* of the *natural operation or exercise of the human will,* which is a property common to human *nature*;
3) But the moral culpability of that choice passes to all his descendants (in whom all have sinned); thus,
4) The *natural operation of the will* and *its personal use* now defines the content of *all persons common to the inherited nature. In other words, **person** has been confused with **nature** on the basis of one, or several, persons using their common faculty of will in the same or similar ways. This common functional use thus implicitly defines the very person itself, and consequently makes possible the conception of a "group" or "corporate" person conceived precisely in terms of this common functional use of the will.* It is this step, in other words, which informs the corporate logic so many people find frustrating, namely, the formation of corporate "group think" cultures. Such a phenomenon is built into, and an inherent component of, the underlying corporate logic of the doctrine of original guilt.

In other words, the distinction between person, operation, and nature has been completely blurred,[4] and what has arisen as a consequence is a kind of "group person"—the Protestant theologians would sometimes call it a federal person or "the federal Adam"—which is defined *by the assumed common functions* of the will and its involvement in a universal guilt. Persons engaged in common functions—in this case, "sin"—defined the group, or corporate, person in this case, all of humanity descended from, or "in" Adam: "in whom all have sinned." It is this step that forms the theological basis of the doctrine of corporate personhood in law.

Finally, in its own way, this doctrine is deeply rooted to the Western Church's understanding of the Atonement of Christ as being the payment of an infinite debt.[5] In one sense, the understanding of "original sin" as an

---

4   It is worth pointing out that this blurring of distinctions *also* occurs in western trinitarian theology, as the Eastern Church pointed out consistently once the peculiar formularies of Augustine of Hippo became known to it. This blurring of the categorical distinctions also played a major role in the recurrent western controversies over predestination and free will. I have outlined these two points previously in my published theological works.

5   See Farrell and de Hart, *Grid of the Gods*, pp. 201–217.

inherited guilt or culpability in someone else's moral choices, by dint of the human nature all share in common, means that "sin," perceived as a "debt" owed to God, begins both to "accumulate," and to be a *systemic* problem. And since God is "infinite" and "infinitely righteous," this means that the debt is infinite, and beyond the ability of mankind to repay, hence God, who is infinite according to this logic, had to become man in the Incarnation, and slaughter himself to himself, to repay the debt in an infinite death to abolish the "principle." Notice that in this version of the doctrine, the ancient "topological metaphor" of the medium, which began as a metaphor of *fecundity* and creativity, as an *open* system of virtually limitless creation of information, was transformed into a zero-sum game and a *closed* system, for no matter how much information was created, that information was always in the form of debt, which only the top echelon of the metaphor—God—could pay off. We will encounter the metaphor, and its transformation within this closed system approach, yet again in this chapter, so for the moment, it is important to note how the closed system interpretation has roots deep within the western theological tradition.

2. The Corporation, or Partnership, in Medieval Italian Law

With this all-too-short and clumsy theological analysis in mind, we return to the main story, for we can see the role of this theological formulation nowhere more clearly than in the high medieval formulations of the liability of corporate partnerships, for it is here that we see clearly how the conceptions previously outlined entered into secular jurisprudence … and finance.

In his superlative study *The Medieval Super-Companies: A Study of the Peruzzi Company of Florence*, Edwin S. Hunt makes the following observations, which are directly germane to our survey here.

1) The medieval super-companies—with which we shall be dealing in the remainder of this chapter—were organized as semi-permanent partnerships;[6]

2) The intended semi-permanent or permanent nature of these partnerships was attested to by their use of a company logo, "such as the golden pears on a blue background in the case of the Peruzzi and the diamond-shaped heraldic design of the Bardi";[7]

---

6 Edwin S. Hunt, *The Medieval Super-Companies: A Study of the Peruzzi Company of Florence* (Cambridge University Press, 1994), p. 76.

7 Hunt, *The Medieval Super-Companies*, p. 76. This point may seem confusing, given the fact that these partnerships were formed and dissolved by the partners. But one may gain an understanding of what is actually taking place by the modern corporate analogue. The partnerships of the

3) These partnerships were formed and dissolved entirely at the whim of the partners themselves, with such dissolutions being normally for the purpose of effecting new shareholdings of the partners themselves. Normally, upon such dissolutions and shareholding realignments, profits (or losses) were distributed among the partners/shareholders on a prorated basis;[8]

We now come to the crux of the matter, and the link to the theological basis of the doctrine of the corporate person. Hunt writes:

4) The "money values" that reflected the stake or share that a partner held in the company "entitled each owner to a share of profit or loss prorated to the percentage of this contribution to total company capital. Thus, the word 'shareholder' can be used interchangeably with the word 'partner.' *The companies were partnerships in the sense that each shareholder was subject to unlimited liability against all of his personal possessions in the case of bankruptcy.*"[9]

Note that *unlike the modern corporation*, the medieval conception still holds the *persons* who constitute the shareholders of the "group person" of the corporation as *personally* liable for the losses or failure of the corporation or partnership itself. In other words, the *theological* doctrine is still fully effective in *secular* conceptions. With this, we may now turn to the financial part of the story, and the rise and collapse of the great Florentine medieval super-companies, and lurking behind it all, the role of the financial oligarchs of Venice. And once again, in doing so, we will encounter in a new guise the "topological metaphor" of the medium.

B. The Financial Part of the Story: The Collapse of the Bardi and Peruzzi "Super-Companies" in the 1340s
1. General Considerations and Aspects of the "Super-Companies"

It is worth noting at the outset that the rise of the great Florentine "super-companies," the Bardi company and the Peruzzi company, in the 14th century

---

various medieval super-companies were formed under the sponsorship of the prominent families—the Bardi, the Peruzzi—forming them. Thus, several formal partnership or shareholding arrangements could be sponsored by the family under the corporate logo and the "company" would constitute, over time, several such realignments of shareholdings. The formation and dissolution of partnerships would be analogous to the sale of shares between shareholders of a modern corporation, the only difference being that in the modern corporation, the corporate charter is no longer formally dissolved and re-registered each time such a realignment of shareholdings occurs.

8   Ibid.

9   Hunt, *The Medieval Super-Companies*, p. 76, emphasis added.

was closely synchronized with the demise of the previous great bankers to western Europe, the Templar order, in 1312. Like the Templars, the Bardi and Peruzzi quickly came to fill the role as "bankers" to the kings and princes of Europe with whose territories their enterprises had dealings. One might go so far as to speculate that there is some sort of connection between the demise of the one, and the rise of the others. Such speculation will, however, have to be tabled until later, when we examine once again the role of the *Serenissima Republica* of Venice in the demise of the great super-companies of Florence. In considering the possible role of Venice in their demise our catalogue of "oligarchical techniques of manipulation" will be considerably expanded, as we shall see.

But why the term "super-company" at all?

Again, in his critical study of this period and of these companies, Edwin Hunt notes that the modern term "multi-national" company would be misleading, since the nation states of that era were themselves not the sprawling bureaucratic edifices we see today, nor, in many cases, were they very large. The same problem holds true with the term "mega-company," which conjures images of corporations with vastly larger amounts of capital, personnel, and other resources than was actually the case. Hence, the term "super-company" simply denotes an entity dealing on an international scale, with sufficient economies of scale to do so, but with a much narrower basis of operating capital and personnel than would be the case with a modern multi-national corporation.[10] In Hunt's own words, "The medieval super-company is defined here as a private profit-seeking organization operating several lines of business in a very large volume in multiple, widespread locations through a network of permanent branches."[11] It is this breadth of operation, sitting on top of a small base of capitalization, that in part tells the story both of their rise, and their collapse,[12] but, as we shall see, only *part* of the reasons. The *other* part of the story must be carefully pieced together from a consideration of the academic monographs. When this is done, the black shadow of conspiratorial competition once more looms over the historical landscape.

There is another aspect that distinguishes these medieval "super-companies" from the modern multinational corporation, and that is that the medieval versions *remained much more tightly* in the control of the families—for our purposes the Bardi and Peruzzi, though there were a few others—that founded them. Indeed, Hunt observes that the company *names* are derived from the founding families, such that it becomes problematical "to distinguish between the activities and motivations of such companies and those of the eponymous

---

10 Hunt, *The Medieval Super-Companies*, p. 2.
11 Ibid., p. 38.
12 See Hunt's remarks on the problems of cash flow that the super-companies had to confront, ibid., p. 65.

families."[13] In the case of the Peruzzi company, though it relied upon many shareholders, control of the company was always firmly in the hands of the family, and the *capo* or "CEO" of the company was always a Peruzzi.[14]

As a matter of course, these medieval super-companies relied upon a careful "philosophy of management," for given the slow nature of communications of the day, this meant that *strategic* decisions effecting the long-term goals of the company remained in centralized family control, *but operational decisions* had to be left in the hands of local factors, or "branch managers," who were trained in the central offices in Florence. In branches of extreme importance, these factors were often members of the founding and controlling family itself.[15]

As a further means of retaining familiar control over the strategic functions of the partnership, all staffing of the branches was overseen by the central offices in Florence, that is to say by the founding and controlling families,[16] and as a further means of retaining control, personnel in the various branch offices and locations were routinely rotated.[17] All of this, of course, also required that the companies maintain consistent intelligence gathering, communications, and courier systems.[18]

In any case, with the Bardi and Peruzzi we are once again perhaps looking at that transference of families from Rome and its environs northward that began during the decline and collapse of the Western Empire. As I have noted elsewhere, this may be significant, for many of these families that moved northward to found the communities that would become the great Italian city-states of Genoa, Florence, Milan, and of course, Venice, were brought to the Roman Empire and to suburbican Italy from "Chaldea," that is, from Mesopotamia, upon the Roman annexation of the region.[19] In the case of the Peruzzi family, the subject of Hunt's study, the family appears to be of ancient Roman descent, *however*, by the same token, its lack of mention in annual lists of Florentine noble families prior to 1280 suggests that it was not an ancient family.[20] Here, as elsewhere, the truth probably lies in hidden family records, though as we shall see, with Venice we are in a slightly more favorable position.

Like the Templars before them, the Bardi and Peruzzi companies of Florence established lucrative trading monopolies over certain commodities within various European states, most notably the England of Edward III in

---

13 Ibid., p. 11.
14 Ibid., p. 25.
15 Ibid, pp. 77, 85, 100.
16 Ibid., p. 89.
17 Ibid., p. 95.
18 Ibid., p. 73, 83.
19 See my *Babylon's Banksters*, pp. 267–272.
20 Hunt, *Medieval Super-Companies*, p. 16.

order to finance the beginnings of the Hundred Years' War, and thus effectively became "bankers" to monarchs. It is here that our story, and our analysis, must begin, for the standard academic interpretation of the causes of the demise of the Bardi and Peruzzi is that when Edward III defaulted on his loans, these companies, caught in a "liquidity crisis," themselves collapsed in the 1340s.[21] But as Hunt observes, this is largely an academic myth that scholars continue to repeat, for the exposure to Edward III by the Bardi and Peruzzi companies was not nearly as large as scholars originally thought, and thus the causes for their demise *must be sought elsewhere*. Hunt's study is an attempt to do precisely that, to find that "elsewhere"[22] and the real reasons for the sudden and spectacular collapse of these companies.

2. A Catalogue of Techniques:
The Rise of the Peruzzi Company, and Mercantilism

A glance—and it can only be a glance—at the rise of the Peruzzi company will demonstrate just how quickly the medieval super-companies mastered all the techniques that many would now ascribe to the conspiratorial machinations of modern banksters, corporations, and groups like the Bilderbergers, the Council on Foreign Relations, the Trilateral Commission, and so on.

One of the standard modern techniques—the winning of special monopolistic concessions from the various governments in whose territories it was conducting business—was practiced by the Peruzzi and other medieval super-companies, and with a vengeance. Hunt makes a very important observation, an observation in which we see a familiar practice of the financial elites beginning to emerge. "The Peruzzi records," he observes, "show that different members of the family followed different career paths—military, diplomatic, political, ecclesiastical, professional, and entrepreneurial—and many generated their own sources of wealth."[23] This penetration into the loci of public power—the church, professional occupations, military, and the organs of domestic and international politics—became the "playbook" for financial elites ever after, and, as we shall discover later within this chapter and have already seen, the Venetians perfected this strategy to a very fine art.

One of the key areas of such penetration was, of course, to gain influence or control over the actual issuance of money itself, i.e., to gain influence or control over the various national mints with which they dealt, beginning, of course, with Florence itself.[24] The Peruzzi company began its rise to power

---

21 Ibid., pp. 1, 6.
22 Ibid., p. 6.
23 Ibid., p., 12.
24 Hunt notes that Tommaso Peruzzi was an official of the Florentine mint in 1311 (see ibid., p. 28).

by exploiting the situation between southern and northern Italy in the late 1200s and early 1300s. Namely, the Kingdom of Naples was, at that time, the grain supplier to the small city-states of northern Italy, and in return, was an importer of textiles and other manufactured goods from northern Italy and the rest of Europe, a fact that required the super-companies to have high capitalization.[25] The Bardi and Peruzzi became the middlemen in this commodities trade, and thus, their corporations made much of their income on the commodities market. As a result of this type of trade, the super-companies, much like their modern counterparts, became involved in all aspects of the trade, from production and manufacturing, shipping, and of course ultimately the issuance and exchange of currency itself.[26]

Thus, by 1316, the Peruzzi company had joined a consortium or syndicate of the other great Florentine companies—the Bardi, and Acciaiuoli, later joined in 1330 by the Buonaccorsi—to operate the mints of the kingdom of Naples, collect the taxes, and pay various bureaucrats and troops.[27] In other words, the Florentine super-companies had essentially formed a *cartel* for the purposes of coordinating and controlling their activities in the Kingdom of Naples, a move doubtlessly induced in part by the need to present a powerful front to the government, and to enforce repayment of loans. This is a point to which we shall return momentarily. But for the moment, one should also note that similarly, for a short period of time, the Peruzzi had gained influence over the mints of France in Paris, Troyes, Tournai, and Sommières.[28]

How was such influence and even control gained?

This may be understood through close consideration of Hunt's research and comments on the relationship between the Peruzzi company and the Angevin kingdom of Naples. Hunt notes that by large loans to the Neapolitan crown, which specified precise details on when, where, and how the payments would be loaned to the crown, and more importantly how they were to be repaid:

> Repayment was achieved mainly by diverting to the lenders certain revenues of the crown designated in the loan contracts, such as general tax receipts from a city, province, or the whole kingdom, or from gabelles and customs. Frequently, repayment was made through the waiver of

---

Of course, similar representation was accorded to the Bardi and other entrepreneurial families in Florence, effectively making the Florentine mint not so much a branch of government but an extension of the companies. This is a pattern, as we shall see, replicated in Venice, and raised to new orders of magnitude.

25 Ibid., p. 39.
26 Ibid.
27 Ibid., p. 49. It should be noted that the Florentine companies, being land-locked, perforce had to lease ships from Venice and Genoa to conduct their business.
28 Ibid., p. 131.

the export tax on grain ... The companies looked to currency exchange and fees for transporting cash for some profit but obtained most of their earnings in the form of "gifts" from the king ... mostly they were in the form of tax exemptions, franchises, and valuable privileges, the most coveted of which was the right to export grain.[29]

This short quotation, summing up the practices of the Peruzzi company, is a textbook catalogue of the standard methods of private financial oligarchy to obtain influence, and eventually control, over the institutions of a sovereign government via economic privilege.

Before we comment further on this, however, let us look at another example of this pattern with the behavior of the Bardi and Peruzzi toward King Edward III's England. The Peruzzi company, like the Bardi company, gained trading privileges from the English monarchy in return for large loans, which were "the price of admission to the wool trade,"[30] at that time under a royal monopoly. At this juncture of history, such nations were too large and powerful for any one company to force an *exclusive* monopoly over such privileges, and indeed, Edward III preferred to disperse such privileges to a narrow group of firms, though, as we saw, a syndicate or cartel of sorts was created by the Florentine companies to present a more united front to the Kingdom of Naples. Thus the pattern is repeated: the "gifts" from monarchs or states that were of the most value to the super-companies were tax exemptions and privileged trading positions in the commodities and manufactured goods that were the core of their business.[31] In the case of the Kingdom of Naples, the large loans advanced to the Kingdom, specifically to King Charles II at the beginning of the fourteenth century, gained for the Peruzzi company various special privileges, among them the ability to open a bank in Naples, control of the taxation of grain exports (!), and the right to have civil cases involving the company "put before the Court of Appeals, not the ordinary tribunals."[32] In other words, they obtained special *juridical* privileges or, to put it somewhat differently, the creation of special courts or special jurisdiction to hear cases involving the Peruzzi.[33] Notably, throughout all of this, there was *no* direct challenge to the maritime powers, Genoa and above all Venice.[34] Note that what has actually happened is that the super-companies had:

---

29   Ibid., p. 54.
30   Ibid., p. 61.
31   Ibid., p. 64.
32   Ibid., p. 134.
33   For further discussion see ibid., pp. 42, 47, 58–59.
34   See the discussion on ibid., p. 55.

(1) negotiated that some of the kingdom's tax revenues had to be specifically earmarked as loan repayments, in other words, they negotiated
a lien on certain revenues of the kingdom, and

(2) negotiated their own tax collection prerogatives in order to ensure
those obligations would be fulfilled. In short, they had negotiated
away the sovereignty of the Kingdom of Naples.

Or, to put all these points more succinctly, they had acquired the sovereignty
of the Kingdom of Naples by achieving control of essential state functions
through the extension of loans and the imposition of what modern international banks call "conditionalities."

Now let us catalogue the "playbook of techniques" of the super-companies
as it has emerged thus far:

1) Retain familial control over the strategic operations of the company by
maintaining controlling interest in the shares of the company;

2) Penetrate or infiltrate the key institutions and operations of the state—
diplomatic, governmental, and above all, the mints or currency
issuance—by training family members and close associates in those
fields, with the goal being to make government institutions and
bureaucracies fronts for corporate activity;

3) Work within existing legal constraints—in this period, the Church
prohibition against usury—by negotiating privileged positions for the
company in trading rights, tax exemptions, and even tax-collecting;

4) Control, or at least influence, the entire range of the company's activities, from shipping, to manufacture and production, to currency and
commodity exchange affecting those operations

In short, what one is looking at is classical *mercantilism*, rather than "capitalism"
per se.

We would err, however, if we assumed this exhausted the playbook of
techniques.

a. Control Both Sides of a (Dialectical) Conflict

Hunt reports that in 1312, the Peruzzi company negotiated a large loan
to the grand masters of the Knights Hospitallers order, for the then-astronom-
ical sum of 191,000 florins.[35]

---

35   Ibid., p. 136.

This money, as Hunt notes, was to be employed for the construction of fortifications and other buildings, with the security on the loan provided by "all the order's possessions in all countries."[36] With this, we may add a very *modern* technique of financial elites to our inventory of techniques:

5) Collateralize the infrastructure of nations themselves, particularly if that infrastructure is being constructed on the basis of loans made by the corporation.

It was inevitable that the super-companies, given their large scale and international base of operations, would be drawn into local or regional conflicts and wars. From 1302–1304, and again in 1314, there were local revolts of the Flemish populations from France. The Peruzzi, of course, found themselves caught in the middle, since their lucrative wool trade involved the looms of Flanders (in what is now Belgium), and we have already seen their penetration and influence in French mints.

They solved this political dilemma by acting as collectors of Flemish debts for the French monarchy, while simultaneously floating loans—with the customary negotiated privileges of course—with local Flemish authorities to "help make the payments possible."[37] Similarly, the Peruzzi, while gaining lucrative privileges in the Kingdom of Naples, were gaining similar privileges from Naples' great rival, the Kingdom of Sicily.[38] To be sure, these were accidents of history and consequences of the international extent of the company, but the Peruzzi response to the Flemish situation demonstrates just how quickly this high medieval financial elite learned the lesson that profits could be made from both sides in a conflict *provided* the corporation maintained the veneer of public neutrality. So we may add to our catalogue of techniques:

6) Maintain careful posture of public neutrality in cases of political conflict, while continuing to act as financial agents for both sides.[39]

---

36 Ibid., emphasis added. Hunt notes on pp. 137–138 that such large sums might indicate that the Peruzzi company was acting as an agent for the papacy. It is also worth noting, though it is a story that can only be taken up adequately in modern times, that the papacy was vital in providing the aura and cachet of probity to the super-companies. See Hunt, op. cit., p. 62. In this, we see a continuation of the pattern of association of financial with religious elites that I first discussed in *Babylon's Banksters*.

37 Ibid., p. 146.

38 Ibid., p. 182.

39 It should be noted that like many prominent Italian families of the era, the Peruzzi had both Guelph (pro-papal) and Ghibelline (pro-imperial) parties, so much a part of the complicated politics of the day, and about which so many reams have been written, that any attempt to survey it here is impossible. See ibid., pp. 19–20. Another way of viewing this is, of course, that behind the public veneer of passionate political differences lay the desire to be on both sides of a conflict.

It is important to notice a significant thing here: at this stage in history, while the super-companies and their intellectual descendants fully appreciated the utility of "being on both sides" of a conflict, they had not yet come to the insight that their modern counterparts would realize later in history, a realization that such figures as the great "closet Hermeticist and Magus" Hegel[40] would make possible, namely that profit could be generated and extended through the *creation* of conflict. In short, the medieval super-companies in this respect, unlike their modern counterparts, are *reactive* rather than *proactive*.

But there were *other* sophisticated techniques as well, and with them, we begin to see the hints of something much darker ...

b. Accounting and Exchange Techniques

As Hunt observes, the Peruzzi company has often been referred to in scholarly histories of accounting, and in particular, of the invention of double-entry accounting, as being in part responsible for its development.[41] Indeed, Hunt devotes a whole chapter to the subject, but our purposes are not a history of accounting but rather an attempt to inventory the techniques of financial and corporate oligarchies and elites as they emerged in the Middle Ages.

In this respect, Hunt makes a number of statements that are well worth *careful* consideration. The first of these is that the Peruzzi company, like the other medieval super-companies, kept "secret books."[42] However, before we spring into the "conspiracy mode" of thinking, it is worth having a closer look at exactly what this means, and to do so we must cite Hunt directly:

> The Assets Book and the Secret Book combine to produce something that at first glance appears broadly similar to the consolidation account of a modern multinational corporation. They contain what look like the opening balances of the new company carried forward from the old company,[43] and they deal with certain items of income and expense, especially interest, not carried in the subsidiary books.

---

40 By referring to Hegel as a closet Hermeticist and magus, rather than simply as a philosopher, I am referring to recent trends in academic analysis. See Glenn Alexander Magee's excellent study, *Hegel and the Hermetic Tradition* (Ithaca: Cornell University, 2001).

41 Hunt, *Medieval Super-Companies*, p. 101.

42 Ibid., p. 7.

43 Lest this point seem obscure, it is to be recalled that the capitalization of each formal organization of the company reflects the relative investments by each partner, and hence, when the amounts of each partner's contribution to the organization of the company changed, the prior partnership arrangement was dissolved (and profits and losses distributed among the partners), and a new arrangement was created and formalized.

But their primary function is to house the individual accounts of depositors and borrowers controlled by the Florence Office, mainly nonshareholders (sic) in the Assets Book and shareholders in the Secret Book.[44]

Thus, with this explanation, the possibility of "double-bookkeeping" and "conspiratorial possibilities" recedes, for the Secret Book was simply the register of shareholders and their capital exposure in the company.

But elsewhere, Hunt reveals precisely what is taking place, using the example of Giotto d'Arnoldo Peruzzi, who maintained a capital investment in the company from 1300 until 1315, when he began to draw on the company for personal needs.[45] On the closing of the books in November 1324, however, Giotto's indebtedness to the company of 22,018 *lira a fiorino* was cleared by crediting it with dividends he was owed and the elimination of "his capital contribution liability"[46] of 11,000 *lira a fiorini*. Hunt comments, "This cleanup has the look of what is now called the year-end 'window-dressing' applied by modern corporations and banks, and might imply that Giotto's normal deep indebtedness to the company was being hidden from the nonfamily shareholders."[47] Similarly, Hunt observes that the company actually handled the disbursements to the Peruzzi "family fund."[48] In other words, the two sets of books really functioned as yet another layer of familial control of the company, for the family's benefit, and as a means, if not of *disguising* family dealings from non-family shareholders, then at least of *obfuscating* them.

But there are even deeper possibilities of obfuscation, and with them we approach, once again, the Venetian part of the story. In the example of Giotto Peruzzi referred to above, the units of money were the *lira a fiorino*, and these were "not a currency at all, *but a fictive unit of account employed by the Florentine business community.*"[49] In other words, given the international extent of operations of such companies and the Bardi and the Peruzzi, special "units of account" were created by which companies converted local currencies and managed their books.

When one considers the addition of the sale and re-sale of bills of exchange, and the bi-metallic ratio of gold to silver bullion, then all sorts of possibilities for manipulation begin to occur, as we shall discover when we

---

44   Ibid., p. 108.
45   Ibid., p. 152.
46   Ibid., p. 153.
47   Ibid., pp. 154–155.
48   Ibid., p. 154.
49   Ibid., p. 7, emphasis added.

consider the Venetian part of this story.

The story of the collapse of the Bardi and Peruzzi super-companies, in 1343 and 1346 respectively, is intimately tied, as we have observed, not so much to the default of Edward III of England, to whom both companies had advanced many loans, but to the machinations of Venice to expand and secure her position as the pre-eminent north Italian city-state and hub of a vast maritime trading empire.

The story—and the conspiratorial possibilities—begins as most such stories do, with "discrepancies." Penetrating beyond the standard academic line that the Bardi and Peruzzi were bankrupted after Edward III's default, Hunt notes that the Florentine records on the Peruzzi company's bankruptcy are "mystifying," and to such an extent that they leave "the impression that we are being presented with a charade."[50] Indeed, Hunt also notes that the Peruzzi family "somehow managed to distance itself from the ruin of the company,"[51] and even to retain their wealth and political power within Florence. (Perhaps those two sets of books had something to do with it, and perhaps there were once records that, for whatever reason—deliberate or accidental destruction—are no longer extant.)

But there are even more anomalies in the collapse of the Peruzzi company, and the deeper one digs, the more anomalies accumulate. These make the standard line that the collapse of the Bardi and Peruzzi was due solely to Edward III's default even more problematic, making the academic bewilderment more acute, and making the ground for speculative possibilities, like deliberate conspiracy, more fertile.

---

50   Ibid., p. 231.
51   Ibid., p. 28.

❧ Eight ❧

FLORENTINE *FERS-DE-LANCE*, PERUZZI PYTHONS, VENETIAN VIPERS, AND THE FINANCIAL COLLAPSE OF THE 1340s

∴

"I have known many bankers in my time. Some of them were lazy; the majority however were very busy, highly intelligent men, indefatigably intent on extending their field of action. They had to, otherwise their banks would have paid no dividend at the end of the year ... In a word, it is stupid to speak of 'the bankers.'"
—Dr. Hjalmar Horace Greeley Schacht[1]

"Venice found distinctive solutions to monetary problems that were common to Western Europe."
—Frederic C. Lane and Reinhold C. Mueller[2]

"The transfer of accounts on bankers' books, or 'giro di partite,' from which the term 'giro bank' derives, was the hallmark of Venetian banking."
—Frederic C. Lane and Reinhold C. Mueller[3]

TO ASSUME THAT THE COLLAPSE of the Florentine super-companies, the Bardi and Peruzzi, was due solely to their over-exposure to England's King

---

1   Hjalmar Horace Greeley Schacht, *Confessions of the Old Wizard: The Autobiography of Hjalmar Horace Greeley Schacht* (Cambridge, MA: Houghton Mifflin, 1956), p. 1.
2   Frederic C. Lane and Reinhold C. Mueller, *Money and Banking in Medieval and Renaissance Venice: Volume 1: Coins and Moneys of Account* (Baltimore: Johns Hopkins University Press, 1985), p. 89.
3   Ibid., p. 81.

Edward III—that is, to assume that their collapse is explainable along "safe, friendly academic lines"—is to assume that nothing else happened, that there were no "dark conspiratorial hands or signatures" evident.

To be sure, those companies *were* over-exposed in their loans to Edward III, and had made those loans to him to advance his purposes in the opening phases of the Hundred Years' War. Those purposes may have been in part financial, for one of Edward's targets was the textile manufacturers in Flanders. These challenged Edward's royal monopoly over English textile manufacturing, and in turn, the Bardi and Peruzzi companies' profits, since they had won, through their loans to Edward, the usual "conditionalities": the right to export wool, and rights, or liens, on certain royal revenues to reimburse their loans. When Edward's campaigns in Flanders floundered, Edward defaulted on his loans, and the Bardi and Peruzzi were caught in a cash flow crisis that rippled across their corporate networks from London to Naples. Eventually, they succumbed.

That, at least, is, or was, the standard line, until Hunt published his now indispensable study. There Hunt points out that the default of Edward III represented a small portion of the dealings of the Bardi and Peruzzi, and that a combination of other natural factors also contributed.

So why bring Venice into the picture at all, much less imply that it had some dark or conspiratorial role to play in the demise of the Bardi and Peruzzi? Briefly, there are two reasons that are rather obvious, and a third not-so-obvious reason that, as we shall see, shows the clear hand of Venetian manipulation. The obvious reasons are that the Bardi and Peruzzi companies conducted much of their international trade—particularly their lucrative grain trade—with the Kingdom of Naples by leasing Venetian ships. This is a very important point, for it means that Venetian intelligence was faultlessly well-informed of the scale of the Florentine super-companies' trading with that kingdom, and thus were well-informed of their major international competitor's *exposure* to foreign trade, and how a disruption of their cash flow could ruin those competitors' business.

The second reason is even more obvious. Much of the Bardi and Peruzzi's trade consisted of seasonal commodities, as indeed, did much of Venice's: grain and wool were both of course subject to seasonal change, and the weather and seasons also determined, particularly in Venice's case, when cargo and war galleys would sortie. The cyclical regularity allowed the Venetian merchant bankers and the Florentine super-companies to make predictions on market behavior of all commodities for these two reasons. Merchants would be most exposed to risk or failure when the ships were outbound, for it was the *returning* cargos and caravans that brought to Florence and Venice the commodities that were sold or marketed to the rest of Europe, and hence, these returning caravans brought the profits on the whole trading system.

But there is a third, much more hidden, reason for the demise of the super-companies, one hidden securely in Venice itself, and in its status as the world's bullion market, a status that allowed Venice to manipulate the value of money itself. To appreciate this, one must dig deeply into the structure of that bullion trade, and even further into the agencies of Venetian oligarchical government.

As a final note before proceeding, as stated in the Preface, the argument that Venice was behind the collapse of the super-companies has made its rounds on the internet, with this or that researcher—some quite famous, such as Tarpley—stating that Venice not only had a hand, but orchestrated the collapse. In some versions of this idea, the Venetian oligarchy is viewed as "taking out" a rival (Florence), before beginning the transfer of those oligarchical families' funds and centers of operation quite deliberately northward, to Amsterdam, and finally London.

In making this case, internet articles often refer to the work of Hunt, and two other scholars of the period, Frederic Chapin Lane and Reinhold C. Mueller, and their magisterial works *Money and Banking in Medieval and Renaissance Venice: Volume 1: Coins and Moneys of Account*, and Mueller's *The Venetian Money Market: Vol. 2: Banks, Panics, and the Public Debt: 1200–1500*. But in referring to these works, those articles and researchers have often committed the standard error regrettably found so much within the alternative research and truth community: they simply *fail to reference with any exactitude*, leaving the reader to "take them at their word."

This "conspiratorial" interpretation of events—that Venice had a hand in the collapse of the Bardi and Peruzzi, and even orchestrated the crisis, that Venice was manipulating the global bullion market, and that its oligarchy (and that of the other northern Italian city-states) eventually transferred their family fortunes or *fondi* and base of operations northward to Amsterdam and eventually London—is far too important an hypothesis to be left to mere assertion, without specific referencing and a closer argumentation.

With that in mind, we may now proceed …

A. Basics of Medieval Monetary System and
the Venetian Bullion Trade
*1. The Structure of Florentine Super-Companies' Trade,
and the Interface with Venetian Bankers*

The first thing we must note is that during the early fourteenth century, when the Bardi and Peruzzi companies were at the height of their power, it was actually *they*, and not the Venetian bankers, who were the "international merchant bankers" of the day. Indeed, these super-companies were *interna-*

tional commodities traders first and foremost, and loans to various royal houses such as the Kingdom of Naples or Edward III's England were made in pursuit of gaining trading concessions or monopolies, and in the hopes of attaching corporate liens on royal revenues and taxes in order to repay the loans that they had advanced. In this sense, they became the defining prototypes of "international merchant bankers." But by dint of their leasing of Venetian shipping to *accomplish* all these goals, they had to deal with the *deposit* bankers of the Venetian Rialto.[4] As a result, insofar as the Bardi and Peruzzi conducted day-to-day business for their shipping, this was done by interfacing with the Venetian banks.[5]

Again, the reasons are relatively simple to appreciate. Europe was at that time, just as it was until very recently in its history, a tapestry of small kingdoms, duchies, and city-states, each with their own coinage, and each system of coinage with its own standards of weight, fineness, bullion content, and so on. Additionally, most of these states were part of a vast trading network flowing through Genoa and Venice with the Middle and Far East, with *their* systems of coinages, weights, fineness, and so on. By the nature of the case, then, Venetian bankers on the Rialto, even when conducting business transactions largely occurring within the city itself, had to be competent at dealing with many different systems of coinage and with exchange rates of gold and silver bullion on a daily basis. For international companies like the Bardi and Peruzzi, they were indispensible.[6] By now the reader will have guessed that *this* is the "soft underbelly" of their business, for as we shall discover, there were available to these bankers a variety of means—all perfectly legal within the Venetian system—of manipulating the bullion supply, and hence, the value of silver or gold-based coinage, and therefore, the value of money.

One must not make the mistake, however, of assuming that the crisis was brought about by the over-use of "fractional reserve banking" on the part of the Bardi or Peruzzi, or, for that matter, by the Venetian bankers. At the time of the super-companies' decline and collapse, ca. 1335–1343, they were not engaged in extending bank money credit, that is to say, they were not engaged in fractional reserve banking (unlike the deposit banks in Venice with which they dealt).[7] Even then, the use of fractional reserve banking and the extension of bank-money credits to governments to finance wars was not a step

---

4   The Rialto was the region in Venice where the deposit bankers principally conducted daily operations and business.

5   Lane and Mueller, *Money and Banking in Medieval and Renaissance Venice*, p. 75.

6   Reinhold C. Mueller, *The Venetian Money Market: Vol. 2: Banks, Panics, and the Public Debt 1200–1500* (Baltimore: Johns Hopkins University Press, 1997), p. 262: Mueller notes that the Bardi company, like the Peruzzi, maintained a permanent factor, or branch manager, in Venice.

7   See Hunt, *Medieval Super-Companies*, pp. 201–203.

taken by such bankers until later, where it made its first appearance in (you guessed it) Venice.[8]

The implications of this interface between the international merchant bankers represented by the Bardi and Peruzzi companies on the one hand, and the Venetian Rialto deposit bankers on the other, cannot be lingered over too long, for those Rialto banks were invariably in the hands of a few small Venetian families, each with their own direct ties to the Venetian oligarchical nobility, but also because the Rialto became not only a nerve-center for banking and international commercial transaction, but accordingly became a nerve center for accurate economic and political intelligence for the world, based on the analysis of the commodities trade flowing between East and West through Venice.[9]

Venice thus provided not only the *ships* by which the Bardi and Peruzzi conducted the lucrative grain trade with the Kingdom of Naples, providing the very lifeblood of food for Florence, but that trade also involved Venetian middlemen in yet another way, since that grain was paid for in gold or silver coins and bullion, and Venice, of course, was by far and away the world's largest concentrated bullion market at that time, about which more in a moment. The point here to be remembered is that if there is a sudden or drastic shift in the relationship of gold and silver bullion or coinage exchange rates, then the value of gold-based or silver-based money will change accordingly, and with it, the Florentine super-companies' ability to conduct their commodities trade.[10] And again, all of this would have been well-known to the Venetian oligarchical noble families through their banks' intelligence gathering capabilities, as well as through their contacts within the Venetian government, for it will be recalled that the agencies of the Venetian government were similarly all controlled by the same families.

To reinforce this point, it is worth noting that prior to 1300, there had been a "silver glut" in Europe, with the result that gold rose in value against silver, leading the nobility in Florence to mint a new gold florin,[11] which quickly became a standard of value in international trade of the day, a kind of equivalent to a modern "reserve currency" in international commercial exchange. The result, so far as account keeping was concerned, provides us our first clue of the looming and sinister hand of the Venetian oligarchical bankers in the Florentine crisis, and it is best to allow Lane and Mueller to state the clear outlines of the shadow:

---

8   Ibid., p. 202, n. 69.
9   Lane and Mueller, *Money and Banking in Medieval and Renaissance Venice*, pp. 146–147.
10   Ibid., pp. 276–277.
11   Ibid., p. 277.

Since Florence was coining gold at the same time, however, whereas Venice coined gold only later, Florence had less need then for a money of account based on fine silver to serve as a standard of value. Its *lira a fiorini* was based on fine silver to serve as a standard of value. Its *lira a fiorini* was based on both gold and silver only very briefly. After 1296 it clung to the gold connection. All the accounts of the Bardi and Peruzzi, great Florentine firms of international merchant-bankers of the fourteenth century, were kept in *lire, soldi,* and *denari a fiorini*, with regular conversions of *fiorini d'oro* into *lire, soldi,* and *denari a fiorini* by use of the equation 1 *fiorini d'oro*=29/20 *lira a fiorini*.[12]

This requires a little unpacking.

Very simply put, the Florentine super-companies, the Bardi and Peruzzi, were still keeping books in terms of *silver*-based coins or "moneys of account"— the *lire, soldi,* and *denari*—while the value of gold continued to rise to the point that it became prudent to coin the gold florin, which became, as noted, an internationally-used standard of exchange and value. *So long as the gold-to-silver exchange ratio remained more or less stable, the calculations on the account books of the Bardi and Peruzzi would remain stable, and so would their liquidity.*

Notably, while the Florentine city-state, equally in the hands of its own oligarchical-financial class as Venice, was coining its new gold florin, Venice was attempting to defend the value of its silver *grosso*, which *had* been, up to that time, the standard of value in international exchange, until mints in the Middle East started to issue close "clones" of the Venetian *grosso* with less silver content but the same stated value. As a result, the "bad" Middle Eastern money began to drive out the Venetian *grosso*, while Genoa, like Florence, began to mint and issue gold coins.

Succinctly stated, there was a wholesale "coinage war" taking place between Venice, Florence, Genoa, and the Middle East at the period the Bardi and Peruzzi entered their prime and decline, as each city-state (and the sultans of the Middle East) struggled to control the bullion trade via the process of making their coinage the standard for international trade.

This is the key, for Venice meant to dominate that bullion and coinage war, and to protect its dominant position in the global trade between western Europe and the Far East that flowed through Venice and the *Middle* East. Venice was attempting to defend its silver *grosso*.[13] It was a gold versus silver war, and given Venice's dominant position in the bullion exchange trade and its ability to *manipulate* that trade, and hence, the value of money,

---

12   Ibid., p. 280.
13   See the much more detailed remarks in ibid., p. 281.

it was a struggle that Florence, like the Middle Eastern mints, was destined to lose.

We must now pause to note yet another contributing factor, and thereby yet another indicator of Venetian manipulation, behind the collapse of the Bardi and Peruzzi super-companies. By the middle to late 1330s Florence was involved in yet another of the many "mini-wars" that so often occurred in northern Italy for supremacy between the various city-states. The Bardi and Peruzzi companies were heavy financial backers of the Florentine cause. Venice was a Florentine ally in that war, until Venice concluded a separate peace, leaving the Florentine companies—the Bardi and Peruzzi chief among them—over-exposed and unable to recoup their loans through war booty. So outraged was Florence that the city-state passed a law forbidding all trade with the Venetians and any of their territories, a law which only made the financial crisis deepen for the super-companies, for after all, their ability to exchange various coins depended in large part on the bankers of the Rialto.[14] The *precise timing* of the Venetian withdrawal from the war suggests quite strongly that the ultimate motivation for its involvement in the war was simply to over-extend the super-companies, as part of a long-term strategy of attack on the value of Florence's money and the basis of its international trade, the gold florin.[15]

This pattern only deepens the more deeply one digs into the details, but we have already pinpointed the soft underbelly of Florentine trade in the quotation of Lane and Mueller on the gold florin, and the silver-based monies of account. The meaning of this two-fold system is revealed by a further consideration introduced by Hunt:

> One other explanation for the reduction in company profitability that deserves consideration is the effect of the well-known changes in the gold-silver ratio in the thirteenth and fourteenth centuries. Grossly oversimplified, this ratio was said to be important to Florentine businessmen because a significant part of their expense, especially wages, was incurred in silver or billon coinage,[16] while their sales in the international markets were mainly in gold florins. An increase in the price of gold relative to silver was thus expansionary and favorable to business interests, while a decrease was depressing and unfavorable to them.[17]

---

14 Hunt, *Medieval Super-Companies*, pp. 205–206.

15 Reinhold C. Mueller covers this war as well. See Mueller, *Venetian Money Market*, p. 260.

16 Billon coinage was the so-called "black money," i.e., money that was an alloy of silver and copper, or simply, copper itself, in the three-fold classification of money in the Middle Ages: yellow money (gold), white money (silver), and "black money," which eventually came to mean everything else.

17 Hunt, *Medieval Super-Companies*, p. 176.

In other words, a change of gold-to-silver exchange rates, if effected quickly enough and in conjunction with other factors (such as embroiling the super-companies in a war, and then suddenly pulling out of that war), could ruin Florentine international trade and greatly magnify its domestic economic problems. And the result, of course, of the collapse of the Bardi and Peruzzi was that Florence never again became the major international competitor to Venice it had been.

Before we can turn to that, however, a final few words about the bankruptcy of the Bardi and Peruzzi companies is necessary in order to properly set the stage for our closer examination of Venice's hidden manipulations during the whole affair.

As we noted in the previous chapter, the logic of the corporate person doctrine was developed in response to a theological doctrine based on a Latin mistranslation of the original Greek of Romans 5:12, and in that secular development, the individual partners of a corporation such as the Bardi and Peruzzi were not exempt from personal liability if the corporation failed. Yet, as we also noted, there are indicators that the whole bankruptcy was a charade.[18] But what are these indicators?

They are quite disturbing, and in them we discover yet another part of the "oligarchical playbook." Hunt observes that when the Bardi and Peruzzi finally collapsed, the Peruzzi company *itself* created the meme that it was the default of Edward III of England that precipitated the crisis. Yet, upon examination of the Assets and Secret Books of the company, there is not a single mention of any advances from the company to the Florentine city-state, nor to Edward III, but simply advances to King Federigo of the Kingdom of Sicily.[19]

One may add to this the unusual behavior of the Peruzzi shareholders after the public disclosure that the company was bankrupt, for they remained in Florence for a full month after the company's collapse,[20] and then suddenly fled. This prompted the government of Florence to issue an amnesty to twenty-two Peruzzi shareholders to allow them to return to the city without threat of prosecution, in order to get to the bottom of what had happened. The terms of the amnesty are themselves illuminating, for they stated that these share-holders "would be free to reenter the city *to defend themselves against charges of having transferred company or personal assets beyond the reach of the syndicate … Some of the names were of men from the foreign branches… .*"[21] While Hunt

---

18 Ibid., p. 231.
19 Ibid., p. 232. It should be noted that the Kingdom of Sicily was the major rival of the Kingdom of Naples. In other words, the Peruzzi, like international merchant bankers ever since, were play-ing both sides, and drawing profits from both sides.
20 Ibid., p. 232.
21 Ibid., p. 233, emphasis added.

does not actually come out and state what is going on here, it is easy to see: the company was being used by the family to transfer its personal assets *out of Florence and to the branches of the family in northern Europe,* and chief among these branches was the English branch.[22] The same phenomenon occurred with the Bardi family, where Philip de Bardi continued to head a powerful and independent Bardi English branch, and Walter de Bardi was Edward III's mint master![23] We shall encounter a *similar* oligarchical pattern of the transference of their family financial fortune, and base of operations, northward once again with Venice. The *head* of the Bardi and Peruzzi hydras in Florence had been severed, but the companies, or rather the familiar power they represented, survived.

2. The Venetian "Grain Office" and the Council of Ten: Tools of the Oligarchs

With these facts and insights in hand, we may now once again turn our attention to Venice itself.

It is worth noting that the infamous Venetian "Council of Ten" was established in 1310, just as the Bardi and Peruzzi were entering their period of greatest growth, and just as the amount of gold and silver on the European market began to shift. One may gain an appreciation of just how incestuous the relationship between this Council of Ten—a combination star chamber with summary judicial powers and intelligence and counter-intelligence agency—and the Venetian banks and oligarchical families really was by noting that by ca. 1390, the Council of Ten allowed bankers to assign silver to the Venetian mint, which was then coined into Venetian coin of the realm and returned to the bankers, who, under the terms of the "arrangement," agreed to loan it to the government![24] In other words, while it is strictly true that Venice had no central bank in the modern sense, the Council of Ten, by granting such favors and privileges to various private banks, served the essential *functions* of one. In its own way, it was a typically Venetian expedient of *appearing* not to favor such direct and open oligarchical practices, while pursuing them behind a byzantine mechanism of councils and committees of the state, all in the hands of the oligarchical class.

The other great tool of Venetian oligarchy was the "Grain Office." While many of the dealings with the Grain Office we shall review *postdate* the period of the collapse of the great Florentine super-companies, they are reviewed here for the manner in which they clarify the operational mentality of the Venetian

---

22 Ibid., pp. 236–237.
23 Ibid., p. 241.
24 Mueller, *Venetian Money Market*, p. 446.

oligarchy that was reviewed in chapters two and three. By 1256 the Grain Office, or *Camera Frumenti*, was in existence,[25] and like the Council of Ten established in 1310, was in full operation during the Florentine crisis. Bankers quickly turned to it to deposit their coins, and thus for the approximate century-long period of its operative power, it functioned, as Mueller observed, as a kind of Swiss bank to the financial elite of Venice.[26] One of the key noble families with large deposits in the Grain Office, and hence, with large influence in its affairs, was the d'Este family, whom we shall encounter again.[27]

The key here is that since the Grain Office was an agency of the Venetian Republic, the state "had use of the money, for its own extraordinary expenses."[28] When one looks more closely at those "purposes," however, one begins to see another oligarchical pattern, for the Grain Office in turn made "occasional loans to Venetian entrepreneurs, mostly but not solely nobles, in sectors involving the common good—mills for grinding wheat and kilns for baking bricks and roof tile, above all … "[29] In this the Grain Office functioned in a manner similar to the American Pentagon today, as the rewarder of lucrative contracts to defense industries for various projects affecting the security of the state as a whole. Mueller puts it this way:

> Alongside loans to the state, this financial institution also made long-term loans to private entrepreneurs, more often than not nobles, upon authorization and in areas of strategic importance for the Venetian economy.[30]

It even made loans to the Byzantine Emperor in Constantinople, with the imperial crown jewels listed on the account books of the Grain Office as collateral.[31] The Grain Office thus functioned not only as a kind of "Swiss bank" but also as a kind of Federal Reserve,[32] since it administered both public and private floating debt,[33] making it also oftentimes the center of various intrigues between the nobles and bankers maintaining deposits, or the entrepreneurs receiving loans. Interestingly enough, and predictably enough,

---

25 Ibid., p. 360.
26 Ibid., p. 360.
27 Ibid., p. 373. Mueller notes that Jacobina d'Este had large deposits in the Grain Office, and the Campagnola damily of Padua held deposits in excess of 60,000 ducats, a considerable sum of money. This is important, for it illustrates Venice's role as a haven for oligarchical money not only for its own nobility but for those of other city-states as well.
28 Ibid., p. 360
29 Ibid.
30 Ibid., p. 402.
31 Ibid., p. 360
32 Ibid., see the comments of Mueller with respect to the public floating debt on p. 363.
33 Ibid., p. 359.

deposits were sought by the state initially to obtain the necessary funds to make grain purchases, with the grain itself—Venice's food supply—being the collateral on the loans.[34]

Finally, emphasizing the ever-present connection in Venetian oligarchical arrangements between the nobility, the financial power, intelligence, and the state, it is also important to observe that the Grain Office was the financial agent to the Council of Ten.[35]

Curiously and conveniently (or perhaps not), the *archives* of the Venetian Grain Office have been "completely lost,"[36] leaving modern researchers to piece together its story from other records and accounts of foreigners seeking permission to make deposits at the Office. In this, too, there is perhaps another footprint of the Venetian oligarchy, deliberately concealing its internal factional strife and activities, while presenting a united front outwardly. It is also interesting, and perhaps also a testament to oligarchical maneuvering, to note that a century later, after the collapse of the Florentine super-companies and when Venice was at the height of her power, that the Grain Office was dissolved, and the bankers of the Rialto stepped openly on to the scene to administer the Most Serene Republic's floating public debt.[37]

One episode highlights the duplicitous nature of the Venetian oligarchy in general, and with respect to the Grain Office in particular. This we may here refer to as the "Cangrande Affair." That we know about this matter at all is due to the fact that records of its resolution were drawn up in Venice by the Procurators of San Marco—yet another important Venetian oligarchical agency of state, which unfortunately time does not permit us to explore in depth—and one Cangrande II della Scala, a nobleman of yet another Italian city-state, Verona. Making a very long and complicated story short,[38] Cangrande made a deposit to the grain bank that was claimed by an heir (a certain Fregano, whose nobility the Venetians disputed), and after much haggling, he managed to press his claim to the point where the Venetian authorities were not able to deny it legally.

The problem was, the claim against the Grain Office and hence against the Venetian state itself had grown, with interest, to the extraordinary sum of some 250,000 ducats,[39] a sum the Venetians clearly did not want (and perhaps did not have the means) to pay. The Venetian disputes over his nobility were doubtless an attempt to evade payment of the massive amount of

---

34 Ibid., p. 364.
35 Ibid., p. 371.
36 Ibid., p. 359.
37 Ibid., p. 360. Mueller also notes that the Grain Office was also the administrator of the office of the papal inquisitor in Venice (see p. 365).
38 Ibid., pp. 375–381, where Mueller presents the detailed story.
39 Ibid., p. 380.

money, and additionally, there were two failed assassination attempts against him which, in Mueller's careful phrasing, "in time involved important organs of the state."[40] When assassinations and delays failed to deter Fregano, a compromise was finally reached, whereby Fregano agreed to quit his claim against the Grain Office, and in return Venice agreed to pay him an annuity of 1,500 ducats, to include 1,000 ducats after his death to his male heirs[41] (heirs, it might be noted, who could easily be subjected to the same tactics of evasion, payment avoidance, and assassination). In other words, the Venetian oligarchs had simply refused to pay what they owed, resorted to threats, violence, evasions, and eventually were able to "re-negotiate" their obligations, doubtless against an exasperated and exhausted opponent who wanted to realize at least *some* beneficial outcome from the ordeal. For the oligarchs, it was a boon, for they had effectively negotiated their obligation down to a few pennies on the ducat, so to speak.

The Cangrande Affair highlights an important function of the Grain Office, for as we have seen, it became the locus of Venetian financial dealings with the "seignorial families elsewhere in central-northern Italy and even in the Balkans."[42] It was, to highlight the point once again, one of the crucial choke points through which the Council of Ten and the Venetian Republic gained the flow of intelligence so crucial to the conduct of their trade, exchange, and empire. By the time that the Grain Office had declined and bank loans to the state were made openly by banks on the Rialto, the functions of the Grain Office in administering the Council of Ten's funds for its various nefarious activities had also been taken over by the banks directly, even to the point of a "new openness in business," such that one request to a Rialto banker from the government was for a loan to offer a reward for the assassination of Venice's enemies (in this case, King Sigismund and Brunoro della Scalla, in 1415)![43]

Before returning to the main theme of the collapse of the Florentine international merchant bankers, and leaving the Grain Office and its eventual replacement by the direct funding of the Venetian state debt by the private bankers of the Rialto—always remembering that these banks in many cases were directly connected to the very same oligarchy running the state—one should also note that the period of the highest lending to the state by the banks was precisely coterminous with the period of Venice's decline.[44]

---

40 Ibid.
41 Ibid., p. 379.
42 Ibid., p. 384.
43 Ibid., p. 429.
44 Ibid., pp. 426–427.

3. The Venetian International Bullion Trade, or, Manipulating the Global East/West Gold/Silver Bullion Flow for Oligarchical Fun and Profit

If one were to rely solely upon academic histories of the decline of the medieval super-companies, or upon more general academic histories such as Fernand Braudel's massive *The Perspective of the World*, or even upon the studies of Hunt, Lane, and Mueller, one would never come away with anything more than perhaps a faint "whiff" of something malodorous, something "wrong" hovering just behind the tidy histories, or just beyond the limits of perception. It is when one reads those studies *closely*, comparing notes, connecting dots, that the pattern begins to emerge.

But one cannot hold one's nose forever, and even academics sometimes notice something is wrong. Hunt perhaps caught some whiff of this odor when he pointed out that one possible, and indeed plausible, reason for the decline of the Bardi and Peruzzi was the relatively sudden shift of silver-gold bullion exchange ratios, as noted earlier in this chapter.[45] Hunt even went further, and pointed out the curious examples of gold and silver bullion exchange ratios cited in Lane's exhaustive *Money and Banking in Medieval and Renaissance Venice*. Let us refresh our memory about what Hunt said:

> One other explanation for the reduction in company profitability that deserves consideration is the effect of the well-known changes in the gold-silver ratio in the thirteenth and fourteenth centuries. Grossly oversimplified, this ratio was said to be important to Florentine businessmen because a significant part of their expense, especially wages, was incurred in silver or billon coinage, while their sales in the international markets were mainly in gold florins. An increase in the price of gold relative to silver was thus expansionary and favorable to business interests, while a decrease was depressing and unfavorable to them.[46]

Hunt went on to say this:

> There is abundant evidence that the price of gold in terms of silver had been rising steadily in Italy from the middle of the thirteenth century until it peaked at around 14 ounces of silver for one ounce of gold (14:1) in Venice and Florence in the late 1320s. Then the ratio began to move firmly in favor of silver during the 1330s and 1340s,

---

45 See pp. 194–195.
46 Hunt, *Medieval Super-Companies*, p. 176.

provoking the severe coinage devaluations in Florence of 1345 and 1347. Lane and Mueller place the turning point in 1327, when the rulers of Bohemia and Hungary agreed to coordinate the coinage of silver groats …

The relationship of the price of gold to silver was of course reflected mostly in currency rates of exchange, although it was just one of many variables involved in determining specific rates between different coinages in specific locations … The florin moved quite strongly against the soldi of Florence, Siena, Pisa, and Genoa, although much less so against the currencies of Naples, England, France, and Venice.[47]

Thus, as Hunt also points out, the relatively quick demise of the gold to silver ratio "contributed importantly to the demise of the Florentine super-companies in three ways."[48] As we already have observed, Florence's international trade was conducted in gold florins, whereas its domestic costs were handled in silver, and thus, the terms of trade for importing commodities, the basis of the super-companies' business, were made higher with the decline of gold relative to silver. Secondly, and even more critically, when the Bardi and Peruzzi made loans, the loans were stipulated in gold, and thus when they were repaid in gold that had diminished in value, they lost money in the transaction. Finally, as Hunt also notes, "the Florentines imported gold and exported the undervalued silver on a large scale in the early 1340s, intensifying an already ruinous deflation. In this connection, the Florentines, unlike the Venetians who were the prime silver traders in the Mediterranean, were not in a position to offset their losses by profitable trading in the Levantine silver markets,"[49] a market to which, of course, Venice had easy access.

But, says Hunt, "These arguments, while persuasive to a point, are seriously flawed as explanations for the downfall of the super-companies."[50] At best, Hunt notes, the gold-silver ratio and the decline of gold "added to the problems of the super-companies"[51] to be sure, but this did not have a "significant influence on their results"[52] in that the Peruzzi companies had sustained heavy losses already from 1331–5, prior to the gold-silver exchange problem.

However, even with all that said, Hunt does acknowledge that *something* was going on, something beyond simple coordination of dates, events, and

---

47   Ibid., pp. 176–177.
48   Ibid., p. 178.
49   Ibid.
50   Ibid.
51   Ibid., p. 179.
52   Ibid.

gold-silver ratios, when he admits that the Florentines were not "great international bullion traders like the Venetians."[53] It would seem, then, that a much closer look is in order, and Hunt himself points the direction where we must look.

We must look, once again, at the research of Frederic Chapin Lane and Reinhold C. Mueller.

a. Coins, Bullion, Mints, and "Seigniorage"

The complicated case of Lane and Mueller lies beneath a mass of details, and these we must unpack very carefully in order to make the case that one contributory factor in the demise of the Florentine super-companies was indeed Venetian oligarchical manipulation.

We will begin with bullion, coins, mints, and the concept of "seigniorage."

Money within medieval and renaissance Europe meant primarily two things: (1) virtual, or "bank" money, created on the ledgers of banks and transferred from one account to another, and by extension, through the trading and discount of bills of exchange from one location to another by international merchants such as the Bardi and Peruzzi, and (2) "real" money, or bullion and coinage, which, as noted previously in this chapter, came in three kinds:

a) Yellow money: gold coinage, used primarily in international trade
b) White money: silver coinage
c) Black money: copper coinage or coins struck with alloys of silver and copper. These latter two kinds of coinage were principally used in *local* and domestic exchange.[54]

Within city-states famous for their banking houses and families, such as Florence, Genoa, and Venice, the variety of coins both foreign and domestic in circulation and being exchanged in the banks (not to mention that within *each* system of coinage there was essentially a "tri-metallic"[55] system) meant that these banks, and the super-companies like the Bardi and Peruzzi, maintained their ledgers in several different moneys of account.[56]

Effectively, however, this "tri-metallic" system was a bi-metallic system, in that even in the so-called "black money," it was the presence of silver in the alloy of the coin that gave it its relative value. The careful reader will now

---

53 Ibid.
54 Lane and Mueller, *Money and Banking in Medieval and Renaissance Venice*, p. 11.
55 The term "tri-metallic" is that of Lane and Mueller, ibid.
56 Ibid., pp. 9–10.

have noted that there are two possibilities for manipulation that immediately open up:

1) the first possibility for manipulation occurs in the accounting of banks and corporations themselves, based on manipulations between various moneys of account, which is in turn based upon
2) the gold-to-silver ratio of bullion exchange.

It will be recalled from chapter six that the value of coins in turn was dependent largely on two factors: first, the bullion content of the coin itself, about which more in a moment, and the *stamp* of value, the mint of the coin itself, which stated a legally *defined* value, often in excess of the intrinsic value of the bullion itself. The intrinsic value of the bullion was measured by weight, and fineness, and this constituted part of its exchange value, which gives rise to the second possibility of manipulation mentioned above. Lane and Mueller put the point this way:

> When differences in bimetallic ratios were large and persistent, merchants collected for export coins of the metal more highly valued *elsewhere. As soon as their market value in bullion exceeded their legal value, they became "good" money* ... and were subject to being driven out by "bad" money made of the metal that was legally overvalued. *With bimetallic ratios changing as much as 20 percent within a decade or two during the Middle Ages, the export of undervalued coins repeatedly destroyed efforts to maintain a stable bimetallic standard.*[57]

For Venice, which controlled the bullion market of Europe, and as we shall see most of Europe's silver production as well, the export or import of gold from or to Europe was a simple matter. By manipulating the supply, Venice could force the value of one or the other forms of bullion, and hence the coins based upon it, to rise or fall, wreaking havoc with the coinage of a putative opponent.

Let us take one simple example. If, say, a silver coin was used in a transaction during a period when the intrinsic value of the bullion in the coin exceeded the legally defined value of the coin in transactions, merchants and bankers could demand that payments to them be made in the *telling*, or *tell*, of coins—"telling" simply being the counting out of coins in payment of an obligation or settlement of a transaction. Conversely, in *paying out* on a transaction, they could insist on *weighing* the coins as the statement of value being transferred during the transaction.

---

57 Lane and Mueller, *Money and Banking in Medieval and Renaissance Venice*, p. 40, emphasis added.

This difference between weighing and telling leads us to the next component of the complexity of medieval and Renaissance money: the mint. During this period, the very act of minting or making coins—"real money"—was still held to be the prerogative of the *state*, not a particular private central bank. As such, mints were expected to *contribute revenue to the state*. A mint, Lane and Mueller note, "paid out for a given weight of silver or gold bullion somewhat fewer coins than the number made from the bullion."[58] This difference was, effectively, a kind of tax on bullion sales to the mint, and this difference was called "seigniorage," representing the profit to the government for coining bullion.[59]

There is a catch in the system, however, since *each prince, and in the case of the Italian city-states in close proximity to each other, each city-state, had its own mint.* Thus, competition would arise between various mints, and mints could be used as a means for attacking the money-minting monopoly of competitors.[60] The method of doing so was relatively simple. Cheaper products, or coins of *lesser bullion purity, or "fineness," could be minted with stamps very similar, or even identical, to that of a competitor.* The result was that the mint issuing such coinage increased the bullion flow and reserves of its mint, since less purity was involved in its coinage issue. Such an act, Lane and Mueller observe, "was considered an act of hostility close to armed conflict."[61] Coinage, in other words, presented limitless opportunities for manipulation, and when coupled to the ability to manipulate the bullion ratio of gold and silver *itself*, the possibilities multiply like rabbits. With this in mind, it is now understandable why Venice required accounting by *tell*, and not by *weight*.[62]

There were other manipulation possibilities. For example, by charging *high* seigniorage, the export of coins out of a particular sovereignty could be inhibited, "because it increased the difference between their exchange value and that of the metal they contained."[63]

b. Banksters, Coinage, and Tactics of Manipulation of the Money Supply

Thus far, we have been dealing with the possibilities open to *governments* for the manipulation of the value of coinage. But in a republic such as Venice, where the functions of government and finance were in the hands of

---

58   Ibid., p. 16.
59   Ibid.
60   Ibid., p. 17.
61   Ibid.
62   Ibid., p. 45.
63   Ibid., p. 22.

an oligarchy, the possibilities for manipulation become even greater when one considers how the banks of the Rialto could *add* their own unique technique to the inventory. This is made even more explicit when one takes note of the fact that the Venetian mint was firmly in the control of its nobility.[64]

Bankers and merchants could deliberately *withhold*, or "cull," coins of relative "newness" or "proof", i.e., coins that had not yet been widely circulated and hence experienced the inevitable wear and tear and reduction of *weight*. They could also "clip" the coins, i.e., shave off a minute portion of the bullion of the coin, collecting a stockpile of such shavings and then melting them down for export or sale to the local mint, whichever was more profitable. Similarly, culling had the effect of reducing the amount of money in circulation, and thus raising the relative stamped monetary *and* intrinsic weight value of the coins that were in circulation.[65]

If this sounds familiar to readers of my previous book, *Babylon's Banksters*, it is, but for those who have not read it, here in essence is how the ancient financial elite managed the transition from those exchangeable clay tablets of credit, to coinage:

1) Penetrate and ally with the temple, to give the financial activities of that elite the aura of probity associated with religion;[66]
2) Issue false receipts, that is, simply circulate *counterfeit* clay tablets, thus destabilizing the money supply and its value;[67]
3) Substitute bullion for letters of credit (i.e., for those circulating clay tablets), as a "secure" measure against counterfeit, or false, receipts;[68] and finally,
4) Create the facsimile of money, new letters of credit against the bullion.[69]

As I pointed out in that book, crucial to this activity is the practice of culling, or hoarding, i.e., the deliberate removal from circulation of competing moneys, namely, the legitimate letters of credit or clay tablets, while substituting into circulation the false ones, and, eventually, the bullion-based ones.

---

64 Ibid., pp. 96–97.

65 See the discussion in Lane and Mueller, ibid., pp. 26–30. It is worth noting Muller's comment in *The Venetian Money Market*, p. 447, concerning the incestuous relationship between the Venetian nobility, the Venetian banks, the government, and the Venetian mint: "A century later, beginning with the War of Ferrara, the Council of Ten adopted a different approach to the granting of favors: it permitted bankers to consign silver to the mint and have it struck into coin, an activity otherwise prohibited, as long as they would make large loans to the government—usually with the very coins struck."

66 Farrell, *Babylon's Banksters*, pp. 202–203.

67 Ibid., p. 203.

68 Ibid.

69 Ibid., p. 204. The relevance of this four-step program in the light of recent financial events concerning the derivatives and bullion markets should be carefully noted.

c. Venice, the East/West Gold/Silver Flow, Moneys of Account, and Indicators of Manipulation During the Bardi-Peruzzi Crisis

We now come to the central issue, the manipulation of the relative amounts of gold to silver bullion in Western Europe, and to the role of Venice in doing so. Venice, by dint of her position astride East-West trade, straddled the European bullion market like a colossus.

And the key here, as so many centuries before with the trade of Rome with the Orient, was how the two regions of the world respectively valued gold and silver bullion. As I pointed out in *Babylon's Banksters*, the West (Rome) tended to value *gold* more highly, and the Orient, silver.[70] Venice, since it virtually controlled most of this bullion flow, represented in this respect a continuation of the "bullion brokers" of ancient times, and in this, one may have yet another loose corroboration that its banking practices—passed down through the ages by the noble families constituting its oligarchy—are themselves a testament or indicator that perhaps those families constitute an unbroken connection to ancient times and similar financial elites.

The relative regional supplies of gold and silver, in other words, could be orchestrated to flood one region with one kind of bullion (thereby reducing its value and the value of coinage minted in that bullion), while causing a "famine" of that kind of bullion in another region, then reversing the process, all the while culling and clipping according to the dictates of the overall trend.

In this respect, Lane and Mueller produce a table in their work showing the best estimates of the gold to silver ratios during the crucial period from 1310 to 1350, the period of the rise and collapse of the great Florentine merchant super-companies. In 1310—the year of the founding of the Venetian Council of Ten—the silver to gold ratio was 14:1. But by 1350, this had dropped, somewhat precipitously, to 10:1.[71] This drop, plus the fact that different moneys of account were in use, all based or attached more or less to units of gold and silver coinage[72]—oftentimes within the same corporate entity—could also present other opportunities to play financial havoc with a merchant or government competitor. Indeed, as Mueller notes in his scholarly sequel to his and Lane's joint work, the bullion trade in Venice peaked sharply, precisely at the time of the Bardi and Peruzzi crisis.

But there was one unique feature of Venetian banking used locally by most merchants in the city, and that was the *banchi di scritta*—banks that would simply transfer, from one account to another, sums of money on their books in payments of transactions, *rather than* the transfer of coins or specie

---

70 Ibid., p. 162.
71 Lane and Mueller, *Money and Banking in Medieval and Renaissance Venice*, p. 39.
72 Ibid., pp. 46–47.

itself. They became, in the apt expression of Lane and Mueller, the "common bookkeepers" for the entire community,[73] and eventually for the Venetian state itself. This had the effect of *freeing* coinage and specie for international trade (and thus, for currency speculations of the sorts we have been outlining), while allowing domestic trade to continue.[74] In effect, they vastly expanded the money supply of Venice, and her ability therefore to draw—to the perplexity of her competitors—on a seemingly inexhaustible supply of money to fund her trade and wars. This transference on the ledgers of the *banchi di scritta* also greatly simplified, and sped up, the pace at which business could be conducted in Venice, since it avoided the lengthy process of telling and weighing coins.[75] With the increased speed and efficiency of circulation, the wealth of the republic expanded.

In other words, with such concentrations of power, of intelligence gathering capabilities represented by the Venetian merchants, banks, government institutions such as the Grain Office or the Council of Ten, and the ability to manipulate the bullion supply and value of money, it is difficult to avoid the conclusion that, all other factors considered, Venice at least played a significant and deliberate role in the demise of the Florentine super-companies.

This conviction can only grow when we look back once again to the duplicitous behavior of Venice during the Fourth Crusade, and to the behavior of the famous (or, depending on one's lights, infamous) "Blind Doge" Dandolo *prior* to the crusading army's departure for what it hoped would be Egypt. It will be recalled that Dandolo, through a combination of skullduggery, blatant manipulation, and Byzantine intrigue (in the literal sense!), managed to divert the Crusade to Constantinople itself. It is a little known fact, often completely overlooked in medieval history textbooks, that Enrico Dandolo caused the Venetian mint to issue—*prior to the Fourth Crusade*—a new silver coin that was a virtual copy of the Byzantine "hyperpyron"[76]—for trade with the Middle East, virtually assuring that the coin would supplant the Byzantine imperial issue, which is exactly what happened, obviously *increasing* both in value and in quantities in circulation after Venice gained outright control of regions of the Eastern Empire after the Fourth Crusade. Eventually, the coin of Dandolo became the "basis for an international standard of value for the region."[77]

Since Venice conducted trade with the Orient, which valued silver as a general "cultural" phenomenon more highly than gold,[78] it became necessary

---

73 Ibid., p. 63.
74 Lane and Mueller note that the use of bank money in Venice was largely a *local* phenomenon, ibid., p. 64.
75 Ibid., p. 63.
76 Ibid., p. 118.
77 Ibid., p. 123.
78 Always bearing in mind, however, that this is subject to regional and local market conditions of

for Venice to control the production of silver in Europe as much as possible. This, of course, was made possible through its relationship to the famous German merchant banking and silver mining family, the Fuggers, who, incidentally, were trained in the techniques of banking and accounting, in Venice.

As silver was flowing Eastward through Venice, gold coincidentally was flowing westward, through Venice, and into Europe, and—again "coincidentally"—in the spring of the year of the Peruzzi bankruptcy, 1343, a very large shipment of gold arrived in Venice from places that ranged from Constantinople, to Tana, the Venetian outpost on the Black Sea, and perhaps even as far away as the interior of Asia,[79] all of which suggest a vast and coordinated effort, requiring a large and extensive intelligence network such as Venice possessed.

But the real clue, the final nail in the coffin so to speak, comes with two observations that Lane and Mueller record in their magisterial study. These observations clearly indicate that the Bardi and Peruzzi companies were caught in a bullion vice of Venetian manufacture:

> Exchange rates used in the account books of the big Florentine firm of the Peruzzi for 1335–37 varied in a range indicating bimetallic ratios of about 13 to 1 to 16 to 1. A more decisive drop came in 1337, when the French minted the gold piece called in England the florin de l'écu. *It was given a price that expressed the ratio 11.5 to 1, the same as the ratio set in Venice a half-dozen years earlier with the coinage of the soldino, in 1331–1332.*[80]

In other words, the Peruzzi ledgers reflected a fantasy world, divorced from the gold glut that Venice was introducing into Western Europe as it was simultaneously exporting German silver to the East![81] It is worth citing the carefully worded evaluation of Lane and Mueller in this respect:

> Although the gold glut cannot be considered the main cause of Florence's financial crisis, the voluminous minting of gold while silver coin was scarce may have made the deflation worse. Although no modern analogy helps explain the conjunction of deepening deflation and increased supplies of gold, monetary conditions of the

---

famine or glut in a particular bullion.

79 Ibid., p. 377.

80 Ibid., p. 437, emphasis added.

81 One may now appreciate the techniques of banks in culling and clipping coins, for over time, a "secret" reserve of this or that bullion could be hoarded, then to be suddenly released into the market. It is worth noting that one liquidator of the rival Bardi company even recorded silver to gold ratios as low as 9.4 to 1! (See ibid., pp. 442–443.)

mid-fourteenth century suggest a connection. The profuse coinage of florins in years when silver coins were scarce may have lowered the exchange value of the gold coins. Previously, for almost a century, 1250–1330, gold had been rising in value compared with silver. Those who had accumulated wealth had found that gold was the best stuff to hoard and that credits stated in gold-based money of account, which was likely to be devalued by the minting of lighter silver … coin … Amid the general loss of confidence and the resulting need for liquidity, they turned to their gold, only to find that gold that had been worth more than 14 times as much as silver in 1330 was worth hardly more than 10 times as much in 1350.[82]

To see even more deeply into just how the Venetian bullion vice had gripped the Florentine super-companies, and thereby Venetian rival Florence itself, one must ask, and answer, a question:

Why had Florence not adjusted earlier its fine silver coinage to the rising value of silver, the value to which the coinage of France as well as that of Venice had been adjusted much earlier, before 1340?

The answer has two sides. On the one hand, the quattrino[83] gave all the needed protection against a draining away of the kind of currency needed for small and local transactions. On the other hand, the profits of the international bankers had come to depend on the exchange rates between florins and various foreign currencies. Where Florentines made loans in florins and collected repayment and interest in a local currency based on silver, they profited from maintaining an exchange rate that set a high value on gold. In England, as the English complained, the Florentines had maintained such a high exchange rate. The vested interest that they as international bankers had acquired in a high bimetallic ratio gave them reason to maintain a high bimetallic ratio also in Florentine coinage.[84]

Or, to put it more plainly, the Florentine super-companies—and with them Florence itself—had simply been wrong-footed, and toppled by the gold glut that gives every indicator of having been orchestrated by the Vipers of Venice. Not for nothing does Shakespeare's play bear the title *The Merchant of Venice*, and not *The Merchant of Florence*.

---

82 Ibid., pp. 454–455.
83 A common coin in circulation in Italy.
84 Ibid., p. 456.

B. A Further Meditation on the Topological Metaphor of the Medium: On the "Financial Pyramid" Version of the Metaphor

We are far, however, from being done with the techniques of financial manipulation, or, for that matter, the Metaphor and how at a deep cultural and subconscious level, it had come to be understood and operate. To appreciate this phenomenon, we must return to a concept that has recurred throughout this chapter, namely, the concept of "moneys of account." These are, simply stated, the units of value in which various accounts were expressed, and hence, in the Middle Ages and Renaissance, were always loosely connected to coinage, even when being transferred as mere ledger entries between various banks.

But almost immediately a philosophical problem occurs, and it is safe to say it probably occurred to the medieval bankers as well (after all, once again witness the hostility of Venice to Giordano Bruno and to the full implications of the Topological Metaphor of the Medium). Lane and Mueller observe that during the 1930s, "just as the gold standard was passing into history," two very different ways of interpreting the problem of the relationship between coins (and therewith, bullion) and moneys of account arose. One version, advocated by Belgian numismatist Hans van Werveke, advanced the idea that moneys of account were always defined in one of three ways:

1) as a definite *weight* of gold or silver, usually as embodied in a particular coin;
2) as a particular coin in general circulation;
3) as "imaginary money, absolutely independent of any 'real money' ... that is, of any coin or fixed quantity of precious metal."[85] This third type, van Werveke maintained, "did not describe any historical reality."[86]

In contrast, Italian economist Luidi Einaudi argued that moneys of account represented a standard of value used in accounting and contracts, and "real" money used in payments.[87]

In other words, as these economists and historians were studying the Middle Ages, they came face to face with the problem we outlined previously in chapter six: did the Metaphor come first, or did coinage?

We gain an appreciation of the importance of this question by noting, once again, that *most* business transactions in Venice itself were conducted on

---

85 Ibid., p. 467.
86 Ibid.
87 Ibid., p. 468.

the basis of ledger transfers using various moneys of account, all more or less abstract, and all circulating much faster than local market conditions reflecting the value of those monies in corresponding coinage. "By creating such ambiguities," Lane and Mueller observe, "the mobility of moneys of account limited or undermined the unity and continuity of monetary standards."[88] This of course was in the control of the Venetian oligarchy that owned the banks, while domestic and foreign exchange, conducted in bullion and coinage, was for everyone else, and there too, the oligarchy virtually controlled the bullion market as well.

All this brings us chin to chin, once again, with the Topological Metaphor of the Medium, and again to the reasons why the Venetians would have so strenuously objected to the construction Bruno put upon it. We may refer to *this* version of the Metaphor as the "Debt Finance Construction."

Here, as always, there are at least two ways to interpret it, one issuing in ever-present debt, and the other, in ever-increasing fecundity.

In chapter six, we saw how the symbolization of the physical medium as the empty hyper-set $\varnothing$ could also represent the bullion substrate of coinage, as well as the physical substrate or *materia prima* of the physical world itself. Thus, coins could represent the resulting instantiations, or derivatives, of that substrate, and as common surfaces of transaction. Suppose we now fix the "value" of that original empty hyper-set at "1." Doing so would mean that all subsequent derivatives have a value of less than one. As derivatives increase, their "value" decreases as fractions of the original.

But, as we have seen in this chapter, as coins circulate, that is, as they change from one context to another, they progressively lose weight, become worn, and so on, thus losing both intrinsic and stamped value. We may express this phenomenon in our topological metaphorical terms as a kind of recontextualizing rule:

$$\varnothing_x \rightarrow \varnothing y - \partial \varnothing x,$$

where the subscript "x" denotes the "coin" in its original valuation in a particular context "x," say, that of its legally defined and minted value, and "y" denotes a new context into which it has moved, represented by the arrow, with a corresponding incremental loss of value, represented by the partial derivative sign ∂.[89] Over time, more and more such recontextualizations will, of course, take their wear and tear on the coin, *such that, the amount of circulating coins will never sum to the original "value" of "1" from which the system began.*

---

88   Ibid., p. 473.

89   A much more formally explicit version of this recontextualizing version of the Metaphor is presented in the appendix to chapter nine in my *Giza Death Star Destroyed.*

No matter how much one culls, clips, hoards, and so on, there will always be an incremental loss in the system. This, briefly put, is how the Metaphor can come to be, by analogy to coinage, interpreted as a Metaphor of perpetual indebtedness. In this instance, positioning oneself closest to the top of the Metaphor will, of course, result in a pyramid of power associated with it.

But as will be evident, there really is no a priori reason to view the metaphor as ever-decreasing *fractions* of the original "value" of 1. One could equally view such derivatives as "countable entities," giving rise to whole numbers. In this view of the Metaphor, information simply increases, with no limit, and no fractionalization or "indebtedness." To the Venetians, ever mindful of their bullion and money, this prospect of a genuinely open system was in itself anathema, for in their closed system understanding, it would only be inflationary, and any inflationary prospect was anathema ...

... unless, of course, they controlled it.

But that control was about to be threatened in yet another fashion, and by a new way of opening the system, one perhaps, as we shall now see, they may have known long before, and suppressed.

It is small wonder that, after centuries of such duplicitous behavior, feigned alliances and sudden withdrawals from them, double-dealing negotiations, coinage war, bullion manipulation, assassinations, and summary secret trials by the Council of Ten, the rest of Europe finally had it, and went to war with Venice during the War of the League of Cambrai. The preamble of alliance for the League is worth recalling; the League was formed, it stated,

> ... to put an end to the losses, the injuries, the violations, the damages which the Venetians have inflicted, not only on the Apostolic See but on the Holy Roman Empire, on the House of Austria, on the Dukes of Milan, on the Kings of Naples and on divers other princes, occupying and tyrannically usurping their goods, their possessions, their cities and castles, as if they had deliberately conspired to do ill to all around them.
>
> Thus we have found it not only will-advised and honourable, but even necessary, to summon all people to take their just revenge and so to extinguish, like a great fire, the insatiable rapacity of the Venetians and their thirst for power.[90]

As noted above, however, the system was about to be opened in a dramatic fashion, a fashion that the Venetians may have even known about for some centuries before events, finally, compelled the secret out into the open ...

---

90   Ibid.

⚡ Nine ⚡

MAPS, MONEY, AND MONOPOLIES:

The Mission of Christopher Columbus

∴

"The one duty we owe to history is to re-write it."
—Oscar Wilde[1]

WE ARE READY TO BELIEVE that conspiracies exist, at least, in modern times. Literature abounds that challenges the promoted "orthodoxies" and the "directed historical narratives" that emanate from the power centers of the world's elites. Many reading this book, for example, would question the promoted orthodoxies concerning the assassination of President John F. Kennedy, the "official story" of 9/11, and so on.

Yet, when we turn to the Middle Ages and Renaissance, we are quick to swallow the standard historical narratives, unwilling to believe that conspiracies—complete with psychological operations, cover stories, false fronts, false flag operations, and so on—could exist in those times. And at the head of this list has been the story of the voyage of Christopher Columbus in 1492. We all know the myth by heart: going before King Ferdinand and Queen Isabella of Spain, Columbus argued he would find a new direct route to the spice islands of the East, bypassing the Portuguese mastery of the route around the horn of Africa and through the Indian Ocean. That, anyway, was the story.

---

1   Oscar Wilde, "The Critic as Artist."

But as will be argued here, the story is just that: *a cover story*, and the truth may be very different. The truth may indeed be *so* different that it boggles the mind.

To see why, we need to step out of the arcane and heady world of finance, philosophy, metals, and metaphors, and into the equally arcane and heady world of navigation and ancient and medieval maps, maps that on close examination demonstrate an unusual knowledge and provenance.

A. The Strange Case of the Piri Reis Map
1. Antarctica

This bizarre story begins with the map of an Ottoman Turkish admiral named Piri Reis (ca. 1465/1470–ca. 1555). The problem of the Piri Reis map may be succinctly stated as follows: it showed something that had not been discovered yet, namely Antarctica, as the following picture shows:

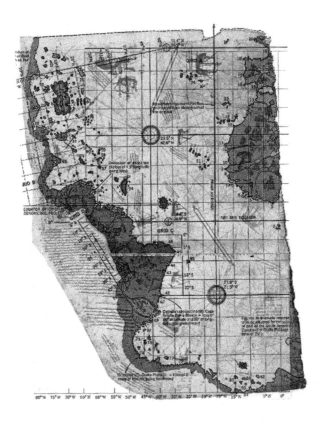

Piri Reis map: Note the coast of South America, the west African bulge, and Spain, then, at the bottom of the map, that of Antarctica

The map immediately caught the attention of science history professor Charles H. Hapgood, [1904–1982] who, with his students, went in search of precedents for this anomaly, searching ancient medieval maps called portolanos and other Renaissance world maps. It was not long before they unearthed the famous Oronteus Finaeus map of 1532, which, like many maps of the period, clearly depicted the *Terra Australis*, as the yet-to-be discovered Antarctic continent was then known.

Right Side of the Oronteus Finaeus Map of 1531 Showing Antarctica[2]

The problem is obliquely admitted by the skeptical website "Bad Archaeology," which notes that "Although there are fairly obvious similarities between the general depiction of the southern continent by Oronteus Finaeus and modern maps of Antarctica, they do not stand up to close scrutiny; indeed, there are more differences than similarities, much as one would expect from a map drawn without genuine knowledge of the southern continent!"[3] In other words, the problem—for those willing simply to *look*—is that long

---

2   Charles H. Hapgood, *Maps of the Ancient Sea Kings* (Kempton, Illinois: Adventures Unlimited Press, 1996), pp. 81–82.

3   "The Oronteus Finneus Map," http://www.badarchaeology.com/ ?page_id=979.

before Captain Cook came close to the continent in 1773, and before actual contact was made in 1820, the continent, in spite of inaccuracies in the map, was being depicted *more or less* accurately, pettifogging tactics of standard academia to deny it notwithstanding.

Hapgood recounts his discovery of this anachronistically accurate map:

> Then one day, I turned a page, and sat transfixed. As my eyes fell upon the southern hemisphere of a world map drawn by Oronteus Finaeus in 1531, I had the instant conviction that I had found here a truly authentic map of the real Antarctica.

The problem with the map as depicted by Oronteus was more than just the general resemblance of the depicted continent to modern cartographic representations; the problem went much deeper:

> The general shape of the continent was startlingly like the outline of the continent on our modern map ... The position of the South Pole, nearly in the center of the continent, seemed about right. *The mountain ranges that skirted the coasts suggested the numerous ranges that have been discovered in Antarctica in recent years.* It was obvious, too, that this was no slapdash creation of somebody's imagination. The mountain ranges were individualized, some definitely coastal and some not ... *This suggested, of course, that the coasts may have been ice-free when the original map was drawn.* [4]

A closer view will allow the reader to see what Hapgood is talking about:

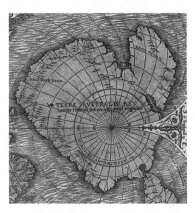

Close-up of Oronteus Finaeus Map of 1532

---

4   Hapgood, *Maps of the Ancient Sea Kings*, pp. 79-83, emphasis added.

Oronteus Finaeus' map was not the only such map depicting the yet-to-be-encountered southern polar continent. Hapgood found others, including the Hadji Ahmed Map of 1559, once again clearly showing the southern polar continent in a Mercator-like projection:

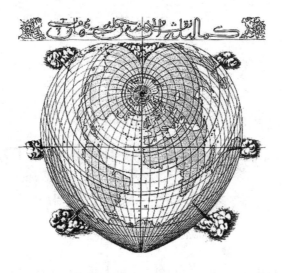

Hadji Ahmed Map of 1559[5]

All of this, as Hapgood noted, led some who had encountered such maps, especially the Piri Reis map, to speculate that portions of the coast on the Turkish admiral's map that lay under the ice and were nonetheless more or less accurately depicted must have been mapped "before the ice appeared."[6]

2. Medieval Portolans

The problem then became much more acute. Pursuing his quest for ancient maps that seemed to embody anachronistically out-of-place accuracy, Hapgood soon discovered the Dulcert Portolano of 1339, produced by Angelino Dulceti, who, interestingly enough, was probably trained in Genoa, the other great northern Italian merchant city-state with its own exclusive trading privileges with the Byzantine Empire, and the great rival of Venice.[7]

---

5   Ibid., p. 100.
6   Ibid., p. 2.
7   For Dulcert, see "Angelino Dulcert," http://en.wikipedia.org/wiki/ Angelino_Dulcert. For Genoa's rivalry with Venice and its trading privileges in the Byzantine Empire, see Robert Crowley's excellent popular treatment, *City of Fortune*, pp. 143, 154–171.

A glance at the Dulcert Portolano, though very faded, will immediately show the problem:

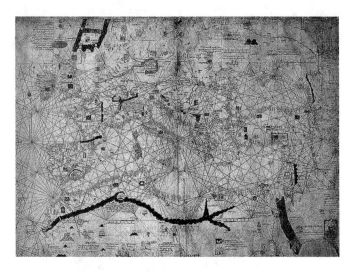

Dulcert Portolano of 1339[8]

While difficult to see, the outlines of Europe, Asia Minor, and North Africa are faintly visible in the above picture, raising the questions: why is this map so *accurate*, and where did this accuracy come from? How did this knowledge come to medieval and Renaissance Europe, to spur the voyages that would confirm that another world existed, unknown to the Europeans?

3. Maps from High Antiquity

Enter Venice once again, and all that it symbolized of the great trading rivalry of Venice and Genoa for the Far Eastern trade flowing through Byzantium.

In Chapter Two, it was noted that the sudden appearance of the Hermetica in northern Italy followed the Council of Ferrara-Florence, which was, we also observed, financially sponsored in part by the Medicis of Florence. We speculated there that the presence of the Byzantine humanists Bessarion and Plethon among the Greek delegation to the council was the contact point for the Florentine merchants who may have been seeking lost knowledge that could only have come from the imperial archives of the East Roman Empire in Constantinople. We thus speculate that this contact may have been one route for the sudden appearance of apparently hidden cartographic knowledge of the Earth during this period.

---

8   Hapgood, *Maps of the Ancient Sea Kings*, p. 8.

But as noted also in chapter three, the contacts of Venice and its rival Genoa with the East Roman or Byzantine Empire predate those of the council of Florence by some two centuries, with the Venetian and Genoese virtual monopolies of ports and tax exemptions within Byzantium. The establishment of the Latin Empire after the Fourth Crusade by Venice would have given Venice access to the imperial archives, and thus to the charts and exemplars from which Piri Reis compiled his map. Similarly, the Genoese access to Byzantium during the period of the Venetian-Genoese rivalry would have given them a corresponding access. The question is, why did Venice not *access and utilize* this knowledge?

As we saw in chapter three, the question is easily answered by a map of the world. Venice could not easily access the Atlantic, for the route was blocked not only geographically but by the warring Moors and Castillians in Spain. Venice, in other words, if it had access to this cartographic knowledge, could not utilize it, and would have had to *suppress* the knowledge of it from being acquired by anyone else lest its favored position astride the trading routes to the Far East be jeopardized, and with it, its whole financial and mercantile empire.

The question that remains is whether or not such exemplars of the Piri Reis map actually existed. If so, then the likelihood of Venetian suppression of knowledge rises. We have already seen that medieval portolanos existed, and that these appear to have been drawn from much earlier exemplars, as Hapgood commented:

> ... (One) of the leading scholars in the field did not believe that the charts originated in the Middle Ages. A. E. Nordenskiöld, who compiled a great Atlas of these charts ... and also wrote an essay on their history... , presented several reasons for concluding that they must have come from ancient times. In the first place, he pointed out that the Dulcert Portelano and all the others like it were a great deal too accurate to have been drawn by medieval sailors. Then there was the curious fact that the successive charts showed no signs of development. Those from the beginning of the 14th Century are as good as those from the 16th. It seemed as though somebody early in the 14th century had found an amazingly good chart which nobody was able to improve upon for two hundred years. Furthermore, Nordenskiöld saw evidence that only *one* such model chart had been found and that all the portolanos drawn in the following centuries were only copies—at one or more removes—from the original. He called this unknown original the "normal portolano" and showed that the portolanos, as a body, had rather slavishly been copied from the original. He said:

"The measurements at all events show: (1) that, as regards the outline of the Mediterranean and the Black Sea, all the portolanos are almost unaltered copies of the same original; (2) that the same scale of distance was used on all the portolanos."[9]

Hapgood notes that Nordenskiöld believed that these measures were derived from Carthaginian and Phoenician sources.[10]

But that was not all. Nordenskiöld also compared the maps of the most famous ancient geographer, Ptolemy, whose maps were introduced to western Europe in the 1400s, with the most famous of the medieval portolanos, the Dulcert Portelano. Notably, *the medieval map was much more accurate,* as Nordenskiöld's comparison of the two clearly shows:

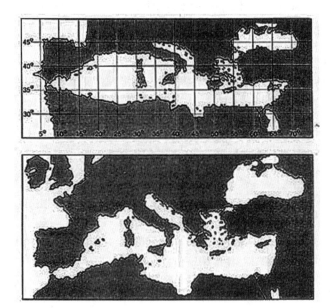

Nordenskiöld's Comparison of the Ancient Geographer Ptolemy's Map (Top), with the Medieval Dulcert Portolano (Bottom)[11]

Hapgood minces no words when stating the implications of this comparison:

Let us stop to consider, for a moment, what this means. Ptolemy is the most famous geographer of the ancient world. He worked

---

9   Ibid., p. 9, citing A.E. Nordenskiöld, *Periplus: An Essay in the Early History of Charts and Sailing Directions.* Trans. from the Swedish by F.A. Bathev. (Stockholm: Norstedt, 1897), p. 24.

10   Ibid., pp. 9–10.

11   Hapgood, *Maps of the Ancient Sea Kings,* p. 10.

in Alexandria in the 2nd Century A.D., in the greatest library of the ancient world. He had at his command all the accumulated geographical information of that world. He was acquainted with mathematics. He shows, in his great work, the *Geographia* ... , a modern scientific mentality. Can we lightly assume that medieval sailors of the *fourteenth century*, without any of this knowledge, and without modern instruments except a rudimentary compass—and without mathematics—could produce a more scientific product?

Nordenskiöld felt that there had been in antiquity a geographic tradition superior to the one represented by Ptolemy. He thought that the "normal portolano" must have been in use *then* by sailors and navigators, and he answered the objection that there was no mention of such maps by the various classical writers by pointing out that in the Middle Ages, when the protolan charts were in use, they were never referred to by the Schoolmen, the academic scholars of that age. Both in ancient and in medieval times the academic mapmaker and the practical navigator were apparently poles apart.[12]

Note carefully what Hapgood is really implying here, for if medieval navigators had no more than crude mathematical techniques and even cruder navigational instruments, then the medieval portolanos, exemplified in the Dulcert portolano, must represent some hidden tradition of secret knowledge, handed down from High Antiquity and antedating even Ptolemy and the renowned library of Alexandria.

However, is there any more evidence to suggest such a notion? Indeed there is, but it is a slightly complicated matter to convey. When Hapgood and his students began to correlate the latitude and longitude positions of Piri Reis' map with actual modern calculations of positions, they discovered that Piri Reis' map was off by some 4 1/2 percent. The source of this error in Piri Reis' map appeared to have stemmed from Eratosthenes' computation of the circumference of the Earth.[13] When Piri Reis' map was redrawn with this correction, an astounding thing resulted, one with profound implications:

> We found that this resulted in reducing all the longitude errors until they nearly vanished.

This was a startling development. It could only mean that the Greek geographers of Alexandria, when they prepared their world map using the circumference of Eratosthenes, had in front of them

---

12   Ibid., p. 11.
13   Ibid., p. 33.

source maps that had been drawn *without the Eratosthenian error*, that is, apparently without any discernible error at all ... suggesting that the people who had originated the maps possessed a more advanced science than that of the Greeks.[14]

In other words, there was a more ancient, and hidden, tradition of knowledge behind the medieval portolanos, and indeed, behind the map of Admiral Piri Reis.

Hapgood summarizes these implications in no uncertain terms:

> To sum up, then, this part of the Piri Re'is [*sic, et passim*] Map suggests that Piri Re'is had a source map of Africa, Europe, and the Atlantic islands, based on maps probably drawn originally on some sort of trigonometric projection adjusted to the curvature of the earth. By default of any alternative, we seem forced to ascribe the origin of this part of the map to a pre-Hellenic people—not to Renaissance or Medieval cartographers, and not to the Arabs, who were just as badly off as everybody else with respect to longitude, and not to the Greeks either. The trigonometry of the projection (or rather its information on the size of the earth) suggests the work of Alexandrian geographers, but the evident knowledge of longitude implies a people unknown to us, a nation of seafarers, with instruments for finding longitude undreamed of by the Greeks, and, so far as we know, not possessed by the Phoenicians, either.[15]

Elsewhere, Hapgood is even more deliberate in pointing out the obvious implications of a lost culture and knowledge from High Antiquity:

> The picture that seems to emerge, therefore, is one of a scientific achievement far beyond the capacities of the navigators and mapmakers of the Renaissance, of any period of the Middle Ages, of the Arab geographers, or of the known geographers of ancient times. It appears to demonstrate the survival of a cartographic tradition that could hardly have come to us except through some such people as the Phoenicians or the Minoans, the great sea peoples who long preceded the Greeks but passed down to them their maritime lore.[16]

---

14 Ibid., p. 33, emphasis in the original.
15 Ibid., p. 49.
16 Ibid., p. 40.

This method of dividing the circle is not modern; it is the oldest way of dividing the circle known to man. Furthermore, since it involves counting by tens, it alone can explain how the ancient source map of the Antarctic, probably drawn ages before either Phoenicians or Babylonians existed, had on it the circle that Oronteus Finaeus took for the Antarctic Circle, but which we have shown may have been the 80th parallel. *The implication from this is that the 360-degree circle and the twelve-wind system were ancient before the rise of Babylonia and long before Tyre and Sidon were built by the Phoenicians. Babylonian science was thus, perhaps, a heritage from a much older culture.*[17]

That is, Piri Reis' map represents the survival of a hidden, ancient tradition, one stemming—as Hapgood notes—from Alexandria, Egypt. This now brings us at last to a consideration of the famous voyage that broke the back of the monopoly of the northern Italian city-states on the trading routes to the East, and particularly the Venetian monopoly. It brings us to ...

B. Christopher Columbus' Voyages and the Hidden Cartographic Tradition

It brings us to the implied *hidden* reasons for it, reasons carefully disguised behind the story—most likely a cover story—that Columbus was merely trying to find a direct oceanic route to trade with the Orient.

1. Piri Reis' Statements on Columbus

Significantly, it is the Turkish admiral Piri Reis who, once again, pries open the door to a significant mystery regarding Columbus and the possible *real*—though very definitely *secret*—purposes of his initial voyage for Ferdinand and Isabella of Spain. On his now famous map there are marginal notes by the admiral himself, and in one of these, Piri Reis states:

This section explains the way the map was prepared. Such a map is not owned by anybody at this time. I, personally, drawn (sic) and prepared this map. In preparing this map, I made use of about twenty old charts and eight Mappa Mundis, i.e., of the charts called "Jaferiye" by the Arabs and prepared at the time of Alexander the Great and in which the whole inhabited world was shown; of the chart of (the) West Indies; and of the new maps made by four Portugueses (sic) containing

---

17   Ibid., p. 185, emphasis added.

the Indian and Chinese countries geometrically represented on them. *I also studied the chart that Christopher Columbus drew for the West.* Putting all these material (sic) together in a common scale I produced the present map. My map is as correct and dependable for the seven seas as are the charts that represent the seas of our countries.[18]

Note that Piri Reis states that he is relying upon a chart drawn by Columbus "for the West." But the questions are, when did Columbus draw this chart, before, or after, his first voyage? And more importantly, what did it show?

The standard answer is of course that Columbus drew his chart "for the West" after his return to Europe from his first voyage. However, in yet another marginal note the Turkish admiral states something truly astounding. Ponder these words closely:

> But it is reported thus, that a Genoese infidel, his name was Colombo, he it was who discovered these places. For instance, *a book fell into the hands of the said Colombo, and he found it said in this book that at the end of the Western Sea (Atlantic) that is, on its western side, there were coasts and islands and all kinds of metals and also precious stones.* The above-mentioned, having studied this book thoroughly, explained these matters one by one to the great of Genoa and said: "Come, give me two ships, let me go and find these places." They said: "O unprofitable man, can an end of a limit be found to the Western Sea? Its vapour is full of darkness." The above-mentioned Colombo saw that no help was forthcoming from the Genoese, he sped forth, went to the Bey of Spain (king), and told his tale in detail. They too answered the Genoese. In brief Colombo petitioned these people for a long time, finally *the Bey of Spain gave him two ships, saw that they were well equipped, and said:*
> 　　"*O Colombo, if it happens as you say, let us make you kapudan (admiral) to that country.*" Having said which he sent the said Colombo to the Western Sea.[19]

Note carefully what we have here, for according to Piri Reis:

1) Columbus possessed a book relating the knowledge of the New World, in other words, Columbus had access to knowledge not generally available, to *secret* knowledge, and therefore possibly had access to a

---

18　Ibid., p, 217, emphasis added.
19　Ibid., p, 220, emphasis added.

secret cartographic tradition as well;

2) That knowledge stated that there was an abundance of bullion and gems, in other words, a source of bullion *not* in the hands of the Orient, nor the Venetians, and thus, a means of breaking the bullion and banking monopolies of Italy; and finally and most importantly;

3) The publicly-stated purpose for Columbus' voyage—the version taught to this day in standard academic histories— namely, that the Genoese navigator was seeking a direct trade route to the Far East, was *not* the real purpose of the voyage; the real purpose *from the outset was to find "Atlantis,"* the lands of the Western Sea, to find the New World, and its riches.

We can see why King Ferdinand and Queen Isabella would back such a venture, for if Columbus' effort to find the New World failed, a direct trade route to the Far East might nonetheless be opened, bypassing the rival Portuguese monopoly routes around the horn of Africa and through the Indian Ocean. If, on the other hand, Columbus *did* discover the New World and thus the potential for vast new sources of spices, bullion, and gems, then again, Ferdinand and Isabella would gain. It was, for them, a win-win proposition, but one whose true purpose—*the testing of a tradition of hidden knowledge*—had to be maintained in deepest secrecy lest Spain lose its jump-started position in the race for those riches. Indeed, it was the historian Las Casas who stated that *prior* to his first voyage, Columbus "had a world map, which he showed to King Ferdinand and Queen Isabella, and which, apparently, convinced them that they should back Columbus."[20]

One can reconstruct a possible sequence of events. Columbus originally approached the Spanish monarchs, and shared with them the details from his book. After several attempts to persuade them had failed, he finally produced what he was holding back in order to convince them: a world map depicting portions of the New World. Such a map would have had to be detailed in other particulars *known* to the Spanish in order to convince them. Is there any evidence of such a map?

Indeed there is.

And it exists independently of any speculative reconstructions surrounding Columbus.

The map, made by Martin Behaim in 1492 *prior* to Columbus' voyage, clearly shows early depictions of the mouth of the St. Lawrence seaway and portions of Newfoundland:

---

20 Ibid., p. 59.

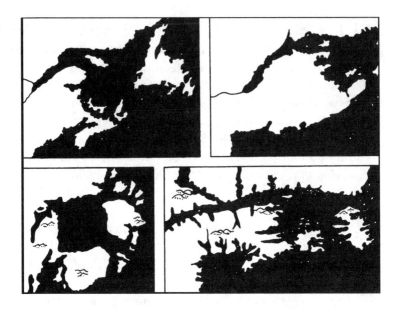

Hapgood's Reproduction of the Modern Cartographic depiction of the St. Lawrence Channel (Upper Left), the map of Sebastion Cabot (1544) in the upper right, the Lescarbot Map of 1606 in the Lower Right, and Martin Behaim's Map of 1492, prior to Columbus' Return, in the lower left.[21]

In other words, Behaim clearly had access to some cartographic tradition depicting the New World before Columbus had even returned, raising the possibility that Columbus had access to such a tradition as well.

But if so, where does it come from?

At the beginning of this section, we noted that Venice is the most likely possibility, since it had sacked Constantinople in 1204 during the Fourth Crusade, and made off with a number of important treasures, some, no doubt, from the imperial archives, which would have likely included *some* remnants from the ancient library of Alexandria. We have also, in other chapters of this book, pointed out that the arrival of the Byzantine humanists at the Council of Ferrara-Florence in the early fifteenth century represents another possible source of hidden, Hermetic, and esoteric tradition and lore. Hapgood himself is alive to all this possibility:

> We have seen that Piri Re'is, in all probability, had ancient maps at his disposal in Constantinople. It is quite possible that copies of these

---

21 Ibid., p. 58.

had reached the West long before his day. Greek scholars fleeing from the Turks brought thousands of Greek manuscripts to Italy before the fall of Constantinople in 1453. Much earlier still, in the year 1204, a Venetian fleet, supposedly intended to carry a crusade to the Holy Land, attacked and captured Constantinople. For about sixty years afterward Italian merchants had access to map collections in Constantinople.[22]

We therefore concur with Hapgood's assessment, an assessment strongly implying that Columbus' original voyage had a covert purpose:

> It is known that (Columbus) traveled widely in Europe, always on the lookout for maps. His voyage was not a sudden inspiration; it was a deeply settled objective, one followed with perseverance for many years, and it required, above all, maps.[23]

C. Some Further Speculations
1. Spain, Genoa, and Venice

With this, we are now in a position to begin to reassemble some pieces, and to construct a speculative scenario of what might have really been going on behind the scenes of Columbus' voyage, and its sponsorship by Ferdinand and Isabella.

1) We assume that at some point, the Italian city-states, and in particular Venice, gained knowledge of the existence of the New World via Greek manuscripts and maps taken when that city sacked Constantinople in 1204;

2) Thus, Venice, at least, had knowledge of the New World, and actively *suppressed* this knowledge for nearly three centuries. The reason for such suppression is abundantly clear, for the New World would represent possible *new* sources of bullion, ending the virtual Venetian monopoly on international bullion trade, and it would also represent an end to the Venetian near-monopoly on trade with the Far East, since Venice, isolated as it was, had no easy access to the Atlantic Ocean and the trading possibilities it represented.

3) *Consequently, one sees two familiar patterns—first appearing in ancient times, and continuing into modern times—of a financial elite that is*

---

22   Ibid., pp. 58–59.
23   Ibid., p. 59.

a) *actively **seeking** ancient sources of information, and*
b) *seeking to monopolize and suppress it, lest that knowledge break out of the closed system of finance that made their power, position, and prestige, possible.*

Columbus' discovery of the New World was the game changer for the closed system of bullion trade and finance that Venice dominated, *and it was meant to be.* Unlike with Giordano Bruno, however, Genoa could not simply arrange for all of Spain to be burnt at the stake for opening the system.

It is worth pointing out yet another speculative possibility as to how this monopoly of hidden knowledge was *broken.* In chapter two, and again earlier in this chapter, I pointed out that *one* likely source for the sudden explosion of Hermeticism in northern Italy was the Greek humanists who accompanied the imperial delegation to the Council of Ferrara-Florence (1438–1439) a mere four decades prior to Columbus' fateful voyage. It is likely *here* that the Venetian monopoly over hidden cartographic tradition—if indeed there was one—was broken, and it is significant that a seaman from Genoa, the great rival of Venice, should be the one to break it.[24]

Indeed, Genoa could not burn all of Spain at the stake for daring to open up the system again, but it is suggestive, and perhaps also significant, that for a brief moment in history, Genoese bankers became the financiers to the Spanish crown, as if in repayment of a "hidden secret protocol" in the negotiations between Ferdinand, Isabella, and Christopher Columbus. After all, it was the Genoan adventurer that they named Admiral of the Atlantic upon his return to Spain, and it was the bankers of Genoa who for that brief moment in history made profit from Spain's new sources of bullion.

Nor can we assume for a moment that the revisionist explanation that Columbus was after a new source of slaves somehow evades the implications of the speculations entertained in this chapter, for slavery, as we know by now all too well, was an integral component of the bullion-coinage-military-slavery complex.

---

24 Another possibility is mentioned by Crowley, namely, that another objective of Columbus "was to find a fresh stock of human beings to enslave," (Crowley, *City of Fortune*, p. 136). Crowley notes that Genoa at the time held more slaves than any other city within medieval Europe. Venice, it will be recalled, also engaged in slaving activity.

⚛ Ten ⚛

CONCLUSIONS

∴

"Italian bankers ultimately managed to free themselves from the threat
of expropriation by themselves taking over governments, and by doing so,
acquiring their own court systems (capable of enforcing contracts) and
even more critically, their own armies."
—David Graeber[1]

IF ANYTHING EMERGES FROM THIS all-too-cursory overview, it is
the strong suggestion that during the high Middle Ages and Renaissance, the
connection between money, the Metaphor (and hence cosmology, physics),
and power began to be consciously, if dimly, perceived. For the financial oligarchies, this connection was, as I have argued, most likely perceived as a
threat to one of the pillars of social manipulation and power they had long
associated themselves with: religion.

Indeed, at a deeper historical level, we discovered that coinage and the
bullion from which it is confected can be viewed as a very close analogue of
the Metaphor itself, and suggestively, while the doctrine of corporate personhood arose from certain theological foundations—in our opinion historically
suspect and doctrinally erroneous ones—it is also possible to see in the activities of medieval Venetian and Florentine merchants and bankers the growing
awareness that the doctrine, allied to the alchemical analogy of money as the

---

1   Graeber, David. *Debt,* p. 291.

Metaphor, could function as a basis for the concentration and accumulation of vast wealth and power in a few hands. Indeed, after the collapse of the Bardi and Peruzzi, we see the Medicis repeating, on a far less grand scale, the same operational strategies and tactics with a new twist: the central office became, in itself, a kind of holding company, directing the branches of its far flung concerns, each in themselves yet another corporation, thus providing another layer of insulation between the partners' personal liabilities and that of the corporation itself.

But most importantly, what *does* clearly emerge from a rudimentary consideration of the strange "coincidences" surrounding the collapse of the Florentine super-companies is that the collapse, while initiated and brought on, perhaps, by factors wholly outside of any human manipulation, the possibility of deliberate Venetian *exploitation* of the crisis is at least possible, and to a lesser extent probable. In short, a case *can* be made that the "internet conspiracy theories" regarding the Venetian oligarchy—and, in some versions, the oligarchies of the other great northern Italian city-states—were indeed manipulating market forces on a global scale, and at least European politics on a continental one.

One thing, however, is abundantly clear, and that is that regardless of where one turns, or from which point of view one examines Venetian practices and institutions, whether one approaches analysis from the standpoint of domestic politics and government institutions, or from the standpoint of banking, or bullion brokering, or even geopolitics, the Venetian oligarchy *did* act consistently, as a class, to cloak any factional divisions within its ranks, and conspired always to protect their own interests, and to make entry into their ranks difficult. The very fact that the nobility itself was distinguished between *longhi* and *curti*, between ancient and more recent houses, strongly suggests that the *longhi* nobility were acutely aware of ancient roots and connections.

It is beyond any question that those oligarchies began to develop their sophisticated "playbook" during the Middle Ages. The Bardi and Peruzzi super-companies, just like the modern International Monetary Fund, World Bank, and other such institutions, established the mercantilist pattern of making significant loans to governments, and exacting as a "conditionality" of their loans dedicated liens on government revenues, and eventually, even the power to oversee the tax collection that repaid these loans, gathering more and more of the powers of the state into their own hands, until, of course, overcome with events and a gold glut that shows every indication of having been engineered by Venetian hands, they were caught in a cash flow crisis from which they could not escape, and they collapsed.

As for Venice, the oligarchical playbook developed forms and methods that would make a member of the modern military-industrial complex proud, for rather than publicly amend the structure and constitution of their government, Venetians simply created new "emergency" agencies to deal with problems as they arose. The most famous, of course, was the Council of Ten, a body whose true importance can only be appreciated if one notes that the intelligence it gathered (on a truly global basis) provided information on future market conditions and trends, allowing Venetian merchants and banks to prosper, or at minimum to manage their losses. Such widespread global intelligence also raises the possibility that Venice was able to confirm the existence of the New World through Oriental, as well as archived Byzantine, sources. Academics may choose to dismiss the arrival of a massive gold shipment in Venice in the same year as the Peruzzi collapse as "coincidental." But such shipments would have had to have been in long planning and preparation, and Venetian agents would have known of the difficulties of the company—after all, it maintained a branch in Venice, and leased Venetian ships to transport its commodities.

Within Venice, too, another technique and tactic arose, the manipulation of "seigniorage" of the mint, itself firmly in the hands of the oligarchical families. This was, so to speak, the same thing as a modern central bank such as the Federal Reserve or Bank of England manipulating the prime lending rate. And as we have also seen, Venice was not above using outright currency manipulation—witness the famous Blind Doge Enrico Dandolo's coinage of a near replica of the Byzantine hyperperon, in an effort to drive the Roman coinage out and replace it with the Venetian one in Middle Eastern trade. The Fourth Crusade, seen in this light, was a continuation by other means of the economic warfare that this step announced.

Finally, we have argued a purely speculative case that in the wake of the Fourth Crusade, Venice may indeed have come into possession of ancient maps that clearly suggested a "New World," and hence an opening of the system of trade that would have endangered Venice's unique and dominant position in East-West trade. Given its geographical, and geopolitical, position, Venice would have suppressed that knowledge, yet another key ingredient of the oligarchical playbook: when knowledge is discovered that for whatever reason can threaten the power of the ruling oligarchy, that knowledge should be suppressed, *until* that ruling elite has positioned itself to take advantage of it (if possible).

In the aftermath of the War of the League of Cambrai, some researchers, such as Webster Tarpley, have argued that the Venetian oligarchy clearly saw the handwriting on the wall: their power could no longer be sustained using Venice as a base of operations. Seeing this, they simply decided to *move* ...

III

EPILOGUE IS PROLOGUE:

The Move Northward: The Annuitary Asps

of Amsterdam and the Collateralized Cobras
of the City of London

---

*"A badly mauled, indebted and humiliated Venice
survived the War of the League of Cambrai ... At the
deepest level, some patricians realized that the lagoon
city could now be crushed like an egg-shell, and was not
a suitable base for world domination. As after 1200
there had been talk of moving the capital, perhaps
to Constantinople, so now plans began to hatch that
would facilitate a metastasis of the Venetian cancer
towards the Atlantic world."*

—Webster Griffin Tarpley,
"The Role of the Venetian Oligarchy in Reformation,
Counter-Reformation, Enlightenment, and the Thirty Years' War,"
Against Oligarchy, pp. 2–3.

❧ Eleven ❧

EPILOGUE IS PROLOGUE:
The Transference Northward to Germany and Holland

∴

"To the towns of the United Provinces, Amsterdam stood in the same position as did Venice to those of the Terraferma. Indeed Amsterdam bore an uncanny physical resemblance to Venice, with the same water everywhere, dividing the city up into islands, islets and canals, surrounding it on all sides with marshes; Amsterdam had her vaterschepen, the little boats which ferried in fresh water, just as the boats on the Brenta did for Venice. Both cities were after all ringed round with salt water."
—Fernand Braudel[1]

VENICE WAS FAMOUS, or better put, infamous, for its sudden, short, sharp applications of military force to bring errant colonies and bases to heel, and in the enforcement of its policies. It is, not surprisingly, a technique that became yet another component of the oligarchical playbook, for we see it in evidence again in the Dutch trading empire, based in Amsterdam, with its ships-of-the-line and grenadiers enforcing its will. The pattern is of course even more in evidence with the British Empire, and updated with the latest technological gadgets—in this case, pilotless drones and stealth bombers—for the American Empire.

---

1   Fernand Braudel, *Civilization and Capitalism: 15ᵗʰ–18ᵗʰ Century: Volume III: The Perspective of the World,* trans from the French by Siân Reynolds (Berkeley: University of California Press, 1992), p. 182.

In this, one could certainly argue that there was at least a continuity of *method* from one mercantilist empire to the next. But the real question that needs to be answered, even if only in the cursory form of "suggestive indications," is the question implied by researcher Webster Griffin Tarpley in the epigraph that began this section:

> A badly mauled, indebted and humiliated Venice survived the War of the League of Cambrai ... At the deepest level, some patricians realized that the lagoon city could now be crushed like an egg-shell, and was not a suitable base for world domination. As after 1200 there had been talk of moving the capital, perhaps to Constantinople, so now plans began to hatch that would facilitate a metastasis of the Venetian cancer towards the Atlantic world.[2]

The fact that the Dutch city of Amsterdam was founded in a similar swamp, and that so many of its cultural institutions seem so peculiarly similar to Venice itself, only adds fuel to the fire for some theorists.

The question implied by such views is this: is there any connection between these mercantilist empires beyond mere resemblance of method? Are there any indicators of actual personal, or *familial*, overlap from the oligarchy of one to the next? Can one indeed maintain at least a *prima facie* case that the rise of the mercantilist empires was not merely the accident of the discovery of the New World and the resulting inevitable eclipse of the northern Italian city-states, and that, at least in part, some of these families simply picked up and moved shop, so to speak?

There are, indeed, indicators that this is the case, and again, they are openly hidden in the history of the period. Let us take one example.

Venice, as noted in previous chapters, dominated the world bullion trade and was indeed the European center of a global bullion exchange market. And as also previously noted, Venice managed to acquire the dominant position in the European production of silver via its close association with the German families mining this commodity. The economic historian Fernand Braudel, whom we just cited, observed that Venice required German commodities traders to come directly to Venice to buy and sell, bringing with them, of course, the silver with which they did so. At the same time, Venice prohibited her own merchants from buying and selling directly in Germany.[3] "That this was conscious policy on Venice's part," Braudel observes, "can hardly be

---

2   Tarpley, "The Role of the Venetian Oligarchy in Reformation, Counter-Reformation, Enlightenment, and the Thirty Years' War," *Against Oligarchy*, http://tarpley.net /online-books/against-oligarchy/ the-venetian-conspiracy. pp. 2–3.
3   Braudel, *Perspective of the World*, p. 125.

doubted, since she forced it upon all the cities more or less dependent upon her." All trade was obliged to pass through Venice, and consequently, "Venice had quite deliberately ensnared all the surrounding subject economies, including the German economy, for her own profit: she drew her living from them, preventing them from acting freely and according to their own lights."[4]

The agents of Venice in this enterprise were yet another famous Renaissance banking and merchant family dynasty, the German family of the Fuggers, who, like the Medici, learned their trade quite literally by being schooled in Venice's markets.[5] The mercantilist arrangements thus connected the Venetian oligarchs, whose power depended so closely upon their ability to control and manipulate the gold-to-silver bullion ratio so vital to their East-West trade, to the northern and central European economy quite directly. Thus, in this context, Tarpley's observations begin to make sense, for any Venetian oligarchical consideration of the deliberate transference of their base of operations would bear this consideration in mind. Equally, they would have to consider the geopolitical realities: the key to future survival, and expansion of their wealth and power, would require a base of operations with direct access to the Atlantic ocean, and this narrowed the possibilities considerably, since Spain and Portugal were already well-established Atlantic trading powers, as was France. This left two relatively less powerful areas open for consideration: the Netherlands and England. So from the standpoint of geopolitical and economic calculation, once again, Tarpley's observations make a great deal of sense. If the oligarchy moved at all, it would have to move north, and west, or perish altogether.

So what sorts of things would one look for to confirm that indeed there was a deliberate policy of such transference occurring?

There are two things: one rather obvious, and the other, not so obvious. Let us begin with the not so obvious one, since the obvious one, once known, is rather stunning.

As we have discovered through the previous chapters, the Most Serene Republic of Venice was indeed an oligarchy, that is to say, the institutions of public government, and private enterprise, were all firmly in the hands of the Venetian nobility, to such an extent that, like the Grain Office, the boundaries between public and private institutions and agencies begins to blur. After the dissolution of the Grain Office, the private banks of the Rialto began to issue and hold the public debt of the Venetian government directly. To use a modern analogy, there was no one private central bank, there were *several*, and each, of course, was directly tied to some family or faction within the Venetian

---

4   Ibid., p. 125.
5   Mueller, Reinhold C. *Venetian Money Market: Banks, Panics, and the Public Debt 1200–1500*, Vol. II of *Money and Banking in Medieval and Renaissance Venice*. (Baltimore: Johns Hopkins University Press, 1997), p. 277.

oligarchy. Mueller notes that ca. 1470–1500, the size of the Republic's indebtedness to these banks was probably somewhere around five million ducats,[6] an astronomical figure for that day, even for governments with much larger territories, much less for one city-state.

Consequently, if there was to be such a transference by any portion of that oligarchy northward, any holdings of public debt of the Venetian state would have to be sold and converted to liquid capital, and the family fortune transferred northward. This is, at least in some cases, exactly what happened. Tarpley observes that

> Under the impact of the War of the League of Cambrai, the Venetian oligarchy realized the futility of attempting a policy of world domination from the tiny base of a city-state among the lagoons of the northern Adriatic.

In other words, Tarpley is expressing the geopolitical reasoning we have outlined in more detail above. He continues:

> As was first suggested by the present writer in 1981, the Venetian oligarchy (especially its "giovani" faction around Paolo Sarpi) responded by transferring its family fortunes (fondi), philosophical outlook, and political methods into such states as England, France, and the Netherlands. Soon the Venetians had decided that England (and Scotland) was the most suitable site for the New Venice, the future center of a new, world-wide Roman Empire based on maritime supremacy.[7]

This represents, for Tarpley, and as we have also suggested in the previous pages, a continuation of a very ancient practice:

> The oligarchical system of Great Britain is not an autochthonous product of English or British history. It represents rather the tradition of the Babylonians, Romans, Byzantines, and Venetians which has been transplanted into the British Isles through a series of upheavals. The status of Britain as the nation foutué of modern history is due in particular to the sixteenth and seventeenth century metastasis into England and Scotland of the Venetian oligarchy along with its philosophy, political forms, family fortunes, and imperial geopolitics.[8]

---

6 Ibid., pp. 429–430.
7 Tarpley, "How the Venetian System was Transplanted into England," *Against Oligarchy*, www.tarpley.net/onine-books/against-oligarchy, p. 3.
8 Ibid., p. 1.

However, this transference did not occur directly, but via a "middle" step or stopover in Amsterdam.[9]

Note Tarpley's statement that there is a direct *family* connection, via their family "fund," in this transference. After liquidating the public debt, which could easily be done through inflation via the mint, which the nobility controlled, important questions arise:

Who are some of the families involved in this operation, and are there real indicators of a transfer northward?

Indeed there are. Let us take just one example, perhaps paradoxically the one most well-known, and yet paradoxically least well-known for its Italian and Venetian connection.

Earlier in this book I noted that one of the d'Este family—a famous Italian noble house and definitely a member of "the oligarchy"—had significant deposits, and hence influence, in the Venetian grain office. This family subsequently split into two branches, with the older branch known as the Welf-Este, or simply, the House of Welf, from the Germanized version of the Italian Guelph.[10] The name Welf-Este was the family name of the Dukes of Bavaria. This family's younger branch produced influential rulers of the city-state of Ferrara in northern Italy, and by 1405, when the whole region fell to Venice, the house became a virtual Venetian satrapy. The origins of the house date to the early ninth century, as far as can be traced, when its first member established himself at Este near Padua.[11] These two branches of the family were reunited, and eventually produced the Electors, and later, the Kings, of Hanover, who, of course, produced the Hanoverian monarchs of Great Britain.

Yet another famous house with Venetian oligarchical roots is the well-known, and very wealthy, German noble family of Von Thurn-und-Taxis. As Tarpley notes, this family's roots stem from Venetian territory, where the Thurn-Valsassina family was known as the della Torre e Tassos.[12]

Intermarriage was, of course, one of the standard techniques of the nobility throughout the ages utilized to cement alliances and maintain power. Thus, in a certain sense, it is to be expected that networks of familial relationships can be traced between the Italian nobility of the city-states in general, and of Venice in particular, to northern Europe, to the Hanoverian House, the

---

9 Tarpley, "Venice's War Against Western Civilization," *Against Oligarchy,* www.tarpley.net/onine-books/against-oligarchy, p. 4.

10 The informed reader will have noted that throughout this book we have steered clear of the complex story of the Guelph-Ghibelline controversy and its role in imperial, papal, and northern Italian politics.

11 *Italian Noble Houses: House of Hohenstaufen, House of Della Rovere, House of Este, House of Candia, Vendramin, House of Bourbon-Parma* (Books LLC, 2010), pp. 55–56.

12 Tarpley, "The Role of the Venetian Oligarchy in Reformation, Counter-Reformation, Enlightenment, and the Thirty Years' War," p. 16.

House of Orange-Nassau in the Netherlands, and of both to Great Britain. But with all such marriages, there is always a movement of money, and power. Here, we have only sketched the threadbare outlines of a vast and complex story that began in the swampy lagoon of Venice, and perhaps much longer ago than that, and ended in the secretive halls and chambers of the Bank of England. Epilogue ...

... is prologue.

As for Venice, with her persecution of Bruno, with his possible role as a Venetian agent until he disclosed to Mocenigo his intentions to found a secret society, with her vast wealth in bullion and from the slave trade, and with the deep currents of the Metaphor running beneath the surface throughout, it is perhaps worth closing with an observation from Roger Crowley. In the year 1500, the Venetian artist Jacopo de' Barbari produced an enormous woodcut of the city of Venice, almost three meters long, portraying the city from almost a thousand feet in the air, and doing so with extraordinary accuracy.[13]

In the midst of it all, at the top of the woodcut map, Venice's titular god, Mercury, the God of Trade and Commerce, presides over it all. In the lagoon itself, Neptune, or Poseidon, is prominent, his trident raised to the heavens.[14]

Mercury, and Neptune. Apollo, and Poseidon, the God of Atlantis. Mercury, the element of alchemical transformation, Mercury, god of trade and commerce, like the Egyptian Hermes.

For those willing to read the hermetic symbolism writ large in de' Barbari's woodcut, the message is subtle, and clear: Atlantis, ancient high knowledge, trade, commerce, and a deeply rooted Metaphor turned into money, with all its associations to the temple of religion, debt, and oligarchical power ...

Small wonder that Bruno, as least as far as Venice was concerned, had to die.

---

13 Crowley, *City of Fortune*, p. 275.
14 Ibid., p. 277.

⚜ Appendix ⚜

THE MISSING DOCUMENTS OF BRUNO'S TRIAL:

Napoleon Bonaparte, Pope Pius IX (Giovanni Cardinal Mastai-Ferretti), and the Implications

∴

"Now then, in order to secure to us a Pope in the manner required, it is necessary to fashion for that Pope a generation worthy of the reign of which we dream ... That reputation will open the way for our doctrines to pass to the bosoms of the young clergy, and go even to the depths of convents. In a few years the young clergy will have, by the force of events, invaded all the functions. They will govern, administer and judge. They will form the council of the Sovereign. They will be called upon to choose the Pontiff who will reign ... You wish to establish the reign of the elect upon the throne of the prostitute of Babylon? Let the clergy march under your banner in the belief always that they march under the banner of the Apostolic Keys."
—Piccolo Tigre, *Permanent Instruction of the Alta Vendita Lodges*[1]

IN THE FIRST CHAPTER, I noted that the documentation surrounding Giordano Bruno's trial and execution remains obscure. And this is for two reasons. Here, it is best, once again, to turn to Frances A. Yates, who provides the intriguing details:

---

1   Piccolo Tigre, *Permanent Instruction of the Alta Vendita*, in Monsignor George E. Dillon, D.D., *Grand Orient Freemasonry Unmasked as the Secret Power Behind Communism* (Metarie, Louisiana: Sons of Liberty Books, no date, original edition published by M.H. Gill and Son, Dublin, 1885), pp. 54–56.

The documents of the Venetian Inquisition on Bruno's case have long been known, also some Roman documents, and are available in Vincenzo Spampanato's publication, *Documenti della vita de Giordano Bruno* (1933). In 1942, a large addition to the evidence was made by Cardinal Angelo Mercati who published in that year *Il Sommario del Processo di Giordano Bruno*. This *Sommario*, a summary of the evidence drawn up for the use of the Roman Inquisitors, was discovered by Mercati *among the personal papers of Pope Pius IX*. This document repeats much that was known from the Venetian archives but adds a great deal of new information. It is not, however, the actual *processo*, the official report on the case giving the sentence, that is to say stating on what grounds Bruno was finally condemned. This *processo* is lost for ever, *having been part of a mass of archives which were transported to Paris by the order of Napoleon*, where they were eventually sold as pulp to a cardboard factory.[2]

Why would Napoleon Bonaparte have Venetian archives, which included the original *processo* of Bruno's Venetian trial, transported to Paris? And more importantly, why would Pope Pius IX (Giovanni Cardinal Mastai-Ferretti), the pope behind the First Vatican Council's decree of papal infallibility, and of papal immediate and supreme jurisdiction, be in the possession of papers relating to Bruno's trial and execution, and found among his personal documents? To my knowledge, no one has attempted an answer to these questions.

And perhaps an answer has not been attempted for good reason, for any attempt to do so will run into some little known, and very murky, facts, which can but compel speculation toward massive conspiracy.

A. BONAPARTE AND THE MASONS

We may easily deal with Bonaparte by pointing out that his foreign minister, Bishop Maurice de Talleyrand, was also the foreign minister for the restored Bourbon monarchy after Napoleon's final downfall, and was a Mason. It may be possible, therefore, that Bonaparte's sacking of the Venetian archives may have had something directly to do with acquisition of the transcripts of Bruno's Inquisition trial.

There is, indeed, some evidence for this, for Napoleon was not only a Mason, but "he owed his first elevation to the Jacobins, and that his earliest

---

2   Frances A. Yates, *Giordano Bruno and the Hermetic Tradition* (London: Routledge, 1964), p. 349, boldface and italicized emphasis added.

patron was Robespierre," a man with strong lodge connections himself.[3] Additionally, the campaign in Italy that led to his looting of the Venetian archives was a campaign that reflected particular brutality to Catholic establishments.[4]

But it is really after his rule commences as Emperor of the French that Napoleon's close ties with Grand Orient Freemasonry become explicit. Alexander Dumas, in his *Memoires de Garibaldi*, outlines the close association:

> Napoleon took Masonry under his protection. Joseph Napoleon[5] was Grand Master of the Order. Joachim Murat second Master Adjoint. The Empress Josephine being at Strasbourg, in 1805, presided over the fete for the adoption of the Lodge of the True Chevaliers of Paris. At the same time Eugene de Beauharnais was Venerable of the lodge of St. Eugene in Paris ... [6]

And of course it was due in no small part to the machinations of the former Catholic Bishop de Talleyrand, himself a Mason, that Napoleon obtained power in the first place. It is therefore possible that Napoleon's plundering of the Venetian archives, and the removal of documents pertaining to Bruno's trial, might have had some connection to the behind-the-scenes maneuverings of French Masonry.

When we turn to the matter of Pope Pius IX, however, the matter is much more murky, and we must deal with it in detail.

B. GIOVANNI CARDINAL MASTAI-FERRETTI (POPE PIUS IX)
1. Brief Notes

Giovanni-Maria Mastai Ferretti was born on May 13, 1792, died February 7, 1878, and reigned as Pope Pius IX from 1846 to his death, the longest reigning Pope in Catholic Church history. He is famous, of course, for being the Pope who pushed for the definition of papal infallibility, and universal, supreme, and immediate jurisdiction of the pope, at the First Vatican Council (1869–1870), over significant opposition from German and Austrian bishops. He also presided over the dissolution of the Papal States under the advance of Italian nationalist armies, which finally destroyed the last remnants of secular papal power in 1870. Pius IX also had the distinction of being the first pope to allow himself to be photographed.

---

3   Dillon, *Grand Orient Freemasonry Unmasked as the Secret Power Behind Communism*, p. 34.
4   Ibid.
5   Napoleon's brother.
6   Ibid., p. 38.

Pope Pius IX (Giovanni-Maria Cardinal Mastai-Ferretti)

It is noteworthy that Pius IX was elected by the liberalizing wing of the Cardinalate, in response to the liberal and revolutionary attitudes sweeping Europe in the mid-1840s, though after a series of assassinations of his ministers, Pius turned increasingly conservative and reactionary, a move culminating in the dogmas of the First Vatican Council. For our purposes, however, we note Pius IX's early liberal attitudes, for these, in turn, would have been a motivation for him to join the many secret societies of Europe championing such causes. Indeed, in the early years of his papacy Pius IX displayed remarkable leniency to revolutionary political prisoners and to the Italian revolutionary secret society, the Carbonari.

We therefore turn to a consideration of statements of the Carbonari leader Piccolo Tigre, "The Permanent Instruction of the Alta Vendita," made in 1849, three years after the election of Mastai-Ferretti to the papacy.

2. The Permanent Instruction of the Alta Vendita Lodge

By the 1840s, Weishaupt's Illuminati had been replaced by the Italian Carbonari lodges as the most obviously revolutionary lodges of Europe, and their manifesto, "The Permanent Instruction of the Alta Vendita," is a distilled essence of Weishaupt's Illuminism. For our purposes, we need only cite those passages dealing with their plans for the Catholic Church:

> Our final end is that of Voltaire and of the French Revolution, the destruction for ever (sic) of Catholicism and even of the Christian idea which, if left standing on the ruins of Rome, would be the resuscitation of Christianity later on …
>
> … The remedy is found. The Pope, whoever he may be, will never come to the secret societies. It is for the secret societies to come first to the Church, in the resolve to conquer the two.
>
> …
>
> We do not mean to win the Popes to our cause, to make them neophytes of our principles, and propagators of our ideas. That would be a ridiculous dream, no matter in what manner events may turn. Should cardinals or prelates, for example, enter, willingly or by surprise, into a part of our secrets, it would be by no means a motive to desire their elevation to the See of Peter. That elevation would destroy us. Ambition alone would bring them to apostasy from us. The needs of power would force them to immolate us. That which we ought to demand, that which we should seek and expect, as the Hews expected the Messiah, is a Pope according to our wants.[7]

The document goes on to outline a plan—reminiscent of Weishaupt's Illuminati—to co-opt the seminaries of the church, and thus to allow

> our doctrines to pass to the bosoms of the young clergy, and go even to the depths of convents. In a few years the young clergy will have, by the force of events, invaded all functions. They will govern, administer, and judge. They will form the council of the Sovereign. They will be called upon to choose the Pontiff who will reign; and that Pontiff, like the greater part of his contemporaries, will be necessarily imbued with the Italian and humanitarian principles which we are about to put in circulation.[8]

It is indeed interesting to observe that Mastai-Ferretti, with his early liberal views and attitudes toward the Carbonari, would seem to fit this bill perfectly. One might go so far as to speculate that there would be no better way to gain

---

7   "Permanent Instruction of the Alta Vendita," cited in Dillon, *Grand Orient Freemasonry Unmasked as the Secret Power Behind Communism*, pp. 52–53.

8   Ibid., pp. 55–56.

power in the Roman church through such a process of subterfuge than to have its primary institution—the papacy—proclaimed infallible, and to endow it with a universal, supreme, and immediate jurisdiction.

While this may sound absurd, there is more ...

3. José Maria Cardinal Caro y Rodriguez, Cardinal Archbishop of Santiago

In a little-known work, *The Mystery of Freemasonry Unveiled* (1928), José Maria Cardinal Caro y Rodriguez, then Archbishop of Santiago de Chile, made some rather breathtaking observations about the pope of papal infallibility:

> For the present I shall tell only of the origin of the imputation made against Pius IX, which is the one the Masons tell most often and with greatest assurance. Here is the way John Gilmary Shea tells and refutes that fable in his *Life of Pius IX*, pp. 291–292, (written in English). "*It began in Germany and the Masons believed that by laying the scene in America, it might help to escape investigation. They declared positively that Pius IX had been received into a certain Masonic lodge in Philadelphia,* they quoted their discourses and declared that several of his autographs were kept in this lodge. Unfortunately for the story, Philadelphia is in the civilized world. The people there know how to read and write. *The claim was investigated and it was found that in that city, there is no Masonic lodge of the name given. It was also found that no lodges in Philadelphia had ever received a Juan Maria Mastai; no trace could be found that he had ever been there, because he never had been*; no lodge had any of his autographed letters; the masons themselves testified that the entire matter was merely an invention. The calumny this refuted has been revived from time to time, and in the last version care was taken not to specify the lodge or the city." (Arthur Press, *A Study in American Freemasonry*, 270–271). To make it more credible they have placed on the photograph of a Mason with insignias, the head of the Pope, cut from his portrait and substituted in place of the Mason's.
>
> The reader will recall the previously cited advice of Weishaupt to be sure that persons of merit belong to Masonry, thereby helping to acquire new members. *That lie involving Pius IX was calculated above all to deceive the clergy so that they might follow the example of one who had been their chief.* I do not know if there could be found in the world a priest so naive that he would allow himself to be deceived by it.[9]

---

9   José Maria Cardinal Caro y Rodriguez, *The Mystery of Freemasonry Unveiled* (Palmdale, CA: The Christian Book Club of America, n.d.), p. 49, emphasis added.

Note what we have:

1) The story about Pius IX's Masonic initiation and membership began to be circulated in Germany;
2) Pius IX was allegedly initiated in a lodge in "Philadelphia;"
3) When lodges in Philadelphia were consulted, no indication of any such initiation or membership was forthcoming, nor was Mastai-Ferretti ever known to have traveled to America; thus,
4) Cardinal Caro y Rodriguez concludes that the story was just that, a story, circulated to deceive other Roman Catholic clergy into accepting Masonic initiation (and also, one may speculate, to confuse or cast doubts among the clergy about the orthodoxy of its own hierarchy and institution).

There is, however, more than just this one problem.

4. A Sidelight from the Bavarian Illuminati

It is known that Mastai-Ferretti did travel to *South* America in 1823 and 1825. More importantly, however, is that at least one secret society with close ties to Freemasonry was known to employ "code names" not only for its members, but also for their *locations*. This was the Bavarian Illuminati of Ingolstadt professor of canon law, Adam Weishaupt (1748–1830).

For example, Weishaupt himself took the name "Spartacus" as his code name, and his close associate Baron Knigge took the code name "Cato." More importantly, however, are the names assigned to provinces and towns. Bavaria, for example, was code-named Achaia, the Tyrol region of northern Italy, the Peloponnese. Similarly, Munich was code-named Athens, Ravensburg was code-named Sparta, Vienna became Rome, and so on, for purposes of coded communications between the society's initiates.[10] The implication is clear, for if other fraternal orders maintained this Illuminist practice, the slim possibility arises that Mastai-Ferretti may have been initiated into a lodge in a "Philadelphia" that was simply a code-name for a European city.

5. Fr. Malachi Martin on "The Bargain"

In his novel *Vatican*, Fr. Malachi Martin outlines the features of what he called "the Bargain," a secret agreement negotiated by the Vatican after the loss of the Papal States during Italian unification with the high Masonic

---

10   Henry Coston, *Conjurations des Illuminés* (Paris: Publications Henry Coston, 1979), pp. 3–4.

powers of Europe, in order to gain access to the financial and banking houses of the West and thereby increase its own financial power. As a component of this Bargain, those powers in return received the right of a secret veto of any candidate elected to the papacy. Later, in his last book, the novel *Windswept House,* Martin wrote of a church hollowed out from within by members of various secret societies with obvious Masonic overtones. This matched in fiction with what some Roman Catholic writers were stating in non-fiction works in the wake of the notorious P2-G scandal, in which Licio Gelli's Masonic Propaganda Due lodge had successfully infiltrated various Vatican institutions, including, according to some, its financial institutions.

All of this would tend, in a very broad fashion, to corroborate the speculation advanced above, that perhaps the association between the Vatican and the fraternal orders of Europe began with Giovanni Cardinal Mastai-Ferretti himself, who, as Pope Pius IX, led the effort to have the Pope proclaimed infallible, and possessed of an universal, supreme, and immediate jurisdiction over and above the Church. It would, in some measure, explain Mastai-Ferretti's interest in the case of Giordano Bruno from a different perspective; instead of just ecclesiastical interest, it was the interest of one initiate in another.

Of course, all of this is highly speculative, and we simply present it for consideration here. It remains my own personal opinion that it is *unlikely* that Mastai-Ferretti was a member of any secret society, but only *slightly* possible that he was such a member. Nonetheless, if he was, the timing of his pontificate and his early liberal attitudes square quite nicely with the attitude outlined in the Permanent Instruction, and if he was an initiate, it would put a unique perspective on his fascination with Giordano Bruno. It would be as if Bruno's Giordanistas had come home to capture the papacy itself.

On the other hand, however, Mastai-Ferretti's subsequent conservatism and ultramontanism would also explain the fascination, as being the interest of someone concerned about the power of the very secret societies that so galvanized the Italian revolution and unification, and stripped him of the last vestiges of power by providing a final end to the Papal States. That too would have been a final manifestation of the Giordanistas sweeping Italy, to the very gates of the Apostolic Palace.

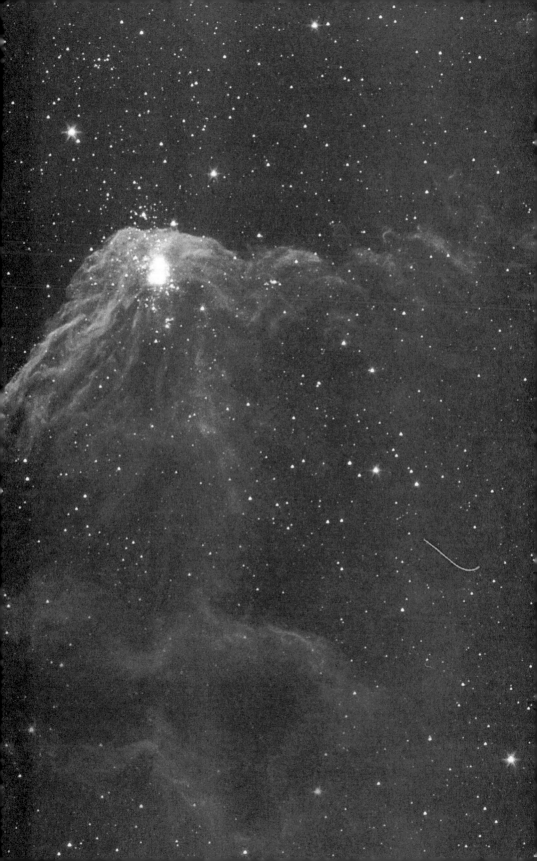

Bibliography

Barrow, John D., and Tipler, Frank J. *The Anthropic Cosmological Principle*. Oxford: Oxford University Press, 2009. ISBN 978-0-19-282147-8.

Barruel, Abbé Augustin. *Code of the Illuminati*. Montana: Forgotten Books, 2008. ISBN 978-160680252-6.

Braudel, Fernand. *Civilization and Capitalism, 15th–18th Century, Volume III: The Perspective of the World*. Translated by Siân Reynolds. Berkeley: University of California Press, 1992. ISBN 0-520-08116-1.

Bruno, Giordano. *Cause, Principle, and Unity and Essays on Magic*. Translated and Edited by Richard J. Blackwell and Robert de Lucca. Cambridge: Cambridge University Press, 1998. ISBN 0-521-59658-0.

Bruno, Giordano. *The Expulsion of the Triumphant Beast*. Translated from the Italian by Arthur D. Imerti. Lincoln, Nebraska: University of Nebraska Press, 1992. ISBN 978-0-8032-6234-8.

Caro y Rodriguez, Jose Maria, Cardinal Archbishop of Santiago, Chile. *The Mystery of Freemasonry Unveiled*. Palmdale, California: Christian Book Club of America. No Date. No ISBN.

Coston, Henry. *La Conjuration des Illuminés*. Paris: Publications Henry Coston, 1979. No ISBN.

Crowley, Roger. *City of Fortune: How Venice Ruled the Seas*. New York: Random House, 2011. ISBN 978-1-4000-6820-3.

de Nicolás, Antonio T., Ph.D. *Meditations Through the Rg Veda: Four-Dimensional Man* (New Edition). New York: Authors Choice Press, 2003. ISBN 978-0-595-26925-7.

Del Mar, Alexander. *Money and Civilization*. 1886. Hawthorne, California: Omni Publications reprint, 1975. No ISBN.

Dillon, Msgr. George E., D.D. *Grand Orient Freemasonry Unmasked as the Secret Power Behind Communism*. Metrarie, Louisiana: Sons of Liberty Books. No Date. ISBN 0-89562-095-2. Original edition published by M.H. Gill and Son, Dublin, 1885.

Ebling, Florian. *The Secret History of Hermes Trismegistus: Hermeticism from Ancient to Modern Times*. Translated by David Lorton. Ithica, New York: Cornell University Press, 2007. ISBN 978-0-8014-7749-2.

Eisenstein, Charles. *Sacred Economics: Money, Gift, and Society in the Age of Transition*. Berkeley, California: Evolver Editions, 2011. ISBN 978-1-58394-397-7.

Farrell, Joseph P. *Babylon's Banksters: The Alchemy of Deep Physics, High Finance and Ancient Religion*. Port Townsend, Washington: Feral House, 2010. ISBN 978-1-93259-579-6.

————. *The Cosmic War: Interplanetary Warfare, Modern Physics, and Ancient Texts*. Kempton, Illinois: Adventures Unlimited Press, 2007. ISBN 978-1-931882-75-0.

Farrell, Joseph P. *The Philosophers' Stone: Alchemy and the Secret Research for Exotic Matter*. Port Townsend, Washington: Feral House, 2009. ISBN 978-1-932595-40-6.

Farrell, Joseph P., and de Hart, Scott D. *The Grid of the Gods: The Aftermath of the Cosmic War and the Physics of the Pyramid Peoples*. Kempton, Illinois: Adventures Unlimited Press, 2011. ISBN 978-1-935487-39-5.

———. *Transhumanism: A Grimoire of Alchemical Altars and Agendas for the Transformation of Man*. Port Townsend, Washington: Feral House, 2012. ISBN 978-1-936239-44-3.

———. *Yahweh the Two-Faced God*. Las Vegas: Periprometheus Press, 2012. ISBN

Ferguson, Niall. *The Ascent of Money: A Financial History of the World*. New York: Penguin Books, 2008. ISBN 978-0-14-311617-2.

Fowden, Garth. *The Egyptian Hermes: A Historical Approach to the Late Pagan Mind*. Princeton: Princeton University Press, 1993. ISBN 978-0-691-02498-7.

Gallagher, Paul. "650 Years Ago: How Venice Rigged the First, and Worst, Global Financial Crash." *The New Federalist; American Almanac*, Sept. 4, 1995.

Gilbert, Felix. *The Pope, His Banker, and Venice*. Cambridge, Massachusetts: Harvard University Press, 1980. ISBN 0-674-68976-3.

Graeber, David. *Debt: The First 5,000 Years*. Brooklyn: Melville House, 2011. ISBN 978-1-933633-86-2.

Grant, Edward. *The Foundations of Modern Science in the Middle Ages: Their Religious, Institutional, and Intellectual Contexts*. Cambridge: Cambridge University Press, 1998. ISBN 0-521-56762-9.

Grant, Edward. *A History of Natural Philosophy from the Ancient World to the Nineteenth Century*. Cambridge: Cambridge University Press, 2007. ISBN 978-0-521-68957-1.

———. *Much Ado About Nothing: Theories of Space and Vacuum from the Middle Ages to the Scientific Revolution*. Cambridge: Cambridge University Press, 2008. ISBN 0-521-06192-X.

Hapgood, Charles H. *Maps of the Ancient Sea Kings*. Kempton, Illinois: Adventures Unlimited Press, 1996. ISBN 0-932813-42-9.

Hunt, Edwin S. *The Medieval Super-Companies: A Study of the Peruzzi Company of Florence*. Cambridge: Cambridge University Press, 2002. ISBN 0-521-89415-8.

Italian Noble Houses: House of Hohenstaufen, House of Della Rovere, House of Este, House of Candia, Vendramin, House of Bourbon-Parma. Books LLC, 2010. No place, no ISBN.

Jammer, Max. *Concepts of Space: The History of Theories of Space in Physics*. Third Edition. Mineola, NY: Dover Publications, 1993. ISBN 978-0-496-27119-6.

"koyaanisqatsi" (username). "Venetian Bankers and the Dark Ages." 2010. www.goldismoney2.com/showthread.php?524-Venetian-Bankers-and-the-Dark-Ages. Reprint of above article by Paul Gallagher.

Lane, Frederic C., with Mueller, Reinhold C. *Coins and Moneys of Account*, Vol. I of *Money and Banking in Medieval and Renaissance Venice*. Baltimore: John Hopkins, 1985. ISBN 978-0801831577.

Lane, Frederic C. "Venetian Bankers, 1496–1533: A Study in the Early Stages of Deposit Banking." No Date. PDF available at mises.org/PDF/venetian_bankers_lane.pdf.

Mueller, Reinhold C. *The Venetian Money Market: Banks, Panics, and the Public Debt 1200–1500*, Vol. II of *Money and Banking in Medieval and Renaissance Venice*. Baltimore: Johns Hopkins University Press, 1997. ISBN 0-8018-5437-7.

Newman, William R., and Grafton, Anthony. *Secrets of Nature: Astrology and Alchemy in Early Modern Europe*. Cambridge, Massachusetts: Massachusetts Institute of Technology Press, 2006. ISBN 0-262-64062-7.

Norwich, John Julius. *A History of Venice*. New York: Vintage Books, 1989. ISBN 978-0-679-72197-0.

Picknett, Lynn, and Prince, Clive. *The Forbidden Universe: The Occult Origins of Science and the Search for the Mind of God*. New York: Skyhorse Publishing, 2011. ISBN 1-61608-028-0.

Rothbard, Murray N. *The Mystery of Banking*, 2nd Edition. Auburn, Alabama: Ludwig von Mises Institue, 2008. ISBN 978-1-933550-28-2.

Schacht, Hjalmar Horace Greeley, with Pyke, Diana. *Confessions of the Old Wizard: The Autobiography of Hjalmar Horace Greeley Schacht.* Boston: Houghton Mifflin, 1956. Literary Licensing Reprint. ISBN 978-1258126742.

Scott, Walter, ed. and trans. *Hermetica: The Ancient Greek and Latin Writings Which Contain Religious or Philosophical Teachings Ascribed to Hermes Trismegistus.* Vol. I, *Introduction, Texts, and Translations.* Montana: Kessinger Publishing Company. No Date. ISBN 978-1-56459-481-5.

Seaford, Richard. *Money and the Early Greek Mind: Homer, Philosophy, Tragedy.* Cambridge: Cambridge University Press, 2004. ISBN 978-0-521-53992-0.

Smith, Paul H. *Reading the Enemy's Mind: Inside Star Gate, America's Psychic Espionage Program.* New York: Tor Books, 2005. ISBN 0-812-57855-4.

Spencer-Brown, George. *Laws of Form: The New Edition of This Classic with the First-Ever Proof of Riemann's Hypothesis.* Leipzig: Joh. Bohmeier Verlag, 1999. ISBN 978-3-89094-580-4.

Tarpley, Webster. *Giammaria Ortes: The Decadent Venetian Kook Who Originated the Myth of "Carrying Capacity."* http://tarpley.net/online-books/against-oligarchy/the-venetian-conspiracy.

———. *How the Dead Souls of Venice Corrupted Science.* http://tarpley.net/online-books/against-oligarchy/the-venetian-conspiracy.

———. *How the Venetian System was Transplanted into England.* http://tarpley.net/online-books/against-oligarchy/the-venetian-conspiracy.

———. *The Role of the Venetian Oligarchy in the Reformation, Counter-Reformation, Enlightenment, and the Thirty Years' War.* http://tarpley.net/online-books/against-oligarchy/the-venetian-conspiracy.

———. *The Venetian Conspiracy.* http://tarpley.net/online-books/against-oligarchy/the-venetian-conspiracy.

———. *Venice's War Against Western Civilization.* http://tarpley.net/online-books/against-oligarchy/the-venetian-conspiracy.

———. *The War of the League of Cambrai, Paolo Sarpi, and John Locke.* http://tarpley.net/online-books/against-oligarchy/the-venetian-conspiracy.

Teichova, Alice, Jurgan-van Hentenruk, Ginette, and Ziegler, Dieter, eds. *Banking, Trade, and Industry: Europe, America and Asia from the Thirteenth to the Twentieth Century.* Cambridge: Cambridge University Press, 1997. ISBN 978-0-521-18887-6.

Yates, Frances A. *Giordano Bruno and the Hermetic Tradition; Selected Works of Frances Yates,* Volume II. London: Routledge, 2001. ISBN 0-415-22045-9.

———. *The Art of Memory, Selected Works of Frances Yates,* Volume III. London: Routledge, 1999. ISBN 978-0-415-60605-9.

THE PHILOSOPHER'S STONE
Alchemy and Secret Research for Exotic Matter

BABYLON'S BANKSTERS
The Alchemy of Deep Physics, High Finance and Ancient Religion

GENES, GIANTS, MONSTERS, AND MEN
The Surviving Elites of the Cosmic War and Their Hidden Agenda

TRANSHUMANISM
A Grimoire of Alchemical Agendas
with co-author Scott deHart